CHAPELON

Genius of
French Steam

CHAPELON
Genius of
French Steam

Colonel H. C. B. Rogers, OBE

LONDON

IAN ALLAN

First published 1972

SBN 7110 0281 9

© Ian Allan 1972

Published by Ian Allan Ltd, Shepperton, Surrey, and printed
in the United Kingdom by A. Wheaton & Co., Exeter

Contents

Acknowledgements

FOR assistance in writing this book, I am indebted primarily to M. André Chapelon himself; for he has supplied most of the information that it contains as well as the greater part of the photographs with which it is illustrated. He has also read, and corrected where necessary, every chapter (though he tells me how embarrassed he is at the praise I have given his work). I am, however, solely responsible for any errors there may be in the book, and it is possible that I have translated some French technical terms into English unfamiliar to British engineers.

I owe much to my friend Mr. R. A. Riddles, CBE, FIMechE (sometime Vice-President of the LMS and former Member of the British Railways Executive for Mechanical and Electrical Engineering), because it was he who suggested that I should write this book and he has taken a keen interest in its progress.

I am grateful to that great steam enthusiast, Mr. R. C. Bond, FICE, FIMechE (formerly of the Midland Railway, and latterly Chief Mechanical Engineer of British Railways and then Technical Adviser to the British Transport Commission) for persuading me as to the merits of the compound locomotives of his old Company, which he has so often driven and fired.

Dr. P. Ransome-Wallis went to much trouble to provide me with suitable photographs from his enormous and magnificent collection, and he has my most appreciative thanks.

Mr. G. W. Carpenter, CEng, MIMechE has given invaluable help in the loan of books, journals, and manuscripts, and in his kindly comments on much of what I have written.

I must thank M. Lejeune, Chef d'Equipe at Le Mans locomotive depot, for his kindness in the trouble he took to show me the many interesting steam locomotives there.

And finally I must mention my wife, who likes steam engines because I do, but who treats with cold disdain any passing interest I might display in trains propelled by other means.

I

The Background

ON October 26th 1892 Andre Chapelon was born in the little *commune* of St. Paul en Cornillon, Loire, amidst the wooded heights of the *Massif Central*. Whilst still a very small boy he acquired a passionate enthusiasm for the steam railway locomotive, an enthusiasm which he says still remains with him today. It was an enthusiasm that was to be the driving force behind a revolution in steam locomotive design; for the little boy who watched the engines of the PLM running along the line that led from St. Etienne to Le Puy was destined to become the greatest of engineers in the last days of steam, and perhaps the greatest of all architects of the steam locomotive. It was to be the tragedy of André Chapelon that in his hands the steam railway engine reached its pinnacle of power and efficiency, combined with (because he is an artist as well) a supreme beauty of line; when it was suddenly superseded by other forms of motive power. And this supersession was due, not to any proven superiority in efficiency or economy, but merely because of a persuasive propaganda that steam was outmoded.

It is probable that Chapelon has exercised more influence on locomotive design than any other engineer since Stephenson. Not only did all other French railways rebuild their principal existing locomotives to incorporate Chapelon's principles to a greater or lesser degree, but in Great Britain engines built by Stanier, Gresley, Bullied, and Riddles incorporated Chapelon's ideas; as did many built in other countries, especially in Belgium, Spain, and Czechoslovakia. In South America today his methods are still demonstrating to those whose eyes are not blinded by diesel oil or the flash from the pantograph that modern steam is a competitive form of railway traction.

In view of the important background that they were to provide to his own future career, it would be appropriate to consider the principal locomotive developments during the time that Chapelon was growing to manhood, and before discussing the main events in his own life.

In 1886 the Société Alsacienne de Constructions Mécaniques built for the Nord Railway a 2—2—2—0 four-cylinder compound locomotive designed by Alfred de Glehn, the British born Chief Engineer of the Alsace Company. (This engine, No. 701, was later rebuilt with a leading bogie and has recently been restored at the Dunkirk Works for

7

preservation). In 1891, the year before André Chapelon's birth, the Nord put into service two 4—4—0 engines, Nos. 2121 and 2122, the first to be designed by M. Gaston du Bousquet, Engineer-in-Chief of the Nord, jointly with de Glehn and incorporating the compound system invented by the latter and applied to No. 701. The two high pressure cylinders were placed outside, immediately in front of the leading driving wheels and drove the second driving axle, whilst the low pressure cylinders were inside, above the bogie, and drove the leading driving axle. Whilst the driving wheels of No. 2121 were coupled, those of 2122 were initially uncoupled, to compare the working of a coupled engine and a 'double single'. To provide extra power at starting a by-pass arrangement allowed the high pressure cylinders to exhaust directly to the atmosphere, and for the engine to be operated as a four-cylinder simple expansion locomotive by admitting live steam into the intermediate reservoir supplying the low pressure cylinders. The engine could also work as a two-cylinder simple expansion locomotive if required, using either its high pressure or low pressure cylinders, thereby enabling it to operate even if partially disabled. Each set of cylinders had its own independently controlled valve gear, so that when working compound the driver could control the admission of steam into the two sets of cylinders independently of each other.

Performance of the two engines was impressive. The coupled engine had the advantage of adhesion, as might be expected, and thirty-five more similar 4—4—0s were accordingly built. At this time the Midi enjoyed excellent relations with the Nord and in 1893 it ordered fourteen compound 4—4—0 express engines which, except for certain standard Midi fittings, were identical with Nord No. 2121 and which became the Midi class 1701. The first two had a fairly short smokebox like the first two Nord engines, but the remainder had the longer smokebox fitted to the subsequent Nord 4—4—0s Nos. 2123–2157, which was intended to reduce the amount of red hot cinders expelled from the chimney when working hard. This was particularly important on the Midi on account of the fire danger in the flat country of the Landes in hot dry weather. The Midi engines began to come into service in 1894 and were put on to the hardest turns, including the "Sud Express" and some of the Bordeaux-Toulouse-Marseilles *rapides*. Nevertheless, although they gave good results and were more powerful and economical than their predecessors, the 1601 class 2—4—0s of 1885, they had little reserve of power with the heavier trains of the Midi, due partly to the low-grade fuel used on that railway. As a result their performance on express services never approached that of the Nord engines which burnt much better coal and could therefore sustain higher power outputs.

However, the Midi were sufficiently impressed to order from the Société Alsacienne 34 similar, though rather more powerful engines. The Alsace Company designed and built these in 1895–1901 and the Midi numbered them 1751–1784. The last ten had a longer smokebox in place of the double spark arresting grid of the earlier engines of the class. The 1751 class displaced the 1701s from the express trains, the latter being relegated to the haulage of slower passenger and fast goods trains. The 1751s had been designed to meet a need for 200-ton trains to be worked at a running speed of 62 mph and 300-ton trains at 50 mph, and they fulfilled this aim so satisfactorily that one of them was tried in 1897 on both the Est and Belgian State Railways. On the Est No. 1760 worked express, goods, and suburban services, with such success that the Company decided to build twenty-four for their own use; these, the 2409 class, were virtually the same as the Midi engines, though a little more powerful. In addition, the Ouest Railway, after carrying out trials between two four-cylinder compounds built in 1894 and their standard two-cylinder simples, had decided that the compound system was superior and ordered sixty engines, Nos. 503–562, identical with this new Midi class. In the meantime the Nord in 1896 purchased from the Société Alsacienne three new 4—4—0s which were very similar to the Midi 1751 class and were sufficiently pleased to order twenty more in 1897, the whole being numbered 2158–2180.

Observing the wide popularity of these compounds, the Paris-Orléans Railway now decided that they too should have du Bousquet de Glehn type locomotives and their Nos. 1–25 of 1899–1900 were nearly the same as the Midi engines. They were put immediately on to the *rapides* and express trains on the Bordeaux and Nantes main lines. However, at that time the excellent Paris-Orleans 2—4—2 simple expansion engines designed by M. Victor Forquenot were amongst the best express locomotives in France; they were also extremely numerous, for between 1876 and 1894 a total of 397 were built in two main classes. With their polished brass-jacketed boilers, outside cylinders and valve chests, and overhanging front end, they looked extremely picturesque and somewhat archaic, but the new compounds could scarcely better their performance except at starting and on the steeper gradients.

In truth these early du Bousquet de Glehn compounds suffered from a relatively restricted steam circuit, so that the running of the engines was rather sluggish at high speeds and, in spite of their much higher boiler pressure, they were unable to pull at speed a weight which, as compared with the 2—4—2s, their nominal power suggested.

The great PLM also built four-cylinder compounds at an early date, for in 1888 they put into service six remarkable four-cylinder compound locomotives, of which two were 2—4—2 passenger, two 0—8—0 mixed traffic, and two 0—8—0 goods. On these the inside high pressure and outside low pressure cylinders drove different axles. In 1892 M. A. Henry of the PLM produced three new express passenger engines which were generally based on the 1888 compounds but with the high pressure cylinders outside and the low pressure inside the frames. Increased power at starting was obtained by admitting boiler steam at reduced pressure to the intermediate receiver, and thence to the low pressure cylinders, where it augmented the pressure of the steam from the high pressure cylinders. The valves of the high pressure and low pressure cylinders were controlled from a single reversing wheel. These engines introduced a new development in that they were fitted with Serve tubes, which had internal ribes to give increased heating surface and which had been the subject of trials on the PLM between 1885 and 1890. Because they increased the heat transfer from the hot gases these tubes could be shortened from the normal length of plain tubes by from three to four feet, with appreciable lightening of the locomotive.

Two of Henry's engines were 4—4—0s but the third was a 2—4—0, showing the still existing prejudice against the leading bogie, though this in fact was one of the greatest advances in express locomotive design. In 1894 the PLM built the first of their forty (Nos. C21–60) highly successful 'wind-cutting' engines; a four-cylinder compound 4—4—0 with a wedge-shaped front to smokebox and chimney and very similar in design to the 1892 engines. This interesting precursor to external streamlining was intended to reduce the resistance against trains exerted by the great *mistral* winds of the Rhône valley.

Superheated steam made its appearance in 1898 when a 4—4—0 simple expansion engine with two outside cylinders, designed by Schmidt and built by Borsig, entered service on the Prussian State Railways. It was immediately apparent that something revolutionary had arrived on the railway because the engine showed an economy over simple expansion engines, using saturated steam, of 30 per cent in water and 20 per cent in coal. A similar engine was shown two years later at the Paris Exhibition of 1900. This superheater was of the smokebox pattern, but Schmidt also designed the earlier superheater with elements housed in the flue tubes, which was fitted for the first time by Flamme in 1901 on the Belgian State Railways.

Perhaps the first engine of real fame in the twentieth century was the Atlantic express locomotive designed jointly by du Bousquet and de Glehn for the Nord, and using the latter's compound system, which was shown at the Paris Exhibition of 1900.[1] The performances recorded

1. Appendix B.1

by locomotives of this type were remarkable. In 1902, for instance, No. 2655, hauling a train of 250 tons, covered the 184.4 miles from Paris to Calais at an average speed of 64.2mph. From 1911 all of them (Nos. 2641–2675) were superheated, the chassis was strengthened, and larger high pressure cylinders with piston valves replaced the previous cylinders with slide valves. After this reconstruction they continued to haul the fastest trains for another 25 years.

In 1901, to cope with heavier trains, the PO ordered some of these Atlantics, but rather larger than those of the Nord with 12 per cent more grate area and 13 per cent more power.[2] The first of these, No. 3001, pulled a test train of 18 four-wheel vans up a gradient of 1/500 at a sustained speed of 70mph. The recorded indicated, or cylinder, horse power was 1,800. Unlike those of the Nord, these PO engines were never superheated. From 1901 the Midi purchased thirty du Bousquet de Glehn Atlantics of similar dimensions to those of the Nord, except that the last fourteen had larger fireboxes and grates to compensate for the lower grade fuel burnt. In 1905 the Etat, too, bought ten Atlantics, which were practically identical with those of the PO, for use on the difficult line from Paris to Bordeaux via Chartres, Saumur, Niort, and Saintes. (One of the admirable features of French railway practice has been the readiness, even anxiety, of administrations to acquire locomotives designed for or by another company if they promised better results than those of their own.)

The Great Western Railway of England, at the instance of G. J. Churchward, its Chief Mechanical Engineer, bought one of the Nord type of Atlantics and two of the larger variety built for the PO. The influence of these engines in Great Britain was remarkable. Churchward adopted the same arrangement of cylinders with dividing drive for his four-cylinder engines, and it was retained by the Great Western for all four-cylinder express locomotives during the whole of its independent existence; in addition Sir William Stanier took the arrangement with him to the LMS for his first Pacifics, and these engines followed the du Bousquet de Glehn pattern even more closely because they had four sets of valve gear. The du Bousquet de Glehn bogie had an even wider application, for it became a standard fitting on the Great Western, the LMS, and British Railways. But Churchward did not adopt compounding. There were probably two reasons for this: firstly, the steam circuit on his locomotives was better than that of the French Atlantics, off-setting the theoretical advantages of compounding, so that engines with his simple expansion system nearly equalled them in efficiency; and secondly, the French engines needed the additional workshop training that French drivers received if the best was to be got out of

2. Appendix B.1

them. Nor did Churchward retain the Atlantic wheel arrangement because for the severe gradients west of Taunton he preferred the extra adhesion that could be obtained from a 4—6—0.

It is a pity that Churchward did not acquire the next du Bousquet express locomotive design for this might have persuaded him to build compounds of his own. In 1907 M. Gaston du Bousquet built his famous 4—6—0s of the series 3513–3537,[3] which were intended to haul the heavy express trains for which the adhesion of the Atlantics was insufficient. At that time engineering work was being carried out on the Nord to permit axle loads of 18 tons, but the existing limit allowed only 17 tons. In order to keep the weight of the new engines down to the permissible loading the coupled wheels would have to be of small diameter and the boiler no heavier than that of the Atlantics. It was decided therefore to use the Atlantic boiler and the cylinders and wheels of the existing 4—6—0 mixed traffic engines. To compensate for the small coupled wheels, M. du Bousquet planned to improve the steam circuit by increasing the cross-sectional area of the steam passages by 25 per cent through the high pressure cylinders and 30 per cent through the low pressure cylinders. The results were astounding. The new 4—6—0s could exert the same tractive effort at 75mph as their mixed traffic predecessors at 60mph, and they could run just as fast as the Atlantics, which had 6ft 8½in coupled wheels.

The next series of these engines, Nos. 3538–3662, built from 1911 onwards, were superheated, and the earlier engines were also superheated when they came in for general overall. In about 1940 the standard Nord mobile cone exhaust was replaced by the Lemaître pattern and the wider diameter of the chimney altered the appearance of the engines. It was these 4—6—0s that might have caused Churchward to have had second thoughts on compounding if only he had tried them; for, with their much smaller wheels, they could have undertaken the duties of the Great Western 'Stars' with greater economy. As it was, the remarkable results obtained by increasing the cross-sectional area of the steam passages, unnoticed by the majority of engineers, struck the perceptive genius of the young Chapelon.

In the meantime the PO had designed for heavy expresses, particularly on the severely graded Toulouse line, a 4—6—0 with boilers and cylinders identical to those of the Atlantics but with smaller driving wheels.[4] It was somewhat similar to the P7 locomotives put into service on the Alsace Lorraine Railway in 1902, though a little more powerful. These two classes, the 3000 class Atlantics and the 4000 class 4—6—0s, were at the time the most powerful express locomotives in France and

3. Appendix B.2
4. Appendix B.3

were very successful. In 1904 M. T. Laurent, an Engineer-in-Chief of the PO under M. Solacroup, applied this standard boiler to a new 5000 class of 2—8—0 four-cylinder compound[5] goods engines, which were derived from the Midi 4001 class 2—8—0s of 1901.[6]

When in 1907 the first Pacifics were built for the PO—the first Pacifics indeed in Europe—the advantages of superheating were still being discussed and they, like most other express locomotives of the time, were not superheated. They had been ordered because of the increasing weight of the trains; for whilst the Atlantics and 4—6—0s, working respectively on easy and heavily graded routes, had been doing well, they were having difficulty in keeping time with trains that were much heavier than those for which they had been designed. It was clear that new engines would need more adhesion and greater boiler power and the Company decided that the natural successor to an Atlantic was a Pacific. But because the long heavy gradients of the Toulouse line needed greater tractive effort than the easier routes, two classes of Pacifics were chosen, one with 6ft 0¾in[7] coupled wheels and the other with 6ft 4¾in.[8] These two classes were designated respectively 4500 and 3500. For heavy goods work a new 6000 class of 2—10—0s[9] was ordered to replace the 2—8—0s. All three classes were to be de Glehn compounds with independent Walschaerts valve gear for the high pressure and low pressure cylinders. But the normal position of the cylinders was reversed on the 2—10—0, the high pressure being inside and the low pressure outside. The firebox on all these engines was of the Belpaire pattern with trapezoidal grate, which was wide at the rear and narrow at the front, and which had been designed by the Société Alsacienne de Constructions Mécaniques in 1906 especially for these PO Pacifics. It was extremely successful, combining, as it did, the advantages of the deep firebox with the increased area of the wide but without lengthening the grate.

The 4500 class, the first of the two types of PO Pacifics, began to enter service in 1907; whilst the 3500 class were working their first trains in 1909. The smooth lines of these handsome engines were more British-looking than French, and when in 1909 they were given capped chimneys they were even more British in appearance. It is of some interest that G. J. Churchward's solitary Pacific, *The Great Bear*,[10] was built in 1908, and one wonders if the publicity that heralded her advent had any influence on French chimney design. It is likely that with Churchward's steam circuit the Great Western engine was better than either of the Paris-Orléans types as originally built. Nevertheless, in that they did the work required of them, the PO Pacifics were success-

5. Appendix B.5   7. Appendix B.6   9. Appendix B.8
6. Appendix B.4   8. Appendix B.7   10. Appendix B.9

ful engines and the Company's express motive power was now amongst the best in Europe. From 1911 new Pacifics of both classes were super-heated.

The PO 4500 class Pacifics heralded an era in this type of locomotive on European railways. They were only just the first because the Baden State Railways produced their IVf class superheated Pacifics only three months later. Within a few years Pacifics were being built for the Ouest, the Midi, the Etat, the Nord, and the PLM, of which the Etat and Midi engines were based on those of the PO. But no British railway followed suit, and Churchward's *The Great Bear* was destined to remain the only example in Great Britain until the construction in 1922 of Raven's and Gresley's Pacifics for the North Eastern and Great Northern Railways respectively.

In 1910 the first Baltic, or 4—6—4, type locomotives were designed for the Nord by M. du Bousquet,[11] but unfortunately this great engineer died two months before the first of these two four-cylinder compound engines was completed. Whilst one of them was built with a wide rectangular grate, the other at first had a water tube firebox; but in 1913 it was given the same pattern as its sister engine because the water tube arrangement needed special maintenance and there was no overall economy to justify the extra cost. The steam circuit of these engines had been well designed, but they were very much in advance of their time with many consequent 'teething' troubles. This perhaps explains why development was prematurely abandoned; for the express loco-motives built in 1912 were Pacifics with a narrow firebox and a grate area of only 34·7sq ft, as compared with the 46·1sq ft of the Baltics.

These Nord Pacifics of the 3.1151[12] class were almost copies of those built in 1909 for the Alsace Lorraine Railways by the Société Alsacienne. They were four-cylinder du Bousquet de Glehn compounds, and were so successful that the next batch of Pacifics, the 3.1200[13] class designed for the Nord in 1914 under M. Asselin, followed the same general principles but with improved steam circuit. Owing to the war these engines were not put into service until 1923, and by then some modifica-tions had been incorporated. They performed extremely well on sche-dules demanding 60mph and over with trains of 550, 600 and even 650 tons, developing maximum outputs of 2,700hp as compared with the 1,900hp of the earlier Nord Pacifics.

The PLM acquired its first two Pacifics[14] in 1909, one of them a four-cylinder compound using saturated steam with the de Glehn cylinder arrangement, and the other a four-cylinder simple expansion with a Schmidt superheater. Boiler pressure on the compound was

11. Appendix B.10   13. Appendix B.12
12. Appendix B.11   14. Appendix B.13

232lbs per sq in and on the simple 174lb per sq in. The results were interesting. On trial the superheated simple expansion engine showed economies in combustion of 16 per cent as compared with the saturated compound (though as the latter was consuming far more than normal the figure was more truly 10 per cent), and 70 more of the simple expansion engines were accordingly built. On the other hand the compound had shown itself to be an easier engine to drive, and so in 1911 20 new compounds were built, but these were superheated. Comparative results were now in favour of the superheated compounds, for they were more economical than the superheated simples, as well as being more powerful. Thinking that the lower pressure of 174lbs was handicapping the simples, the PLM in 1912 built some four-cylinder simple expansion engines with 203lbs pressure. Although better than the earlier simple Pacifics, they were still inferior to the super-heated compounds by 11·5 per cent. No more simple expansion engines were therefore built and after the First World War all the existing ones were converted to compounds. All engines kept their original boiler pressure, but the rebuilding of the simple engines as compounds resulted in average fuel savings of about 10 per cent. All future PLM Pacifics were therefore compounds. The advantages of superheating, however, were by this time clear and on the PO, for instance, all Pacifics built from 1910 onwards were superheated.

Meanwhile, whilst all this intensely interesting development was going on in the locomotive world, the young André Chapelon was watching it, and thinking, and forming opinions. He was particularly interested in the work of Gaston du Bousquet on the Nord and G. J. Churchward on the Great Western—two great engineers who between them laid the foundations of efficient locomotive performance.

In July 1909 Chapelon took the 1st Part of his *Bachelier* examination, in Latin and the Sciences, and passed with the comment *Assez-Bien*. In July 1910 he passed in Elementary Mathematics in the 2nd Part. There now followed preparations at the *Ecole Centrale* as a pupil in Special Mathematics, and he was admitted to the School after his success in the examination of June 1913.

Chapelon was now subject to the Military Law of 1905 which provided for an engagement of five years for pupils at the *Grandes Ecoles*. Of these five years, two years were spent in military service and three years in study. The two years' military service could be taken either together, after leaving the School, or else one year could be undertaken before entering the School and the other year after leaving. Of the two years one was spent as an Artillery Officer Cadet and one year as a Second-Lieutenant in the Artillery, before becoming an officer of the Reserve. Chapelon chose the second method and in October 1913 he joined the 6th Fortress Artillery Regiment at Toul, which was then one of the French frontier fortresses. There, with six others, he was posted to the platoon of Reserve Officer Cadets from the *Grandes Ecoles*.

War broke out in the following August and Chapelon's hopes of returning to the *Ecole Centrale* faded into an indefinite future. On September 2nd 1914 the cadets were commissioned as Second-Lieutenants of the Reserve in the same Regiment and were posted to the Fire Control Section of Toul Fortress. Before joining for duty, however, they had to attend a short course in topography and artillery survey.

Chapelon was allocated to the south-western sector of the fortress and was directed by the staff to determine the coordinates of the various batteries and works, in order that the records of the Governor of the Fortress might be brought up to date. He was also ordered at the same time to undertake the instruction of NCOs selected to direct the fire of the batteries to which they belonged.

Chapelon profited by the proximity of the Technical Section of the Toul Fortress Artillery to make use of its comprehensive records and to study the regulations for fire control. From the knowledge thus acquired he joined with a friend who was commanding a battery of two 75-mm anti-aircraft guns to compile calculating tables which, as compared with the existing unsuitable fire tables, resulted in increased speed and precision of fire.

Chapelon was not however left long at Toul. He had made his mark quickly as a very promising officer and in December 1914 he was appointed staff officer to the commander of the 16th Infantry Division Heavy Artillery. There his commanding officer made him responsible for fire observation, for the flash spotting sections, for plotting batteries and observation posts, and for the artillery telephone network. Not only did he carry out this comprehensive task with great efficiency, but for gallantry during the operation of April 22 1915 at the '*Tête à Vache*' near St. Mihiel he was awarded a citation in the 16th Divisional Orders of May 6th 1915.

Soon after these operations some of the Heavy Artillery was reorganised. The two batteries of 155-mm guns forming the 1st Group of Heavy Artillery of the 61st Artillery Regiment became the nucleus of the 106th Regiment, which was placed under the command of the old Commander Heavy Artillery 16th Division. The mounted personnel came from the 61st Regiment, but the rest of the men and the additional equipment were provided by the 6th Fortress Artillery Regiment at Toul. Chapelon was posted to this new regiment and appointed Fire Control Officer.

In September 1915 the 106th Regiment took part in the Champagne offensive as part of the artillery of the XIV Corps. By this time Chapelon was the Lieutenant of one of the batteries. After taking part in other operations in Champagne, he volunteered at the beginning of 1916 for the not very popular job of observer in captive balloons. After attending a course for aerial observers at Mailly, he was appointed to a balloon section and was an artillery observer in June and July 1916 during the offensive on the Somme. This experience suggested to him a method of fire control by a single balloon observer. The classic method of ground observation was to bracket the target by long and short shots and for the observer to correct the fire for range. This was not a practicable method for a single balloon observer owing to the angle from which he observed, and who saw shots as a deviation from the target rather than as a short or over. By Chapelon's method the battery did not attempt to bracket and he announced shots as falling to the right or left of the target from the position of the observer. The battery corrected in relation to the position of the observer and the line of fire. As Chapelon was able to demonstrate later, this system was a great improvement on previous practice. It was necessary, of course, that the angle formed by the lines observer-target and battery-target should be sufficiently large; if it was not the ordinary bracketing method was used.

After spending more than sixteen hours a day in a balloon basket during this intensive battle, Chapelon was worn out. He was awarded another citation, this time in the Orders of the Aeronautical Section of the Sixth Army. He then rejoined the 106th Heavy Artillery Regiment as a staff officer to the Lieutenant-Colonel commanding, who was then Chief of the South-West Sector of the Fortress of Verdun on matters affecting heavy artillery. Here Chapelon used his off-duty time in writing a paper setting out, with examples, his method of fire control by unilateral observation. His Colonel submitted his treatise to the Artillery Improvement Centre. It was examined there by the mathematician Emile Borel, who could find no fault in the system. A practical demonstration was then given at the Artillery Training Centre at Mailly camp. During a practice carried out with 75-mm guns the average point of impact with 50 shots practically coincided with the target. As a result Chapelon's new system was embodied in Artillery Regulations.

In January 1917 Chapelon was appointed to the Fire Planning Section of the Third Army as Chief of the Topographical Department. Here he was given the task of reconstituting the artillery survey network; for the old one had been entirely displaced by the move forward of the Army when the Germans retreated to the Hindenberg Line. Chapelon's new survey was built up on a base of 80 kilometres in length, following the front line but at a standard distance in rear of it.

Into the resulting network were tied all the Third Army's batteries, observation posts, and sound and flash spotting sections to a depth of some 60 kilometres. Chapelon constructed his system by sun observation and he used ruined bell towers for most of the ground fixes. The centre of the whole network was the bell tower of St. Quentin Cathedral. When he had finished there was an error of only about one metre from the true coordinates.

At the beginning of 1918 Chapelon was appointed an Instructor at the School of Officer Observers, but when the German offensive started towards the end of March he was recalled to the Fire Planning Section of the Third Army.

In spite of the deep thrusts of the German attacks, and the consequent fluidity of the front, Chapelon's survey, because it was oriented by the sun, could be adapted to the moving battle and he was able to provide bearing points for the Army's heavy artillery fire plan to batteries, observers, and plotting sections. The resulting effectiveness of the heavy artillery played a notable part in the slowing and halting of the German advance on the Third Army's front.

In April 1919 André Chapelon removed his horizon blue uniform for the last time and rejoined the *Ecole Centrale* more than five years after the planned date. However, the course for returning pupils was fixed at two years instead of three, and early in 1921 he graduated as *Ingenieur des Arts et Manufactures*. He then joined the Rolling Stock and Motive Power section of the Paris-Lyon-Méditerranée Railway as a probationer.

2

Rocket Centenary

CHAPELON gained much valuable knowledge in the Rolling Stock and Motive Power section of the PLM. The instructor under whom he was placed, M. Etienne Tribolet, was a senior mechanical inspector at the Lyon-Mouche depot, and he arranged that Chapelon should have practical experience with most of the various classes of locomotive in the district of both old and recent manufacture.

During the time that he spent with the PLM the aspect of the railway's operation which impressed André Chapelon most unfavourably was the manner in which the engines were driven; particularly the four-cylinder simple expansion Pacifics of the 6100 class. The drivers normally ran their engines with 50 per cent cut-off and partly opened regulator; a practice which had the appalling result of reducing a 170lbs per sq in boiler pressure to about 57lbs per sq in in the cylinders. It was a practice which was in contravention of all the convictions that Chapelon had reached during his studies at the *Ecole Centrale*, and it was totally opposed to the principles annunciated by the founder of the science of thermo-dynamics, the eminent Frenchman Nicholas Sadi Carnot (1796–1832). Carnot's teaching had had a very great influence on Chapelon's thought, and the realisation that a great railway company should be so ignorant of the elementary economics of locomotive operation led him in later years to place emphatic importance on using full boiler pressure and eliminating throttling throughout the steam circuit.

Tribolet was very impressed with Chapelon's abilities. In a letter to him on April 14th 1923 he said: ". . . Immediately I return I will write to you to give you the necessary information and I can assure you in advance that all the criticisms that you have made in your interesting letter are true . . . and I must always say, as regards you M. Chapelon, that you interest yourself to the highest degree in the design of the steam locomotive."

Because he had been born and brought up on it, Chapelon regarded the PLM as his native railway. Indeed, when he first mounted the footplate in 1903, it was on one of the picturesque PLM 0—8—0 locomotives of the 4000 class. But after a short time it was apparent that there were few openings for promotion and little scope for a disciple of Carnot. In the autumn of 1924, therefore, he left locomotive work altogether and joined the *Société Industrielle des Telephones* on satisfactory terms. Here his ability was so marked that he became Assistant Manager the following year. But he was not happy in his work because, as he says, he suffered from 'steam locomotive nostalgia'. His professor of thermodynamics at the *Ecole Centrale* had been M. Louis Lacoin, who had formed a high opinion of Chapelon's technical ability and who was well acquainted with his distinguished war service as an officer of the Heavy Artillery. Louis Lacoin was a cousin of M. Maurice Lacoin, Engineer-in-Chief of Rolling Stock and Motive Power on the Paris-Orléans Railway, and thanks to the former's help Chapelon was appointed on January 12th 1925 to the Research and Development Section of the PO.

It was an appointment for which he was particularly well fitted because he had made an intensive study of the steam locomotive for years and had read practically every book and paper of importance that dealt with it. As a result of this study he had formed his own opinion on the improvements that were needed before he had even joined the PLM.

On the PO Chapelon came under the orders of a most remarkable engineer, M. Paul Billet, who had created the Research and Development Section as an adjunct of the Design Office, which he had accused of being too absorbed by work in connection with existing equipment. At his direction Chapelon was put on to work in connection with trials and charged particularly with the improvement of the exhaust systems of the Pacific and other locomotives.

For the PO was not satisfied with the performance of its impressive and good-looking compound Pacifics. If it had not been for the admirable Atlantics, which had been copied from those of the Nord, it is probable that the Pacifics would have been accepted as satisfactory because they performed as well as those of most other railways. But in the light of the oustanding performance of the Atlantics it was clear that design had not kept pace with dimensions. Indicator diagrams of cylinder performance showed throttling of the steam at admission to the cylinders, high back pressure at the exhaust, and a considerable drop of pressure in the intermediate receiver between high pressure and low pressure cylinders—all in much greater degree than on the Atlantics. Superheating increased the power of the Pacifics by at least 20 per cent, but even then they could not develop more than 2,000 indicated horse power, whilst the Atlantics could attain a peak of 1,600ihp, or even 1,900, and they were not superheated. The problem was to get engines of sufficient power to haul the heavier postwar trains at the express schedules of 1914. The normal solution would have been to build new express engines of modern design, but this would have been expensive, and because the decision had already been taken to electrify the PO main lines new steam locomotives could expect only a short life. It was decided therefore to see what could be done to improve existing stock.

This is not a technical work, but in order to understand what Chapelon was engaged on and to appreciate what he achieved, it would be advisable for the benefit of non-technical readers to try and outline in simple terms the elements of draughting in a steam loco-motive. As most people know, the power of an engine depends in the first place on its ability to boil water, and the bigger the boiler the larger should be the supply of steam. Again, it is elementary knowledge that the bigger and hotter the fire the quicker will the water boil. But to produce a big and hot fire two things are necessary, a large enough grate and an adequate draught. In fact, provided that the boiler is well designed, the heating surface is of less importance than the size of the grate. But a large grate is itself ineffective unless there is a draught sufficient to draw the hot gases through the tubes to boil the water. Much therefore depends on the arrangements by which the exhaust from the cylinders is used to provide the draught. It is easy enough to produce a fierce draught by narrowing the blast pipe exhaust nozzle to restrict the exit of the steam, but this will cause a high back pressure on the pistons and so hinder the steam in the performance of its work and reduce the power of the engine. It is necessary, indeed, to arrange that the steam has as free and unobstructed a flow as possible from the boiler, into and out of the cylinders, through the exhaust blast pipe nozzle, and out through the chimney into the open air, if the engine is to develop its maximum power. The design of the exhaust in a steam locomotive is therefore of the greatest importance; it is primarily a matter of arriving at the best compromise, that is the lowest possible back pressure combined with the maximum possible draught. And this latter entails so mixing the exhaust steam with the gases of combus-tion that they are expelled from the chimney at the same speed.

Owing to the limit imposed by the loading gauge the chimney of a large locomotive is necessarily very short. Ideally a chimney should have a height equal to three times its narrowest diameter; but it is generally less, even though its extension downwards into the smokebox may compensate for the lack of external height. Research having demonstrated that the chimneys in general use were inadequate for big and powerful locomotives, many large engines were provided with chimneys of almost double the normal diameter. But, because this reduced the height-to-width ratio, the benefits, with the short chim-neys which large boiler barrels dictated, were doubtful. To try and remedy this M. Legein of the Belgian State Railways achieved considerable success in 1925 with double chimneys.

Blast pipe nozzles may be fixed or variable, the latter having a mechanism that permits the size of the orifice to be varied. The former are generally preferred because the exhaust of a steam locomotive has the property of automatically adapting the draught to the requirement. As many drivers of steam locomotives know, ordinary exhausts can be improved by placing a bar across the middle of the blast pipe, thus dividing the steam into two jets; a practice viewed with marked disfavour by some locomotive administrations because it increases the back pressure on the pistons.

The PLM used a variable exhaust of a pattern known as 'trefoil'. It had a central core, which could be moved up or down, and three openings to steam of different diameters, of which the one in use depended on the height to which the core had been raised. It was a great improvement on the ordinary blastpipe which it replaced, for engines fitted with it could haul 14 per cent greater loads. By the middle of 1925 2,400 PLM locomotives and from 300 to 600 on other French railways had the trefoil exhaust.

On some locomotives there is mounted a sleeve of large diameter between the blastpipe and the chimney with a bell-shaped opening at the bottom, which is known as a 'petticoat'. The object of this piece is to draw a large part of the hot gases from the boiler tubes through it and mix them with the steam to produce a flow at the same speed before exhausting through the chimney. This results in an improved draught and an even flow through the boiler tubes.

To operate efficiently an exhaust assembly requires very precise dimensions, and the difficulty of establishing these is shown by the number of different types that were designed and used. M. Chapelon speaks highly of the 'Vortex' blastpipe which was designed by William Adams in 1885 and fitted not only to more than 500 engines of the London & South Western Railway but also to many locomotives on the Nord and Ouest Railways. He comments that perhaps it did not receive sufficient attention at the time. It had an outer annular orifice for steam and an internal circular opening for the gases; the latter forming the upper portion of a bell-mouthed scoop which was open to the bottom rows of boiler tubes.

A notable exhaust gas and steam device was invented by a Finnish engineer named Kylälä in 1919; and from this M. Chapelon derived his Kylchap (KC) exhaust in 1926. This was so designed as to produce an adequate draught over the whole smokebox and to mix the gases so well with the exhaust steam that the mixture might be expelled with the minimum of effort. From the top of the exhaust standpipe, leading from the cylinders, the exhaust steam passed through a conical blast pipe nozzle fitted with four radial wedge-shaped inserts. These inserts divided the steam into four jets which, drawing some of the hot gases with them, passed into the four lobes of the Kylälä spreader which was mounted a short distance above. This division of the exhaust steam into four jets improved still further the entrainment of the hot gases above the exit from these lobes where more of the hot gases circulated; the mixture then being carried upwards through a petticoat to a final mixing with the remainder of the gases and out through the chimney.

The pattern of Kylchap described above was designated 1K/1C. In a variant, the 1K/T, a downward extension of the chimney, swelling into a trumpet shape, replaced the intermediate petticoat.

On very large locomotives there is not sufficient height within the loading gauge to allow proper proportions to the draughting assembly. For these, two complete Kylchap exhausts are usually provided together with two chimneys placed one behind the other, and on the most powerful locomotives there are three of such assemblies.

In 1926 trials of the Kylchap exhaust were carried out on the compound Pacifics of the 4500 and 3500 classes, the simple expansion Pacifics of the 3591 class, and other large PO locomotives. The results were most encouraging, for there was a significant improvement in steaming and a reduction of back pressure. On Pacific No. 4597 there was such an increase in draught that the exhaust pipe had to be so widened that the back pressure was reduced by 41 per cent. Carnot's principles were verified by the performance of the same engine, for on trial with the regulator wide open there was a pressure of 224lbs per sq in, instead of the previous figure of 112lbs, and this was with cut-offs of 40 per cent HP and 60 per cent LP, as compared with the previous 60 per cent HP and 70 per cent LP. In addition the engine showed an economy in coal consumption of 16 per cent. Similar results were obtained with No. 4528 (which, unlike No. 4597, was unsuperheated) and with the simple expansion superheated Pacific No. 3638.[1]

It was apparent to Chapelon that even better results could be obtained by increasing the cross-sectional area of the steam passages and, to be on the safe side, he considered that it would be advisable to double it. At the same time he would eliminate the sharp bends in the steam pipes and increase the volume of the steam chests. By these measures he would reduce the losses from throttling which were occurring in the steam circuit from the regulator through to the HP and LP cylinders.

It is rather strange that the first to appreciate the importance of large steam passages was that eminent British locomotive engineer Thomas

1. Appendix B.14

Russell Crampton, whose first two engines were built in 1846. The most notable feature of Crampton's locomotives was the single pair of driving wheels behind the firebox with four to six small carrying wheels in front. Crampton's object was to obtain a large heating surface combined with a low centre of gravity; but in Great Britain, at any rate, no locomotive engineer, not even that keen student of locomotive affairs E. L. Ahrons, seems to have noted the easy steam flow that did so much to make the Crampton engines the success they were in France (for in England their popularity was short). It was fifty years before the next advance. In 1897 the Nord Company carried out experiments with express locomotive No. 2158, as a result of which steam circuit proportions were established which ensured the success of the Atlantics. These included large steam chests to regulate the flow of steam between boiler and cylinders and so lessen the losses from fluctuations in pressure due to throttling. This was another discovery that was insufficiently appreciated by most engineers, but it had been fully noted by Chapelon who deduced that to obtain the correct proportions in the LP steam chests of the PO Pacifics it would be necessary to quadruple them in size to equal approximately the volume of the cylinders. The principle behind the Nord experiments was not indeed new for, as Chapelon was well aware, it had been annunciated by D. K. Clark (later Locomotive Superintendent of the Great North of Scotland Railway) in his *Railway Machinery* of as long ago as 1850; but it had long since been forgotten by the majority of locomotive engineers.

Chapelon's proposed improvements to the exhaust and steam circuits should (according to a theoretical diagram), with a 40 per cent cut-off in the HP cylinders and at a speed of 60mph, result in an increase in the indicated horse power of 1,936 (obtained with an unmodified engine) to 2,406; that is, a gain of 25 per cent in both power and efficiency.

However, there was more to come. Chapelon had measured the temperature in the intermediate receiver of one of the superheated locomotives and had found that the degree of superheat in the LP cylinders was practically nil. It was evident therefore that if the condensation in the LP group could be eliminated there would be a still further gain in the efficiency of the engines. The improvement in economy of the superheated over the original saturated engines was about 20 per cent, and this was with 300 deg C (572deg F) of superheat; but the gain was practically entirely in the high pressure cylinders. If the low pressure cylinders could be made to contribute their proper share it seemed reasonable to anticipate a further 10 per cent. Chapelon estimated that to obtain such a result it would be necessary to raise the temperature of the superheat by 100deg C (180deg F) at the admission to the HP cylinders. The provision of oil and castings suitable for this higher temperature presented a potential problem, but Chapelon was able to solve it satisfactorily.

From these calculations André Chapelon now assessed the overall improvement that could be expected from a Pacific engine rebuilt in accordance with the principles he had established.[2] Taking the average ihp of a superheated Pacific locomotive of the large-wheeled 3500 class running at high speed to be 1,850, he reckoned that his proposed improvements in the steam circuit would raise the ihp by 20 per cent to 2,200, and that the increase in superheat should raise it a further 10 per cent to 2,400. On top of this the improved draughting with the Kylchap exhaust should increase the boiler output by 25 per cent above its previous limit and so raise the ihp to 3,000.

Put simply like this, the sheer brilliance of the argument is rather obscured. It is sufficient to say that no previous locomotive engineer had reasoned on these lines. Chapelon, who is an extremely modest man, argues that he only followed in the footsteps of his predecessors and built on the work of such eminent engineers as Anatole Mallet of articulated compound fame, Henry of the PLM, du Bousquet of the Nord, G. J. Churchward of the Great Western, Nadal of the Etat, and Wilhelm Schmidt the superheater celebrity. In this he is at one with R. A. Riddles, who holds that all sound engineering progress builds on what has gone before. But the art, of course, lies in the ability to build; and the long years of Chapelon's thinking and study bore fruit in the greatest advance of all time in steam locomotive engineering.

As a result of Chapelon's argument and in the light of results obtained in the tests, it was decided in November 1926 to rebuild one of the 3500 class Pacifics completely. Because of the high superheat envisaged the locomotive chosen was one on which it had already been intended to try the Lentz poppet valve system, and for which arrangements had been made with Messrs. Paxman & Co. of London, licensees of the Lentz patent. Rotary cams were at first proposed, but it was eventually decided that it would be better to keep the existing Walschaerts valve gear and to actuate oscillating cams with it.

In May 1926 Chapelon received a letter from M. Louis Lacoin, in which he said, "My cousin Maurice Lacoin told me a few days ago how satisfied he is with you and your enthusiasm for work. I am telling you this to encourage you and to let you know what pleasure it gives me".

The first engine to be rebuilt was No. 3566 (which was about the worst of the whole class, and so bad that the enginemen nicknamed it

2. Appendix A

Cholera). It emerged from Tours Works in November 1929. This lengthy period between the decision to rebuild the locomotive and its completion was due to the dislocation caused by the unfortunate death of M. Billet and the retirement of M. Lacoin, who was succeeded by M. de Boysson. The main reason for this was that nobody believed in Chapelon's engine, the conception of which was considered to lie in the realm of fantasy rather than to merit consideration as a practical project. Ultimately Chapelon had to write a note to M. de Boysson drawing his attention to the great interest which had been taken in the rebuilding plan when it was originally approved. As a result de Boysson asked him for a full explanation of the whole project and at length agreed to its continuation.

As completed the rebuilt engine incorporated, in addition to the improvements mentioned above, an ACFI feed-water heater and a Nicholson thermic syphon; the purpose of this latter equipment being to improve the circulation of the water in the boiler and accelerate the increase in pressure after lighting up and after closing the regulator. A double Kylchap exhaust was fitted with two chimneys.[3] (It is of interest that the idea of two or more chimneys was first tried by Nozo and Geoffroy in 1860 on a Crampton engine of the Nord.)

No. 3566 ran her first trials on November 19th 1929, almost exactly a hundred years after the triumph of Stephenson's *Rocket* at Rainhill. The results obtained were remarkable. Chapelon's calculations were exactly fulfilled, for No. 3566 developed about 3,000ihp at a speed of between 75 and 80mph hauling a heavy train, and with an economy over the unrebuilt engines of 25 per cent at normal power outputs. The new locomotive sprang to immediate fame, not only in France but in most other countries of the Western world.

Extensive trials were carried out with No. 3566 on ordinary and special trains on the Paris-Bordeaux main line south of the end of the electrified section at Les Aubrais (near Orleans). On April 4th 1930 the engine covered the 70.6 miles from Poitiers to Angoulême with a train of 368 tons at a speed which remained absolutely constant at the legal limit of 75mph, irrespective of the gradient. On the engine was M. Edmond Epinay, who had just taken over from de Boysson as Chief of Rolling Stock and Motive Power, and who described the run as the most remarkable event of his career. It was this performance which in due course led to the timing of one hour between Poitiers and Angoulême which M. Epinay pressed on a reluctant Traffic Department. (His confidence was justified, for no driver ever lost time on this schedule.)

Another notable trial took place on March 24th 1931, when with a

3. Appendix B.12

457-ton train the run of 365 miles from Paris to Bordeaux was performed in 5 hours 48 minutes at the overall average speed of 62·5mph without exceeding the 74mph limit, and including the change from electric to steam traction at Les Aubrais. No. 3566 backed on to the train at Les Aubrais and then ran to Bordeaux (286 miles) in 4 hours 26 minutes, including a stop of 8 minutes at Poitiers. The run included average speeds of 65mph between Les Aubrais and Poitiers and 64·4mph between Poitiers and Bordeaux, in spite of numerous slacks impose by the permanent way department. The passengers on the train included representatives of other French railways, and on arrival at Bordeaux M. Marcel Bloch, Engineer-in-Chief of Rolling Stock and Workshops (under M. Epinay) said, "Chapelon you have certainly done something (*Vous avez fait quelque chose*)".

This run was undertaken to ascertain the practicability of a scheduled time of 5 hours 50 minutes between Paris and Bordeaux. It was clear that not only was this possible but with this power at the disposal of the engine other accelerations of between one hour and one and a half hours could be made between Paris and Bordeaux. M. Epinay, who had himself experienced such timings with trains often loaded to over 800 tons, insisted on them being put into effect as more engines became available. For in the light of the startling success of these trials it had already been decided to rebuild Pacifics No. 3501–20 of 1909 which were still using saturated steam. All were rebuilt at Tours in 1931–32 and were ready for the 1932 summer service. No. 3566 was now renumbered 3701 and the other engines became 3702–20 (though not consecutively according to their old numbers). There were slight differences from the original rebuild; the boiler pressure was raised from 232lbs to 246lbs per sq in, the Robinson superheater was replaced by the Houlet type which gave higher superheat, and there were other minor alterations. All these locomotives were allocated to Tours depot and worked heavy express trains and *rapides* between Les Aubrais and Bordeaux and between Tours and Nantes.

Trials on the western main line from Tours to Nantes and beyond had taken place in 1932. On March 12th No. 3701 took over a train from Paris to Redon (317 miles) at Les Aubrais. Departure was delayed owing to a faulty coach having to be detached from the train, reducing the load from 475 to 345 tons. Redon is an important junction, beyond Nantes, on the line to Brest. In spite of 4 stops and 15 slacks No. 3701 completed the journey at a speed which made the overall average from Paris 61·3mph. The average running speed between Les Aubrais and Redon was 78·8mph, with a specially authorised maximum for the trial of 84·3mph. M. Lancrenon, Engineer-in-Chief of Rolling

Stock and Motive Power on the Nord Railway, was on the train and it was as a result of this run that he decided to order 20 similar rebuilt engines from the RO and to have 28 others built new by private industry.

This decision by M. Lancrenon was confirmed by trials carried on the Nord later on in 1932. The locomotives participating were Chapelon Pacific No. 3715, a PLM 4—8—2, an Est 4—8—2, and a Nord 3.1250 class Pacific. It would have been difficult to collect more interesting engines for comparative tests, each supreme on its own railway and probably together regarded as the best that France had. The Nord was always on the lookout for more powerful and efficient locomotives to work their extremely sharply timed and heavy *rapides* and expresses. The Company's traffic manager operated on the apparently para-doxical principle that Nord trains were punctual because they were hard to work.

The Nord Pacific belonged to a class of 1931 which was a modified version of the 3.1200 series built in 1923.[3] These latter engines when new were some 30 per cent more powerful than any other French Pacifics and were aptly nicknamed "Superpacifics". Certain defects, however, resulted in costly maintenance and the modifications intro-duced in the 3.1250s were designed to rectify these. The Est 4—8—2 was one of a class built in 1925.[4] In 1928 the Etat Railway wanted to run their boat trains over the very difficult 231 miles between Paris and Cherbourg (with an intermediate stop) in $4\frac{1}{2}$ hours and to load them to 600 tons. As they had no engines that would do the job, the Etat arranged trials with a 3.1200 class Nord Pacific and one of the Est 4—8—2s. Its substantially larger grate and increased adhesion favoured the Est engine and the Etat accordingly ordered 40 of this type—a very considerable order, for the Est themselves only had 41. The PLM 4—8—2, No. 241.C.1,[5] was a solitary example which had been completed on December 30th 1930. It was a successor to the earlier 241.A class of 1925[6] (but with 6ft 6¾in coupled wheels instead of 5ft 11in) and the prototype of the later 241.P class built for the SNCF in 1948 (though these latter embodied many Chapelon-type modifications).

There was another interesting aspect of these engines in that, as Baron Gérard Vuillet has pointed out in his book *Railway Reminiscences in Three Continents*, they represented two schools of locomotive design. The main lines of the Est and the PLM mostly follow the valleys of the great rivers and are therefore routed in long sweeping curves. In consequence these railways always built their locomotives with rather thin frames so that they could flex to the curves. In addition, because

4. Appendix B.16   5. Appendix B.17   6. Appendix B.18

their gradients were long but not severe, short periods of high power working were not required of them. The main lines of the Nord and the PO, on the other hand, generally cut across the valleys and were characterised by a number of short steep climbs and consequent difficult starts from many of their stations. Their locomotives had thick frames and were strongly built to meet the heavy demands for power over their often switch-back routes.

On the footplate of No. 3715 were Head Driver Réné Gourault and Fireman Léonce Miot. The tests took place during the winter 1932–3 and entailed the haulage of special trains with frequent stops between Paris and Boulogne, firstly of 660 and later of 750 tons, and also the working of the "Golden Arrow" service between Paris and Calais with its load increased to 650 tons. As had been foreseen, the engines with eight-coupled wheels showed to advantage with trains of 750 tons making frequent stops, the Pacifics suffering from too little adhesion. Nevertheless, even with 750-ton trains No. 3715 put up a very good performance, returning from Boulogne in a time 5 minutes 39 seconds quicker than the PLM 4—8—2 and 16 seconds quicker than the Est engine. The Nord Pacific was unfortunately below the form for its class and was not therefore tried at all on the 750-ton trains. The Est 4—8—2 was not only inferior in power to the Chapelon Pacific but had the heaviest consumption of all the competing locomotives. Actually, three of these Est engines were tried, for first one and then another fractured those long slender frames on the gruelling Nord main line. The big PLM 4—8—2 produced the highest drawbar horse power but at the cost of twice the expenses in running maintenance as compared with the other competing locomotives. By far the best was Chapelon's Pacific. It had the lowest average consumption of coal and water and it had to its credit the finest of all the performances recorded by the competing engines, when it hauled the "Golden Arrow" over the summit of the 24·9 miles long Gannes bank (1/333–1/250) at 74·6mph. The Nord locomotive men were very impressed with its performance, particularly Locomotive Inspector Cugnet who was with Chapelon on the engine on this occasion. Cugnet had not been able to conceal his enthusiasm when he saw the train pass Gannes at this speed with 650 tons; the engine having its regulator fully open, cut-off at 60 per cent in the high and 58 per cent in the low pressure cylinders, pressure high, and water level held. (The same inspector was equally enthusiastic when invited a long time afterwards to the trials of No. 242.A.1 between Paris and Lille.) It was a great triumph for Chapelon and also for those devoted enthusiasts Gourault and Miot. (When he retired from the railway service Miot wrote a farewell letter to M. Chapelon in which he said how much he had earned the appreciation of firemen for the comfort that the Kylchap exhaust had brought them; it was a tribute that Chapelon valued as much as any he had received.) After these trials the Nord went ahead with its order for 20 Chapelon-type Pacifics from the PO, and in 1936–7 28 new ones were built by private firms.

For its own needs the PO rebuilt at Tours ten more engines which embodied still further improvements[7] and on trial one of these produced 3,700ihp and 3,400dbhp at 87·5mph on the Vitry test bank. As Chapelon says, these figures proved that he had succeeded in the aim of most designers of compound locomotives in getting as much work out of the LP as the HP cylinders. Eventually there were 102 of these locomotives, of which 31 were rebuilt for the PO, 23 were rebuilt for the Est, and 48 were rebuilt or built new for the Nord.

Having obtained such outstanding results from a complete rebuilding, it was decided to try a modified and cheaper improvement of those 3500 class Pacifics which had been superheated at the time of their construction and which had slightly larger cylinders. No. 3583 of this series, therefore, was fitted with a Kylchap exhaust, its original superheater was replaced by the Houlet type, and the slide valves of the LP cylinders were replaced by piston valves designed by M. Willoteaux (PO Chief of Design), with double admission and double exhaust, in order to get steam passages of a volume comparable to those obtained with poppet valves. The rebuilt engine showed such a marked improvement that 15 more were similarly modified during 1932 and put into service at the Limoges Depot to accelerate the night trains between Paris and Narbonne.[8] On this line, with long gradients of 1 in 100, it was now possible to cut the timings of these trains by from one hour to one and a half hours.

Soon after No. 3566 ran her first trials Chapelon enjoyed a singular triumph on another railway. In 1927 the *Societe Suisse pour la Construction de Machines* at Winterthur built a trial 2—6—2 tank locomotive with three simple expansion cylinders on the Stumpf system. The engine had a water-tube boiler with the very high pressure of 840lbs per sq in. The Central Office of Design (OCEM) had asked for this engine to be tried with brake locomotives on the Est Railway; however neither the constructors nor the OCEM could cure the very poor steaming of the locomotive. Chapelon was approached and he designed a Kylchap exhaust specially for it. On December 10th 1929 the engine was given its first test with the new exhaust. The trial run was from Chalons-sur-Marne to Reims, a hump-backed route starting with a steep climb from Chalons. To the astonishment of all the pressure not only did not drop during the initial acceleration but even rose to such an extent that there was much lifting of the pop safety valves during

7. Appendix B.15   8. Appendix B.19

the ascent. Chapelon could only express his feelings at this astounding result by a fervent thanksgiving for having the inspiration necessary for the solution of such an apparently hopeless case. On the arrival at Reims, Chapelon's feelings were shared so much by those present that the representative of the Winterthur Company could not stop himself from embracing the engineer who had saved his engine.

3

Eight-Coupled Revolution

In 1930 the PO Company began to seek means of both accelerating and increasing the weight of its trains on the Toulouse main line, particularly over the difficult section between Chateauroux and Montauban, where the long 1 in 100 banks combined with the limited adhesion of the smaller-wheeled 4500 class Pacifics prohibited any cutting of existing schedules and limited the maximum weight of the trains to 500 tons. It is true that the modified rebuilding of the superheated 3500 class Pacifics (designated 3800 class) had resulted in a great increase in overall speeds, but their adhesion was insufficient for the haulage of heavier trains. What was wanted was an engine which would work a train loaded to 700 tons on these accelerated schedules.

M. Epinay at first thought of buying such locomotives as the PLM C class 4—8—2, which had the eight coupled wheels needed to give the extra adhesion, or of rebuilding the two-cylinder simple expansion 2—8—2s of the PO (most of which had been built in the United States) as three-cylinder 4—8—2 engines. However André Chapelon suggested to Epinay that a way out of the difficulty might be to rebuild the 4500 class Pacifics on the same principles as the larger-wheeled 3500 class, but to convert them into 4—8—0s.[1] M. Epinay agreed to this suggestion and Chapelon was charged with this task in October 1931. It was clear that the existing 4500 class boiler with its trapezoidal grate would not do, and that a long narrow firebox would be necessary to fit between the rear coupled wheels. Chapelon decided that the excellent boiler fitted to the Nord Pacifics of the 3.1200 class would suffice and he asked the Nord Railway for the drawings. However, he selected the longer Belpaire firebox with the 40·4sq ft grate of M. Asselin's original design of 1914 rather than the modified firebox of 1923 with only 37·7sq ft grate area, and he incorporated a Nicholson thermic syphon. These Nord Pacifics had always been able to give results that were 30 per cent better than other pre-Chapelon French Pacifics, and, although they had a better valve gear arrangement and a better designed steam circuit, the narrow firebox contributed to their better performance. The original frames of the 4500 class engines were cut

1. Appendix B.20

32

behind the third coupled axle and then prolonged to the rear by plates welded on and of the same thickness.

Rebuilding of the first engine, No. 4521, started at Tours in October 1931, and the engine in her rebuilt form ran her first trials nine months later in August 1932—a very different speed of construction as compared with No. 3566! The firebox was 12ft 6in long, though general opinion held that the maximum length should not exceed 10ft. But Chapelon was satisfied that stoking a narrow firebox of this greater length did not present the fireman with any great difficulty. Furthermore, he had established that this type of firebox lent itself to a combustion rate which was higher than that of a wide firebox of similar grate area. In fact, it was easier for a fireman to maintain a good fire on a narrow grate than on a wide one, on account of the difficulty with the latter of reaching the back corners. An additional advantage of the narrow firebox was that the automatic trimming forward of the coal tended to stop any clogging of the grate, with the wide firebox the fireman had to watch every part of the grate to stop this happening.

On the first run with the rebuilt No. 4521 it was apparent that this was a giant amongst locomotives, for her performance was superior even to that of the rebuilt Pacifics. Nevertheless there was an amusing aspect to the first trial in 1933, with the engine hauling a heavy train of 730 tons on the line between Vierzon and Limoges, on which were a number of interested observers as passengers. Between Vierzon and Chateauroux, running with a short cut-off, the engine suffered steaming trouble; to the undisguised satisfaction of those who had already criticised the grate area of the engine as being too small. At Chateauroux, as already planned, the load was reduced to 654 tons for the heavily graded section on to Limoges. There was some delay before the train started again. After a fast run over the level stretch to Argenton, the engine started to climb the 1 in 100 banks and here the steaming suddenly became superabundant and so remained, thus confounding the unhappy critics. In fact the engine surmounted these heavy gradients at such an astonishing speed that Limoges was reached at the scheduled time, wiping out all the delay that had been incurred up to the time of leaving Chateauroux. Subsequent examination showed that the double exhaust column was not functioning properly at low cut-offs, and this was soon rectified by a minor adjustment.

On May 16th 1933 No. 4521, hauling a 575-ton train, covered the heavily graded 125 miles between Vierzon and Limoges at an average running speed of 61·25mph; and on subsequent tests she was shown capable of maintaining continuously 3,800ihp at 56mph and 4,000ihp at 70mph, powers considerably in excess of, for example, those available to the diesel-electric 'Deltic' locomotives of British Railways.

Following these astounding results, eleven more engines were rebuilt in the same way; No. 4521 was renumbered 4701 and the others 4702–4712. They were put into service at Brive depot to pull the heavy express trains between Vierzon and Narbonne, and easily met the PO requirement by working 700-ton trains at the accelerated schedules. They also showed themselves to be remarkably flexible, because they were equally at home hauling fast and heavy passenger trains over easily graded lines at speeds up to 94mph, passenger trains of over 700 tons up 1 in 100 gradients with 500-yard radius curves at 30–50mph, and freight trains over routes of the latter type of a greater weight and at a higher speed than those worked by the 6000 class 4-cylinder compound 2—10—0 locomotives of 1910. Tried at a constant speed and cut-off, No. 4701 maintained a dbhp of 3,030 at 62·5mph. On this occasion Fireman Marty, refusing any assistance, achieved the remarkable feat of shovelling four tons of coal into the firebox in one consecutive hour, whilst at the same time keeping such mastery over the fire that the boiler steamed perfectly during the whole period.

No. 4707 (by then renumbered 240.707) was tried successively on the Nord and the Etat, and on both railways confirmed the reputation that the type had established on the PO. On the Nord, on February 18th 1935, the engine hauled a train of 650 tons from Paris Nord to Calais Ville, with a stop at Amiens, at an overall average speed of 68·8mph. The actual running speed was 74·4mph, and over practically the whole of the 62½ miles between Amiens and Etaples the specially authorised maximum speed of 87·5mph was maintained. On the return journey to Paris the average running speed throughout was 77·25mph. Running from Paris to Boulogne with a train of 750 tons, steam-heated throughout, and making frequent stops, No. 240.707 produced remarkable steaming. The power outputs recorded included 3,200dbhp at 53mph on the Neufchatel gradient of 1 in 143 and a sustained dbhp of more than 2,750. As regards this latter figure, No. 241.C.1 of the PLM had only managed 2,350–2,450dbhp on a similar train, PO rebuilt Pacific No. 3715 produced 2,150–2,250dbhp, and the Est 4—8—2 1,960–2,000.

No. 240.707 then went to the Etat and worked several times over the heavily graded and curved 231 miles between Paris (St. Lazare) and Cherbourg with a 607-ton train of 14 coaches. The minimum time taken was 3 hours 32 minutes including a stop of 6 minutes at Caen. On March 21st 1935 the two highest officials of the German Reichsbahn were on the train to observe the working of the locomotive. As far as Caen Doctor Fuchs was on the footplate and Professor Nordmann in the dynamometer car. Fuchs congratulated Chapelon on dismounting from the engine; and Nordmann, before leaving the Gare St.

Lazare, said, "I shall have to revise my opinions on the compound system." For the two of them had seen the dbhp rise to 2,900 at the summit of the 1 in 125 Bernay Bank, which was far higher than they had expected from this locomotive, which had appeared to them at the Gare St. Lazare before their departure as 'a very small engine'.

On its home railway on October 4th 1935 No. 240.710 pulled between Bordeaux and Angouleme a train of 1,000 tons at the speed of the "*Sud Express*", which was 13 min faster than the schedule for heavy express trains.

In November 1936 No. 240.705 was tried on the Est working *rapides*, heavy expresses, stopping passenger trains, and freight trains, and gained considerably on the schedule of all of them. For example, with a 823-ton passenger train 26 minutes were gained on schedule between Chalons and Paris, and with a 1,228-ton freight train the engine gained 38 minutes over the 98 miles from Pantin Yard (Paris) to Troyes on a run scheduled at 30mph. On December 30th 1936 No. 240.705 took over a 1,024-ton near Reims which was normally worked by the Est 5200 class 2—10—0s of 1925 (derived from the Saxon XIII-H class). The test entailed stopping the train twice in the middle of a 1 in 100 gradient and on each occasion the engine started again without hesitation, very quickly reaching a speed of from 16 to 17mph; and in spite of these stops the train passed the summit of the bank 3 minutes early.

In 1938, at the request of the PLM, No. 240.705 was tried out on that railway between Paris and Lyon. After working expresses for about 2,500 miles between Paris, Dijon, and Lyon, the engine worked trains Nos. 11 and 12, the fastest on the railway, over the 332½ miles which separate Paris and Lyon without change of engines, for nine trips, thus running 2992·5 miles without any adverse incident. With train No. 11 it gained an average of 25¾ minutes, with a maximum of 30 minutes, and with No. 12 it had an average gain of 22·6 minutes and a maximum of 29 minutes. The average running speeds were 67·4mph and 66mph, as compared with the 61·5 and 61·2mph, respectively, required by the timetable. One outward and return journey was carried out with 345 tons, and the others with the weight increased to about 400 tons by the addition of a dynamometer car. On July 6th, with train No. 12 loaded to 398 tons, No. 240.705 passed Blaisy tunnel at 71mph; the average equivalent power on the level being 2,600dbhp up the bank of 1 in 125 between Velors and Baulme la Roche with a maximum of 2,840. On July 18th with 15 coaches weighing 672 tons, running on the timings of the 320-ton P1 *train de luxe*, the "Cote d'Azur" Pullman, and after a ten-minutes-late start from Laroche, No. 240.705

was on time at Arcy le Franc (35 miles) and 5 minutes early at Blaisy (18·7 miles farther on).

It was as a result of these trials that the SNCF (which has been formed in 1938) decided that the PO should rebuild for the PLM (now the Sud-Est Region) 25 of its 4500 class saturated steam Pacifics. In these new rebuilds M. Chapelon incorporated a number of improvements, such as an increase of 10 per cent in the volume of the LP cylinders (as in the PO Pacifics 3722–3731), the fitting of a mechanical stoker, and strengthened frames. In addition external pipework was largely concealed within an enlarged boiler outer casing, the running plate was raised above the coupled wheels so that wheel splashers were eliminated, and the cab was fixed to the boiler instead of to the chassis, thus reducing vibration and providing the crew with greater comfort. Chapelon had got the artist, the late Emile André Schefer, to assist him with the external outline and a most attractive looking engine resulted. The new engines were classified 240.P and numbered 240-P.1–240.P.25.[2] They were put into service from the beginning of June 1940 and all were in service by the end of 1941, hauling fast and heavy trains on the line Laroche-Dijon-Lyon.

The mechanical stoker is frequently regarded as very extravagant in coal. It was first used in America on locomotives having a grate area of some 60 sq ft. and burning an average of about two tons of coal per hour. Through using a stoker it was possible to increase substantially the boiler evaporation rate and also the weight behind the tender by sometimes as much as 25 per cent. As regards the consumption of coal, efficiency was lowered in respect of water evaporated per pound of coal at higher rates of working, but expense per ton/mile was less because of the better utilisation of the power of the engines. However, it was necessary to accept the inconvenience of having to cut the coal down to a size suitable for the stoker, and this could lead to expulsion of cinders from the chimney and consequent loss. In M. Chapelon's application of the mechanical stoker the firebox brick arch was lengthened to burn the small coal particles which would otherwise have been ejected, and the consumption of heat in the 240.P class, for the same steam production was only 10 per cent more than that of the 240.700s, and this was accounted for by the steam required to operate the mechanical stoker.

The Nord Railway got very interesting results with a mechanical stoker on their 2—10—0 locomotives of the 5.1200 class, which had a boiler identical with that of the 'Super-Pacifics' and a narrow grate of 38sq ft area. With carefully selected fuel they obtained boiler efficiences comparable to those experienced with hand firing on the

2. Appendix B.20

same engines. The fitting of mechanical stokers to the 240.P class gave similar favourable results.

One of the 240.P class engines (No. 240.P.5, Driver Chartier and Fireman Jarry) produced what is probably the finest steam locomotive performance on a power-to-weight basis ever recorded anywhere. The train hauled weighed 800 tons and consisted of 17 coaches; and on May 31st 1941, with this load and under the scrutiny of the senior Motive Power officials of the Sud-Est, the engine maintained an average speed of 66·3mph and developed 3190 estimated dbhp, up the 19½-mile gradient between Les Laumes and Blaisy, which averaged 1 in 188 with a maximum of 1 in 125. A speed of 71mph was reached up the 1 in 213 immediately after Thenissey, and Blaisy at the summit was passed at 61mph. The gross power (i.e. neglecting acceleration and gradient) developed at the drawbar, as registered in the dynamometer car, increased steadily over the whole of the section; it was 2,500 passing Les Laumes, 2,900 at Thenissey, 3,300 at Verrey, and no less than 3,300 at Blaisy. The last two kilometres on a rising gradient of 1 in 125 were covered at a speed of 61·2mph with a dbhp of 3,175, corresponding to 3,600dbhp at a uniform speed on the level. The pressure in the boiler was kept constant during the whole of this run, and the water level in the gauge still stood at 6cm when the regulator was closed at the end of this effort. It is a performance which at the time of writing, nearly 30 years later, no single diesel locomotive in Europe could equal.

On May 7th 1941 No. 240.P.3 had made a very fine run. With 12 coaches weighing 512 tons the engine covered the distance between Les Laumes and Blaisy in 15 minutes 36 seconds at the average speed of 75mph with a maximum of 81mph at Thenissey and 68·8 at Blaisy. The average dbhp sustained throughout was equivalent to 2,682 on the level.

Chapelon regarded the 240.Ps as his favourite engines, and, as a class, they were probably the most brilliant steam locomotives ever to have been built. At Laroche depot on the old PLM section of the SNCF they were received with enthusiasm by drivers and firemen because, with their great power and good steaming, they were not only the most capable express engines that had ever run on the line, but with their strong reinforced frames they gave little trouble in maintenance. Their predecessors at Laroche, the PLM 4—8—2 locomotives of the 241.A class, had the inadequately braced frames already referred to, and the continual flexing of these caused many overheated driving axle boxes and sometimes broken connecting rods. The only mechanical trouble ever experienced with the 240.Ps occurred later in the war when they were allocated to a depot of the Sud-Est Region where maintenance standards had declined and only inferior oil was available. Some of the engines then suffered from heating of the bogie axleboxes due to clogging of the oil pads which prevented oil from reaching the bearings. However, a new chief, M. Merlan, of the depot concerned found the cause of the trouble and stopped it by periodically changing the lubricator pads, and later cured it by using a more suitable pad. Up till the time that the line was electrified in 1949–50 the Chief of the Motive Power department of the Sud-Est expressed his great satisfaction with these engines. The boilers remained in an exceptionally good condition and in their latter days the percentage of 240.Ps immobilised was only 4, a figure which was much below the normal for steam locomotives.

During the war, and immediately after it, the 240.Ps were hauling vast trains. When for instance, the main line in Dijon was closed by war damage they were working trains of from 22 to 28 coaches weighing 1,100 to 1,400 tons on the only day service to the south over the Bourbonnais line via Nevers and were sustaining a speed of 53mph on level track and 25mph up gradients of 1 in 166. They also worked vital coal trains of over 2,000 tons from the Pas de Calais coalfield in the difficult period immediately following the end of the war.

The Nord Region of the SNCF became intensely interested in these engines and, when they were becoming redundant owing to electrification, the Nord made urgent application in 1951 for some of both the 240.Ps and the earlier 240.700s to work the heavy express trains on the steeply graded Lille-Valenciennes-Charleville line. However, the headquarters of the SNCF were under the mistaken impression that the 241.P class 4—8—2 locomotives, which had been developed from the PLM 241.C.1, were better for the task and the application was turned down. But in 1952 this route was selected for conversion to electrification on the new 25kv 50cs system and no new steam power was therefore acquired.

There was a further possibility of using the 4—8—0s on the Paris-Cherbourg line of the old Etat, for the motive power engineers of this region, remembering the sparkling performance over their railway by No. 340.707, applied for them. Unfortunately the late Engineer-in-Chief for Rolling Stock and Motive Power of this railway had opposed further use of eight-coupled express engines on the light and heavily curved track of the Cherbourg line owing to the derailment in 1933 of one of the Est type 4—8—2s which had, at that time, deficient bogie lateral control. And so Chapelon's magnificent 4—8—0 locomotives, which had excellent lateral control, went prematurely to the scrap heap. There had been in all 12 of the 240.700s and 25 of the 240.Ps.

The performance of the 4—8—0 rebuilds set the seal on Chapelon's status as the foremost locomotive engineer in France. On January 9th 1934 another great locomotive engineer of an earlier generation wrote to him. M. Edouard Sauvage had designed in 1887 a 2—6—0 which was the first three-cylinder compound locomotive in France. This engine was built in the works of the Nord Railway on which Sauvage was an Engineer-in-Chief. He was subsequently Engineer-in-Chief on, in succession, the Est and the Ouest, and after his retirement from railway service he became Professor at the Academy of *Arts et Métiers*. In 1894 there was published the first edition of his great work *La Machine Locomotive* which was written specially for the motive power personnel of the railways. Nine separate editions were brought out up till 1935, and then after Sauvage's death M. Chapelon brought it up to date for a tenth and last edition in 1945. In his letter to Chapelon Sauvage wrote: "My dear Engineer, your kind remembrance gives me great pleasure, and I thank you. For my part, I wish you a continuation of the same success in your work on the locomotive, and I take the opportunity to tell you how much I admire the scientific method which has led you to such remarkable practical results".

In July 1934, for his outstanding work in connection with locomotives, Chapelon was honoured with the appointment of Chevalier of the Legion of Honour. This was not the only honour. Also in 1934 he was awarded the Plumey Prize of the *Academie des Sciences* and the Gold Medal of the *Société d'Encouragement pour l'Industrie Nationale*. In 1935 he received the Medal for the *Conferences au Conservatoire des Arts et Métiers*, in 1937 the J. J. Meyer Prize of the *Société des Ingenieurs Civile de France* for his 1936 memorandum on improvements to the steam locomotive, and in 1950 the A. Mallet Prize from the same Society for his memorandum entitled *The Centenary of the Crampton Locomotive and a Century of Progress in Steam Traction*.

But Chapelon modestly insists that his success would not have been possible if he had not always been so well supported by his admirable team. These men, he says, were full of enthusiasm for the work in which they were participating, and the results achieved gave them great satisfaction and pride. This team was formed right at the start of Chapelon's work from Paris-Orléans personnel and showed a devotion to and confidence in him which increased as time went on. With such men, he says, one could work miracles. Through the excellent administrative organisation of the PO, too, the ideas of the Chief reached all levels of the staff, and it was the consequent understanding of the work that enabled Chapelon to complete the rebuilding of No. 4521 (prototype of the 4700 class) in nine months from the start of design—a speed which he was able to verify some years later as equal to the best the Americans had been able to achieve, cutting out all sources of administrative delay.

In spite of the national, and indeed international, recognition accorded to his work and the pre-eminent position in design which he now occupied on the PO (or perhaps because of it, through jealousy of this young engineer), Chapelon had to climb laboriously up the promotion ladder through each successive step of the locomotive hierarchy: from 2nd Class Inspector, to 1st Class Inspector, 2nd Class Divisional Inspector, 1st Class Divisional Inspector, Assistant Engineer, and then Engineer of the Rolling Stock Design Section. This took him up to 1938 when the PO (from 1934 amalgamated with the Midi) was absorbed into the nationalised SNCF. But whatever his official rank, his actual duties remained the same, though with increasing responsibility. He dealt with the design of locomotives and their development trials; first as attached to the Section of Research and Development of the PO, next as its Chief, and then as Chief Engineer for Rolling Stock Studies on the PO-Midi.

During this period up to the formation of the SNCF Chapelon was not only doing the practical work entailed in his steam revolution, but he was writing on locomotives and particularly on the rebuilding of the PO engines. For the *Revue Général des Chemins de Fer*, for instance, he contributed four major articles: the first, of August and September 1928, was concerned with locomotive exhaust, as illustrated by tests carried out on the PO; in July 1929 he wrote of research into the best means of countering exhaust steam and smoke beating down on locomotives; in July 1931 he described the rebuilding of the 3500 class PO Pacific locomotives by modifying the steam circuit, increasing the superheat, and fitting Kylchap exhaust and poppet valves; and in February and March 1935 he dealt with the rebuilding of the smaller wheeled Pacifics of the 4500 class into 4—8—0s in similar fashion.

In 1938 André Chapelon's great book, *La Locomotive á Vapeur*, was published, with a preface by Edouard Sauvage. This tremendous work (of which a second and revised edition appeared in 1952) is without question the most outstanding study of the twentieth century steam locomotive which has ever been, or is ever likely to be, written. It is fitting, if unusual, that the best book on steam railway engines should have come from the pen of such an eminent designer of them.

4

The Doctrine Spreads

THE PERFORMANCE of Chapelon's rebuilt Pacific No. 3566 aroused great and immediate interest in Great Britain, and in no person more so than Mr. H. N. (later Sir Nigel) Gresley, Chief Mechanical Engineer of the London & North Eastern Railway. Gresley had sent his Principal Assistant, O. V. S. Bullied, to Tours to watch some of the trials, and before the end of 1925 he went himself to France and visited Chapelon. As an immediate result of this visit Gresley decided to fit a Kylchap exhaust to one of his Shire class 4—4—0 engines, and, supplied by Chapelon with the drawings, a single Kylchap was made and fitted by the LNER. The Shire class had been built at Darlington for medium express duties in the North Eastern and Scottish areas of the LNER and the first of them had been completed in September 1927. They were three-cylinder simple expansion engines with Walschaerts valve gear, and the drive to the valves of the middle cylinder derived through the LNER conjugated gear. In 1930 Chapelon rode on the footplate of the engine fitted with the Kylchap exhaust between London and York. It ran quite well, but a mistake had been made in the construction of the Kylchap assembly with the result that the performance was not as good as it should have been. The four lobes of the Kylälä spreader, instead of being entirely separate from each other, had been connected just below the top by iron ties, thus creating an obstruction which impeded the gas flow through the centre of the apparatus and prevented it from functioning properly. Chapelon pointed out the defect and suggested that it should be put right, but he does not know whether this was ever done.

In 1929 Gresley had built his remarkable 4—6—4 engine No. 10000, a revolutionary design which embodied a four-cylinder compound system together with a Yarrow water tube boiler pressed at 450lbs per sq in. The engine did not come up to expectations and both Gresley and Bullied had discussions with Chapelon on what could be done to improve it. Chapelon pointed out that the degree of superheat was insufficient to avoid condensation in the low pressure cylinders and that it should be increased; he added that even better results could be obtained by re-superheating (as used in his own No. 160.A.1, which is described later), and that the fitting of a Kylchap exhaust would help. Gresley applied re-superheat and used the double Kylchap exhaust, with resulting improvement in performance and efficiency. Problems such as lack of air tightness in the boiler walls and short-circuiting of gases with consequent lowered boiler efficiency remained unsolved, and No. 10000 never produced economies or perform-ances to justify its unconventional design. In 1937 it suffered the indignity of being converted to a simple expansion engine with conventional boiler (of the same type as that fitted to *Cock o' the North*), retaining its double Kylchap exhaust.

The next occasion on which Gresley consulted Chapelon was in connection with his 2—8—2 express locomotive No. 2001 *Cock o' the North*, which was built in 1934.[1] It was a three-cylinder simple expan-sion engine with a double Kylchap exhaust, rotary poppet valves, wide steam passages, and high superheat; all of which Gresley had copied from the rebuilt PO Pacifics. Indeed, Gresley, in his second Presidential address to the Institution of Locomotive Engineers in 1936, said, "I did not hesitate to incorporate some of the outstanding features of the Paris-Orléans Railway's engines, such as the provision of extra large steam passages and a double blastpipe. There was no real novelty in these features but the French engineers had worked out the designs scientifically and had proved them by the results obtained in actual service."

At Gresley's request arrangements were made for *Cock o' the North* to be tested on the Vitry test plant. In December 1934, therefore, the engine ran to Harwich for embarkation, pulling some 40-ton wagons loaded with the coal with which she was normally fired. Engine and wagons were shipped to Calais from whence they ran to Vitry-sur-Seine, where Bullied also arrived to watch the tests. The tests were disappoint-ing because, like many other engines, *Cock o' the North* could not be driven hard on the test bank without the axle boxes heating. A worried Gresley visited Chapelon at his Design Office, showed him the plans of the engine and asked what he should do. Examination did not reveal any particular fault and Chapelon, who had seen several engines per-form badly on the test bank, proposed that the LNER locomotive should be tried out on the line with a test load. This, in accordance with normal PO practice, consisted of a dynamometer car and three 'dead' (i.e. out of steam) four-cylinder compound counter-pressure brake locomotives (in which water is admitted to the cylinders and pumped against pressure in the boiler). This test took place between Les Aubrais and Tours and was satisfactory; there was no heating of the axle boxes and the engine showed itself capable of producing a drawbar horse power of 2,000 at 70mph. This was, of course, consider-

1. Appendix B.21

ably inferior to the power developed by Chapelon's own 4—8—0s. One trouble lay in the firing of the engine (which was carried out in turn by the LNER fireman and by the No. 3566 trials fireman, Léonce Miot). The firebox door was too small to allow of the back corners of the wide grate being properly covered. This resulted in the steaming being so hampered that the working pressure in the boiler fell whilst the steam production rate remained practically constant. Another peculiarity of this engine was that, contrary to other engines of the same class which were fitted with piston valves, it was necessary to increase the diameter of the exhaust pipe by 50 per cent to avoid having too great a draught. This singularity could be attributed to the excessive temperature of the exhaust steam, which was probably due to its being re-heated by contact with a partition separating it from the live steam. This lowered the efficiency of the engine and a re-design of the cylinder block would have been necessary to rectify it.

Bulleid claimed in a discussion at the Institution of Locomotive Engineers in 1947 that *Cock o' the North* compared favourably in her coal consumption per dbhp with the French engines; but Chapelon gives figures which show that the engine was far from being as econonomical, in both coal and water, as his own compounds. It was, of course, a simple expansion engine and the poppet valves may not have been perfectly steam tight. Comparative test figures obtained from one of Chapelon's rebuilt Pacifics and Gresley's 2—8—2 were:

	P.O. Pacific		*Cock o' the North*
Speed	68mph	56mph	68mph
dbhp	1910	2700	1910
Water per hp/hr.	7·5 kg	8·20 kg	10·45kg
Coal per /hp/hr	1·05kg	1·22kg	1·48kg

A bad fault displayed by *Cock o' the North* lay in the design of the leading pony truck which resulted in the engine being very hard on the track, because the first coupled axle of the rigid wheel base encountered any change in the direction of the track too roughly. Chapelon had noticed this during the trials, particularly at the junction of Montlouis which was taken rather harshly even by his own Pacifics. The trouble could have been avoided by using an Italian bissel bogie (i.e. an arrangement by which a displacement of the leading truck was followed by a lateral movement of the leading coupled axle) as fitted to the later 141.P class 2—8—2s, which rode as well as the French Pacifics whilst having all the advantages of superior adhesion. Edward Thompson's solution of building the *Cock o' the North* class as Pacifics certainly made them more flexible but they lost adhesion. Both classes of 2—10—0 engines designed by R. A. Riddles, on the other hand, could traverse sharp curves far more readily than could Gresley's 2—8—2s.

Gresley and Bulleid were in France for three weeks whilst the tests were conducted on the LNER engine. Although Gresley had incorporated so many of Chapelon's ideas in the design of his 2—8—2, it was clear that he had failed to build an engine equal in either performance or efficiency to the French rebuilds. Indeed he told the Institution of Locomotive Engineers that the first *Cock o' the North* would be the last and that any subsequent P2 class engines would embody the lessons learned in France. The second of this class, No. 2002 *Earl Marischal*, was completed, however, in October 1934, before the despatch of No. 2001 to France, and differed from the latter only in having Walschaerts valve gear with piston valves. The final four, Nos. 2003–2006, had the even larger steam passages that were being fitted with such success to the A4 class Pacific locomotives which were being built at about the same time. From 1937 the A4s also had the double Kylchap exhaust and one of these, *Mallard*, on July 3rd 1938 achieved the so far unbeaten record for steam of 126mph.

These later Gresley Pacifics and 2—8—2s were all streamlined, and this was an era when streamlining was extremely popular on many of the world's railways. The streamlining craze was one of the more curious episodes of locomotive history, and one suspects that on many railways the addition of a streamlined casing was intended to impress the public rather than to facilitate the movement of a train at speed. It must have been, for instance, on only rare occasions that the streamlined Pacifics of the Iraqi State Railways ever attained such a wild burst of speed as 40mph.

The idea of streamlining was not new. In 1888 M. Ricour of the Etat Railway had sought to reduce air resistance by providing engines with an exterior offering less opposition, and at speeds of 60mph he achieved a gain in power of 10 per cent. In 1894 the PLM put into service the first of its famous wind-cutting locomotives, mentioned in Chapter 1. In 1934 the South Manchurian Railways, at Japanese instigation, introduced the first regular service of entirely streamlined trains to operate an express service of 8 hours 30 minutes over the 441 miles between Dairen and Ilsiking (Harbin).

Many studies have been made to ascertain the best streamlined form for a locomotive. Tests have been carried out on small models to ascertain the most suitable shapes to reduce the resistance of air at high speeds; and from these tests calculations have been made to determine the gains to be obtained. However, these calculations gave an exaggerated estimate of likely power savings because, as experience has shown, air resistance to the movement of small models is nearly always relatively greater than to the full-scale locomotives. Only comparative trials carried out on the line can really show the advantages of a streamlined casing. The PLM carried out such tests in 1935 by streamlining a complete train consisting of one of the old 221.A class Atlantics of 1907 and four normal bogie coaches, and running it in competition with a train of precisely similar make-up but unstreamlined. The savings achieved by the streamlined train were 275hp at 75mph and 450hp at 87·5mph. Of these figures, 155hp and 260hp respectively were saved on the engine and 120hp and 190hp on the coaches. If the streamlined train, on the other hand, were pulled by an unstreamlined locomotive the respective savings were only 50 and 90hp. It was therefore more worthwhile streamlining the engine than the carriages. A comparison between these two otherwise identical trains was made between Les Laumes and Paris. At an average speed of 67mph the streamlined train showed a saving over its rival of 28 per cent in coal and 23 per cent in water.

In 1936 one of the PO-Midi rebuilt Pacifics, No. 231.726, was streamlined (probably the most attractive streamlining of a steam locomotive ever carried out). In test hauls of brake locomotives No. 231.726 showed a saving over the unstreamlined Pacifics of 60hp at 56·2mph, 80hp at 62·5mph, 105hp at 68·7mph, 130hp at 75mph, and 150hp at 81·2mph. These figures show that at high speeds there are undoubted advantages in streamlining. But when one remembers that the rebuilding of the PO Pacifics increased their dbhp at 70mph from 1,450 to 2,650, or by a total of 1,200hp and that this was achieved by merely modifying their exhaust, degree of superheat, and steam circuit, it is apparent that the gain provided by external streamlining is comparatively small. It is all the more curious that in designing steam locomotives for high speed, thermodynamics have often been neglected whilst emphasis has been placed on aerodynamics.

In practice external streamlining does not appear to be profitable at speeds below 75mph. It was for this reason that in the projected standard classes of the SNCF it was intended to streamline only engines intended to operate the very fast expresses running at 95mph and over. For other express locomotives it was considered sufficient to clean up the exterior, as had been done for the 240.Ps, to reduce to a minimum the losses which arise from the lateral friction of the air against the engine—an important part indeed of the total resistance. Very high speeds, however, were recorded with Chapelon Pacifics without either streamlining or 'smoothed' exterior. In September 1935 No. 3.1174, rebuilt for the Nord, reached 108·7mph with 400 tons down the 1 in 250 gradient towards Chantilly. In 1956, to test the interaction between a pantograph and the overhead wire, a number of test runs were made on the Nord with electric locomotives propelled by Chapelon Pacifics, There were two sets of trials; the first in February using No. 231.E.35. and the second in June with No. 231.E.9 (ex-3567 of 1912) rebuilt for the PO at Tours in 1934. Both engines belonged to the Fives depot and together they ran 70 trials covering a distance of nearly 200 miles at speeds between 100 and 110mph without any special preparation and without experiencing the slightest trouble. The fastest run was made by No. 231.E.9 pushing an electric locomotive and pulling an inspection saloon and coach—an equivalent of 220 tons. With this load the engine attained a speed of 110·6mph down a gradient of 1 in 117.

Many locomotives of other French railways were rebuilt between 1932 and 1936 on the lines advocated by Chapelon. His old railway, the PLM, rebuilt many of its Pacifics.[2] The first to be taken in hand was No. 231.F.141 which was given an improved steam circuit and new cylinders and piston valves. A double blastpipe was fitted of the same dimensions as Chapelon's but with a variable double clover exhaust instead of the Kylchap pattern. A new boiler was provided with a pressure of 292lbs per sq in and an improved superheater, together with an ACFI feed water heater. The engine was renumbered 231.H.141 and the results obtained were so good that she became the prototype of 30 231.H class locomotives, rebuilt from 231.B and 231.E classes, which themselves had been rebuilt as compound engines from the four-cylinder simple expansion Pacifics of around 1912.

Other PLM Pacifics were also rebuilt, though on a more modified scale than the 231.Hs, and of these there were 12 classified 231.K and no less than 118 of class 231.G. As compared with the 231.H class, the 231.Gs retained the original and larger HP cylinders, and the original boiler with its pressure of 232lbs per sq in, whilst the 231.Ks were similar to the 231.G class except that they had a slightly shorter boiler and independent HP and LP valve gears.

The Etat rebuilt a number of their 231.500 class Pacifics.[3] These had appeared in 1914 and construction of them continued during and after the war. Many were running on other French railways; for in 1920 the Ministry of Public Works ordered 400 of them, of which 280 went to the Etat, 40 to the Est, 40 to the Alsace Lorraine, and 40 to the PO. They had been designed by M. J. Nadal and were almost identical with the PO 3500 class Pacifics, except that they had a round-top firebox, because of the restricted Ouest loading gauge, and the Ouest type bogie. The Etat rebuilt 187 engines on Chapelon principles, of which 134 had Lentz poppet valves to the LP cylinders (class 231.D), 23 had Willoteaux slide valves to the LP cylinders (class 231.F), and 30 had Lentz poppet valves to both HP and LP cylinders

2. Appendix B.13   3. Appendix B.22

(class 231.G). The poppet valve engines had the Kylchap 1K/1C double exhaust whilst the Willoteaux valve engines had the Kylchap 1K/T single exhaust. Another 82 engines had less extensive alterations which included a larger superheater, large section steam pipes, Kylchap 1K/T single exhaust, and modified valve setting (class 231.H). The remaining engines were not rebuilt. The most powerful of these rebuilt Pacifics were the 231.Gs. In addition to this extensive rebuilding, the Etat also modified some of their four-cylinder compound 4—6—0 locomotives on Chapelon principles and built more of them new.

On the Est some of the 4—8—2s and all of the Etat-type Pacifics were rebuilt on Chapelon lines. The 4—8—2 engines were much more powerful as a result and one of them developed 3,500hp at the wheel rim during trials on the test bank at 68mph. Also on the Est many of that railway's 4—6—0 locomotives, the mainstay of its passenger services, were rebuilt.[4] All of the last 50 built in 1925 were given trefoil exhausts with six jets, wide chimney, and Est pattern LP double admission and double exhaust piston valves. 174 engines received the whole or part of these modifications.

The results obtained through modifying compound locomotives encouraged a number of railways to search for improvements of the same order in simple expansion engines. The LNER has already been mentioned in this connection and Gresley's selection of the double Kylchap exhaust for express passenger engines was continued by his successor Edward Thompson and to a certain extent by A. H. Peppercorn, who followed the latter. In 1934 the Société Nationale des Chemins de Fer Belges built some large four-cylinder simple expansion Pacific locomotives with a boiler casing identical with that originally fitted to *Cock o' the North*. Some of these engines had the double Kylchap exhaust. In 1933 the Alsace Lorraine Railway, noted for its preference for simple expansion engines, had two two-cylinder simple expansion Pacific locomotives (designated Class S.16) built for it by the Société Alsacienne de Constructions Mécaniques which had the double Kylchap exhaust, a boiler pressure of 280lbs per sq in and Caprotti poppet valves. One of them also had a booster.[5]

But perhaps the most notable Alsace Lorraine engines were the two great three-cylinder simple expansion G.16 class 2—10—2 goods locomotives of 1936.[5] Like the Pacifics they had Caprotti poppet valves and boiler pressure of 280lbs per sq in. The boiler was similar to that of the PLM 151.A class 2—10—2 engines, and was in turn practically identical with PLM 241.A class 4—8—2 boiler. They had an ACFI feed water heater and the Kylchap variable double exhaust system—the inserts in the blastpipe nozzle being movable vertically. On the

4. Appendix B.23   5. Appendix B.24

gradient of 1 in 100 from Thionville to Hargarten the G.16s showed a remarkable capacity in the haulage of heavy loads. In normal service they worked 1,650-ton trains and they could take as much as 1,800 tons. On the same stretch the PLM 151.As were limited to 1,450 tons, and the fine 5.1200 class 2—10—0 engines of the Nord could only manage 1,350 tons. Tried in comparison with the 151.A between Dijon and Les Loumes the G.16 could develop the equivalent of 2,800hp on the level at a uniform speed of 30mph as compared with 2,670 by the 151.A. However, the advantage of the compound locomotive was shown by its consumption of 12·6 per cent less water than the G.16 at 2,000-dbhp. None of these four A.L. engines survived the war.

In the United States of America the success of Chapelon's methods led to the Pennsylvania Railroad modifying one of their K4s class Pacifics of 1924, No. 5399. The improvements carried out included the fitting of poppet valves, as improved superheater, and an increase in the steam pipe diameter. The result was a considerable increase in power. At 75mph the modified engine developed 4,200ihp as compared with the 3,500ihp of an unmodified engine; and at 100mph the respective figures were 4,100 and 2,800.

In Spain and Czechoslovakia the Kylchap exhaust was fitted with great success to both simple expansion and compound locomotives. The Norte Railway in 1938 rebuilt a 4—8—2 four-cylinder compound locomotive with poppet valves, large steam passages and double Kylchap exhaust. The increase in power was so great that 28 new 4—8—2 engines were constructed to the same design as the rebuilt locomotive.

Numbering of French locomotives has received considerable mention in this and previous chapters, and it is perhaps appropriate to discuss here the various systems used. The first system adopted in France was to use a four-figure number of which the first digit denoted the number of coupled axles; e.g. a 4—6—0 would have a number in the 3000 series, a 2—8—0 one in the 4000 series, etc. This soon broke down, and the PO Atlantics, for example, were numbered in the 3000s and the contemporary 4—6—0 engines in the 4000s.

In 1908 the Etat evolved a better system by using two groups of figures, of which the first denoted the axle arrangement and the second the serial number of the engine. Thus, the first class of Pacific locomotives were numbered 231.011 to 231.060, whilst the second class were 231.501 to 231.783. The Nord used a modification of this method by replacing the first group with a figure for the number of coupled axles only, and the first batch of Nord 'Superpacifics' were numbered 3.1201 to 3.1240. When the PO was amalgamated with the Midi the Etat system was adopted by replacing the first digit of the old four-

Left: The double Kylchap exhaust assembly which was later fitted to the rebuilt Pacific No 3566.

[PO

Below: Rebuilt Pacific No 3566 after taking over the train at Les Aubrais on March 24, 1931 from an electric locomotive, and being examined by representatives from other French railways.

[Chapelon collection

Top : No 3566 on March 24, 1931 with a trials train at Poitiers. Representatives from various French railways were on the train.

[Chapelon collection

Above : Edmund Epinay, E-in-C of Rolling Stock and Motive Power, stepping over the track in front of the trials train at Poitiers on March 24, 1931. On the left of the group in front of the engine is Louis de Boysson, Epinay's predecessor and Assistant Director of the PO.

[Chapelon collection

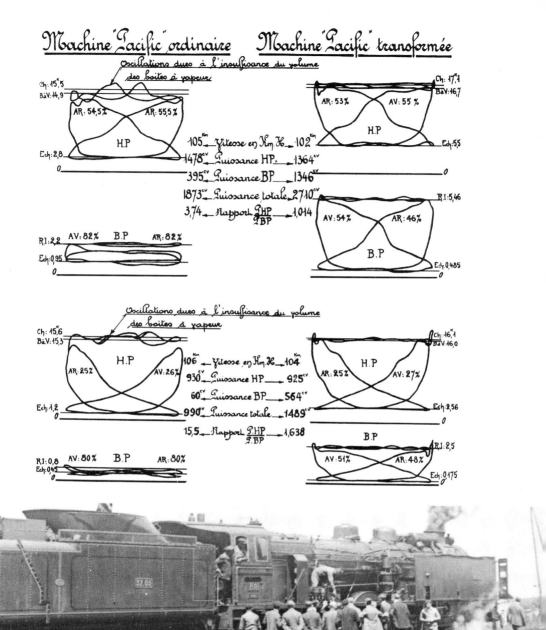

Top: Indicator diagrams before and after rebuilding 3500 class Pacifics of the Paris–Orleans Railway.

[PO

Above: Trials before the technical commission of the OCEM. Rebuilt Pacific No 3705 at the head of a 750-ton train about to depart from Angouleme.

[Chapelon collection

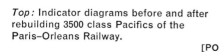

Above: Chapelon rebuilt Pacific of the Nord No 231.E.19 (ex-3.1190) waiting to back on to the 'Golden Arrow'.

[Nord

Left: No 3715 at the Calais depot during the 1932–33 trials on the Nord. Standing beside the engine is Head Driver Réné Gourault.

[Chapelon collection

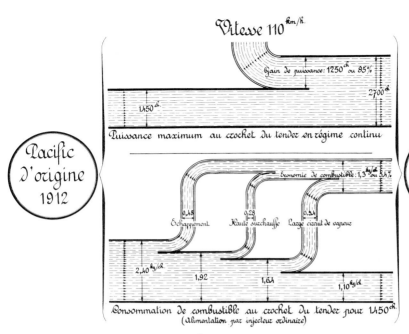

Top: Diagram showing the improvements effected between the superheated 3500 class Pacifics of 1912 and the last 3500 class of rebuilds of 1934.

[Sud-Est

Above: Another of the Chapelon-type Pacifics built new for the Nord, No 231.E.46, on the down 'Golden Arrow' at the Gare Maritime, Calais.

[Chapelon collection

Top: No 4521, rebuilt from a Pacific into a 4-8-0, on the occasion of its first appearance in steam on August 16, 1932. Standing round the engine are the staff of Tours Works with Alfred Renaud in front of the cylinders.

[Chapelon collection

Above: No 4521 at Cahors station during a trial run on May 11, 1933, hauling a train of 658 tons between Vierzon and Toulouse. Representatives of other French railways are discussing the performance of this remarkable 4-8-0 on the platform.

[Chapelon collection

Top: No 240.P.4, off-side view.

[Pouillet

Centre: No 240.P.4, near-side view, with tender.

[SCNF

Above: No 240.P.15 with Union Pacific type tandem rods, at Laroche depot.

[Sud-Est

figure number by the axle arrangement. Thus 4—8—0 No. 4706 became 240.706.

But whilst the Etat system showed the type of engine, the serial numbers did not so readily show the class. The PLM in 1918 improved the Etat method by inserting a letter to signify the class, leaving the serial number to indicate only the engines in that class. The first PLM simple Pacifics built in 1912 were then renumbered 231.A.2 to 231.A.71, the first compound Pacifics became 231.C.2 to 231.C.86, the 231.Bs were the 231.As with higher pressure converted to compounds, and so on. It was this system that was adopted by the SNCF when it was formed in 1938 (though the old numbering was retained by some Regions for locomotives of the old Company). As an example of consequent renumbering, Etat Pacific No. 231.011 became 231.A.011. New SNCF engines were given the letter P to denote, in conjunction with the axle arrangement, the class; e.g. 141.P was the class designation of the 2—8—2 four-cylinder compound engines built for the SNCF from 1941, and Chapelon's 4—8—0s for the Sud-Est Region of the SNCF were 240.P.

5

Six Cylinders

ANDRÉ CHAPELON's last locomotive design for the PO-Midi was completed in 1940, some time after the railways of France had been absorbed by the SNCF, and, owing to the war, no trials took place until 1948. Although in a later chapter Chapelon's great 4—8—4 No. 242.A.1 is stated correctly to have been the greatest steam locomotive of all, the subject of this present chapter was perhaps the most remarkable of steam locomotives; for it went far to prove two things, firstly that a compound locomotive could be built of such unquestioned superiority to any simple expansion locomotive as to convince the most enthusiastic supporter of the latter system, and secondly that the maintenance and running of such a locomotive would be so low that no juggling with figures could make a change to diesel traction economically attractive. But the final evaluation of its results came too late.

In 1909 the Paris-Orleans repeated its 'first' with Pacifics by introducing the 2—10—0 wheel arrangement to France with its 6000 class freight locomotives. In Europe they were second only to the Austrian engines of this type built in 1907. The 6000 class[1] were four-cylinder superheated compounds built by the Société Alsacienne de Constructions Mécaniques and were very similar to the PO Pacifics of the 4500 and 3500 classes; but in order to keep the axle load below $15\frac{1}{2}$ tons they had a shorter boiler, smaller grate, and rather lighter frames. Their general arrangement was derived in part from their predecessors, the 5000[2] class 2—8—0 goods engines of 1904. The 6000 class were intended primarily for the haulage of heavy goods trains on the main lines, particularly between Paris and Bordeaux; but they were also used to work all kinds of traffic over the sharp curves and terrific gradients of the lines running across the Massif Central. After 1920 many were given trefoil exhausts, and from 1926 15 were provided with Kylchap 1K/T exhausts, with resulting economy of 14 per cent over the trefoil fitted engines. From 1931 a large number of them received feed water heaters of one of the three types, ACFI, Worthington, or Dabeg. The four cylinders were in line; the HP inside, driving the second coupled axle, whilst the LP were outside and drove the third coupled axle.

1. Appendix B.8   2. Appendix B.5

In 1936 Chapelon started design work on the rebuilding of one of the 6000 class as a 2—12—0. His aim was to produce a locomotive with great tractive effort and with the ability to run economically at low speeds. Because the average steam locomotive is at its most extravagant when running slowly, the solutions to the problem was not easy. The main difficulties were the cooling effect of the cylinder walls and leakages. In an express engine the main problem is throttling, whilst in a slow engine it is the increased expansion that is necessary to achieve economy; and it is at slow speeds, particularly when working hard, that cooling by cylinder walls and leakage of steam militate against expansion.

The trials of the 240.700 class 4—8—0s had shown Chapelon that even with very high superheat the HP cylinder diagram showed very considerable condensations during expansion at short cut-offs when running slowly. It appeared, therefore, that the high superheat was being badly used, and that the excess calories contained in the steam situated in the middle of the cylinders were not moving to replace the deficiency caused by contact with the cylinder walls. It was the desirability of heating the cylinder walls that gave Chapelon the idea of using steam jackets; thereby making the superheated steam do some work before, as well as after, entering the cylinders. In other words, the excess calaories would be used to heat the cylinders walls from the outside as they would not do it from the inside. The jackets would be part of the active steam circuit, so that the steam would brush at speed around both HP and LP cylinders. Because the latter would be re-superheated it would be possible to achieve this aim without having HP temperature higher than the castings and oil could withstand. In addition Chapelon decided on chrome steel for the cylinder sleeves to reduce the wear on the piston rings and consequent leakage.

Poppet valves having been selected, there was no need to take account of leakage due to wear of piston valve rings. But, on the other hand, the poppet valves would have to be absolutely steam tight and not be liable to distortion under pressure. Trials were therefore made of various types from which it was found that the Lentz poppet valves were the least liable to distortion. To counter the tendency to distortion from expansion, poppet valves with conical seats were chosen. A trial with this kind of valve had previously been made with success on a 240.700 class 4—8—0 locomotive. The valves were actuated by oscillating cams driven by Walschaerts gear with independent operation. All the valve gear was mounted outside the frames and the movement of the inside LP valves was derived from the outside mechanism.

To obtain a large expansion combined with a high tractive effort, it was essential for economical operation to have cylinders of the largest possible volume. But two low pressure cylinders of the requisite volume would have been so large that they would not have fitted inside the loading gauge. Chapelon therefore decided on a six-cylinder engine with two high pressure and four low pressure cylinders. The two HP cylinders were towards the middle of the engine, between the second and third coupled axles, and inside the frames; of the LP cylinders, two were inside, and of the same diameter as the HP cylinders, and two were outside, and they were all in line in front of the first coupled axle. The HP cylinders drove the fourth coupled axle whilst the inside LP drove the second and the outside the third.

Re-superheating was applied to the LP cylinders, that is to say, the steam was superheated, not only before its entry into the HP cylinders, but also during its passage to the intermediate receiver. The HP superheater was of the Houlet type to obtain the maximum efficiency with the minimum number of elements. A considerable number of superheater tubes had to be reserved for the LP superheater which, contrary to the HP, had to have the maximum number of elements to reduce the loss of pressure in the transition from HP to LP (a vital point in re-superheating which had been neglected in its previous applications by the Belgian Etat and French Est Railways) and had to be of reduced efficacy so as not to produce excessive re-superheating temperatures. To effect this double aim Schmidt elements were adopted, coupled in parallel with two in each large tube; a solution which was found perfectly satisfactory.

To increase the intensity of the thermic exchanges between gas and water in the boiler, the barrel was separated into two parts by an intermediate tube-plate which was fixed 6ft 7in from the smokebox tube-plate. Chapelon had here adopted the Franco-Crosti principle but instead of a separate drum or drums for the pre-heater, with an ugly and inconvenient chimney in front of the cab, the pre-heater was the front part of the boiler barrel. This front part was always full of water and the feed water was introduced into it by an ACFI pump driven by exhaust steam, with an injector as stand-by. From the pre-heater the water was fed to the boiler proper by a simple overflow. There was a second reserve injector to supply direct feed to the boiler proper in case of emergency. This arrangement was found satisfactory.

The PO 2—10—0 from which the engine was rebuilt had a trapezoidal firebox like the same railway's Pacifics but with a smaller grate of 41sq ft area. This firebox was modified, as in the case of the 240.700 class 4—8—0 locomotives, by lengthening the grate to 12·5ft and thus increasing the area to 44·5sq ft—an increase which provided a very large surface of direct heat and made it easy to keep the fire in good condition.

The engine had, of course, a double Kylchap exhaust and steam passages which were all of large cross-sectional area. At starting live steam was admitted to the LP cylinders at 140lbs per sq in; direct exhaust from the HP cylinders to the atmosphere being unnecessary.

The chassis of the engine was considerably reinforced to give it sufficient rigidity. But owing to the long wheel base with six coupled axles, special arrangements were necessary to ensure easy entry into curves. This was easily achieved, however, by having only three of the coupled axles fixed—the second, third, and fourth—and these had thin flanges. The leading coupled axle had a lateral movement of 20mm, the fifth one of 10mm, and the sixth axle 30mm. The result was so good that the engine rolled easily out of Tours Works over lines which had a reputation of being difficult for engines with a far shorter wheel base.

The engine, No. 160.A.1,[3] was completed in June 1940, and although conditions of the time were critical, for German troops were advancing rapidly southwards, Chapelon hastened to save his precious new engine by despatching it to Brive, the depot to which he had in any case intended to send it. By that time the Operating Section were in such difficulties for motive power that no light engine running could be permitted. No. 160.A.1 did indeed run light to Limoges, but there a heavy freight train of 1,200 tons was waiting. Without any trial running, therefore, the engine had to pull this formidable load over the 1 in 100 gradients between Limoges and Brive. The driver was René Gourault who had driven No. 3566 on its first trials in 1929, and with this expert the engine never dropped below 25mph on the most difficult of the banks. On arrival at Brive No. 160.A.1 was hidden away in the sheds, and there it remained until the end of the war.

With all its apparent innovations, Chapelon's 2—12—0 was in fact a perfectly logical development of the classic, or conventional, steam locomotive. But it embodied many features that he wanted to try out with a view to their incorporation in a future generation of locomotives. No. 160.A.1 was, in fact, particularly rich in the lessons which it produced. It was, says Chapelon, a veritable laboratory. Nevertheless, the analysis of results proved very laborious with the measuring apparatus available, and if Chapelon had had more means at his disposal for research he would, he believes, have made better use of these results. However, he is convinced that important principles were brought to light which could not have been established without practical test.

A particularly difficulty was encountered in measuring the temperature of the steam at different points of its circuit, because, when different arrangements of the measuring apparatus was used to check a set of

3. Appendix B.25

figures, different results were obtained. The reason, it appears, was the very bad coefficient of conductibility of superheated steam. This was suddenly revealed on a day when the engine was tested using saturated steam throughout. On that day all the suspected apparatus reported, in exact agreement, the same temperatures. At the same time this showed the mistake made by the Vitry test bank because they had fixed a reservoir on the engine fed with saturated steam to verify *in situ* the accuracy of the measuring apparatus. But this verification was insufficient because, with superheated steam, the temperature depends essentially on the type of apparatus and its position on the engine.

The initial testing at Vitry-sur-Seine could not take place until after the war and it was not till 1948 that No. 160.A.1 was ready for trials on the line. By that time Chapelon's great 4—8—4 locomotive No. 242.A.1 had been under trial for two years (see Chapter 9), the plans for the new range of steam locomotives had been formulated (see Chapter 11), and these plans had been cancelled owing to the decision to stop steam locomotive construction and to electrify the main lines (Chapter 11). Any lessons derived from No. 160.A.1 would therefore have been applied by Chapelon, not to the next generation of locomotives which he had already designed, but to the generation after that. As it was these lessons could only be used in the rebuilding of existing stock. In fact no such rebuilding ever took place and in November 1955, two years after Chapelon had retired from the SNCF, his 2—12—0 was scrapped; though it would be difficult to think of an engine more worthy of preservation.

Chapelon's arrangements of the cranks is of interest. Those of the two inside HP cylinders were placed at 90deg from each other. The cranks of the inside LP cylinders were set at 180deg apart, and those of the outside LP cylinders were at 120deg from each other and from the joint thrust of the inside LP. The effect of this disposition was that the LP group acted as a three-cylinder engine with six exhaust beats for each turn of the wheels. It also allowed of a single direct admission of live steam to the LP cylinders which made for extremely energetic starting.

An advantage peculiar to the Franco-Crosti pre-heater was that the water could be replenished without any appreciable fall in boiler pressure, and this was of considerable value if the water level in the gauge had to be re-established when working hard on lines with heavy gradients.

In spite of having only 4ft 7in coupled wheels, the engine showed itself capable of running at comparatively high speeds and thus suitable for working express trains over the more difficult routes. On test a speed of 59mph was recorded.

It was of greater importance, however, that no fall in thermal efficiency at slow speeds was observed. As compared with other types of locomotives, on which fuel consumption increased when the speed (with wheels of similar diameter) dropped to about 21mph, the consumption per horsepower at the tender drawbar of No. 160.A.1 continued to fall with decrease in speed. It was, indeed, another most notable addition to the locomotives which the enginemen designated as *chapelonisées*.

Tests took place during May and June 1948 on 17 trains in ordinary service with dynamometer car attached, over lines with varying ruling gradients and with medium to very heavy loads. The lines concerned, with their ruling gradients, were Villeneuve St. George-Laroche, (1 in 200), Laroche-Dijon (1 in 125), Roanne-St. Etienne (1 in 83), Baden-St. Etienne (1 in 33), Lyon-Roanne via Tarare (1 in 38). On these lines the engine was always able to pull without any help the heaviest loads allowed, which were 1,650 tons between Laroche and Dijon, 1,000 tons between Roanne and St. Etienne, 850 tons between Badan and St. Etienne, and 575 tons between Lyon and Roanne via Tarare. The equivalent on the level of tractive efforts of 20 to 22 tons were sustained at speeds between $12\frac{1}{2}$ and 20mph, corresponding to 1,800–2,300dbhp. At a higher speed of about 28mph the tractive effort was 16·5tons and at 37mph it was 12 tons, corresponding to 2,650–2,750dbhp.

Consumption was relatively low for trains in ordinary service. Thus, between Laroche and Dijon, pulling a train of 65 vehicles weighing 1,660 tons, with a sustained average tractive effort of 21,340lbs on the level at a speed of 30mph (corresponding to 1,702dbhp), and over a prolonged period of $2\frac{3}{4}$ hours, expenditure per horsepower/hour at the drawbar was 15·37 pints of water and 2·7lbs of coal. Up a gradient of 1 in 125 between Dijon and Les Laumes, with a train of 1,510 tons (64 vehicles), the average tractive effort sustained at the drawbar (adjusted to the equivalent on the level) was 31,680lbs at a speed of 24·16mph, corresponding to 2,062dbhp. Consumption was 16·72 pints of water and 3·466lbs of coal per hp/hr. In spite of an increase of 50 per cent in the sustained effort the consumption of water only increased by 6 per cent.

Between Badan and St. Etienne, with a train of 32 vehicles weighing 993 tons, the equivalent average tractive effort sustained at the drawbar was 34,540lbs at a speed of 18·6mph, corresponding to 1,612dbhp. Consumption was 18 pints of water and 3·32lbs of coal.

Consumptions of the same order as with the last two trains were recorded when pulling the LO Express, of 13 vehicles weighing 575 tons between Lyon and Roanne via Tarare, with an average tractive effort of 17,710lbs at 32mph. On June 8th 1948, hauling this train, with the speed limit raised by the Permanent Way Department from 37·7mph to 43·5mph, the engine gained 5½ minutes on schedule, maintaining speeds of 37 to 40mph up 1 in 83 gradients and 20mph up the Sauvage gradient of 1 in 38, without the customary banking engine at the rear of the train.

At Beuchaille, between Dijon and Blaisy, on a curved gradient of 1 in 125, No. 160.A.1 started a train of 1,660 tons; the tractive effort recorded in the dynamometer car was 36 tons.

In all these trials, in spite of the great tractive efforts developed, a noteworthy feature was the excellent condition maintained in all parts of the engine. This was probably due in part to the distribution of effort with a six-cylinder drive.

The tests on the line, working trains in ordinary service, were followed by those with brake locomotives. The first series of these took place on the easily graded line Moret-Montargis-Cosne. But the tractive effort developed by the engine was so great that from five to seven brake locomotives were needed. It was considered, therefore, that it would be more convenient to continue on a more heavily graded line. The section chosen was that between Givers and St. Etienne with gradients of 1 in 167 and 1 in 71 where, working trains in normal service, one 2—8—2 brake locomotive would suffice. The trials went very well but there was a surprising aspect. The engine consumed from 10 to 15 per cent more water and coal per dbhp on the St. Etienne trials than it did on those based on Montargis. Research was undertaken to find how this had happened. The influence of curves on the resistance to movement of the engine was investigated by rearranging the coupling of the driving axles to that they operated in two separate sets of three. This investigation supplied no solution to the problem. It was then suggested that there was greater wear in the mechanism over the difficult route at St. Etienne than over the easy gradients operated from Montargis. A return was made to test this hypothesis, but it broke down immediately, for the consumption figures were exactly the same as they had been before the move to St. Etienne.

The solution, when it eventually was found, was extremely simple. The trials at Montargis had been carried out over a longer route than at St. Etienne, and when journeys of the same length were run over the two routes the consumption figures were exactly the same. This showed the extreme importance of ensuring that comparisons are exact; and this, says Chapelon, is a point over which too little care is generally taken and one which removes much of value from many published results.

The trials at St. Etienne were carried out with up to 23 tons of tractive effort at the drawbar, and they were complete enough to allow of a full analysis to be made of the functioning of the engine. It was tried first with complete superheat and re-superheat, secondly with the HP superheat reduced by one-third, thirdly without any HP superheat, and finally without superheat for either the HP or LP cylinders. The results were extremely interesting and enlightening. Without the HP superheat the engine consumed only 1.5 per cent more at 37·5mph and 3 per cent more at 12·5mph. Running with saturated steam only, it consumed 6 per cent more at 37·5mph and 13 per cent more at 12·5mph. This last figure is explained by the increase in throttling of saturated steam, even at low speeds. These results were far from the generally accepted differences between superheated and saturated engines.

For a similar cut-off in the HP and LP cylinders, and the same speeds, the engine, running with saturated steam only, registered an average of 93 per cent of the indicated horsepower achieved in super-heated and re-superheated conditions throughout the whole power scale.

These trials thus brought to light an aspect of the functioning of a compound locomotive which had hitherto been completely unknown; that is, that by applying superheat only to the low pressure steam and by having steam jackets on the high pressure cylinders, one could obtain the same efficiency from an engine as by superheating the high pressure steam to a very high temperature. This remarkable discovery arose from the use of steam jackets which Chapelon had introduced for quite a different reason. Its principal value was that it was no longer necessary to use the very high temperatures which are so injurious to castings, oil, piston rings, and the general maintenance of an engine. Furthermore, because the discovery was only applicable to compound engines, it would make these far cheaper to operate and maintain than simple expansion engines of equivalent power. Had the war not broken out when it did, it is probable that such compound engines would now be running, perhaps not only in France but also in Great Britain and elsewhere. Chapelon says that his 141.P class 2—8—2 locomotives (see Chapter 6) would have been designed as compounds with LP superheat only and steam-jacketed HP cylinders. But the evaluation of the results obtained with No. 160.A.1 came too late—too late even to be included in the 1952 edition of his own book *La Locomotive à Vapeur*.

In discussing Chapelon's revolutionary 2—12—0 we have run a long way ahead of our timetable. But of course No. 160.A.1 was designed whilst the PO-Midi was still an independent railway and was intended to meet that railway's needs. In his future designs Chapelon would be considering the locomotive problems of all Regions of the SNCF. On the formation of this new organisation he was posted as

Chief of Studies in the Division specifically concerned with steam locomotive design, and he ultimately became Chief of the Division. He progressed through the grades of Engineer and Principal Engineer to Engineer-in-Chief.

As on British Railways, nationalisation posed the problem of how far to proceed with existing designs, and, alternatively, the extent to which requirements should be met by entirely new locomotives of either new designs or modifications of existing ones. In meeting the problem, France had one advantage over Great Britain, because there was not that innate hostility to locomotives of another railway, which was one of the reasons which influenced R. A. Riddles in his decision to build locomotives of a British Railways design rather than to develop those of one of the old railway companies. Of French railways only the PLM seemed a little reluctant to accept 'foreign' engines, but even they asked for Chapelon's magnificent 240.Ps.

Chapelon was of course a convinced compound enthusiast and his selection for the SNCF appointment signified approval of his views. Indeed, comparison between compound and simple expansion loco-motives had been universally in favour of the compound. Before the war, for example, a very interesting series of trials had been carried out between two engines built on Chapelon principles, one a compound and the other a simple expansion locomotive. These were a four-cylinder Etat Pacific of class 231.DD (later re-designated 231.G, and the most powerful of the Etat rebuilds), and a two-cylinder simple Alsace-Lorraine Pacific of the S.16 class (with a pressure of 292lbs per sq in instead of 232) mentioned in the last chapter, and which had been specifically designed with the object of achieving expansion ratios similar to those of equivalent compounds. The trials took place between Paris and Le Havre, a line which included the Motteville vank with an average gradient of 1 in 182 for 19 miles. The S.16 climbed this with a load of 560 tons at an average speed of 55mph. With a much heavier train of 690 tons the Etat Pacific maintained an average speed of 63mph up the bank, developing the equivalent of 2,470dbhp. On the mainly level section between Paris and Rouen the 231.DD sustained a speed of 82–86mph and its fuel consumption over the whole run was about 30 per cent lower than that of the S.16. Tests with brake locomotives between a rebuilt PO Pacific, No. 231.726 (with 245lbs per sq in pressure), and the S.16 produced similar results.

It has been argued that, because hardly any other country in the world followed France in building compound engines, there can have been little overall advantage in compounding. The simple answer to that argument is that the Chapelon compound engine was far in advance of any other steam locomotive design in the world.

6

After the War

In 1945, not long after the end of the war, Chapelon gave a remarkable address to the members of the *Association Francaise des Amis des Chemins de Fer* (AFAC) on projects for future steam traction on the SNCF. Because this address covers the whole subject so comprehensively, it will be used as the basis for the story of the remainder of Chapelon's career on the French railways, and the various locomotives will be discussed in detail as they occur in the course of the address.

At the start of the war there were on French railways 9,137 steam tender locomotives of 114 main types and 2,726 tank locomotives comprising 63 main types. (Each of these types included all engines in each of the original companies of the same wheel arrangement and driving wheel diameter.) The most numerous of types, or groups of classes, was that of the PLM with 692 2—8—2 locomotives having coupled wheels of 5ft 5in diameter, built from 1918 onwards. The PLM had the large number of 370 Pacific express locomotives, all with coupled wheels of 6ft 6¾in diameter; though they were surpassed by the Etat, on which the 340 6ft ⅞in Pacifics for its services had been followed by an order for 140 identical engines from the Minister of Public Works, which, paid for as war reparations, were delivered to the AL, Est, and PO Railways from 1920. In their original form (i.e. before Chapelon-type rebuilding) the PLM and Etat designs dated from 1909 and 1914 respectively.

By 1945 the average age of tender engines in service was 34 years. They were divisible into two main groups; one of about 1,200, principally 4—6—0 engines, dating from 1910, and the other of some 1,500 engines built from 1923 onwards and consisting mainly of Pacifics and Mikados. Of tank engines, which averaged 32·3 years of age, there were four main groups, numerically much smaller than those of the tender engines. There were about 300 0—6—0 engines, of which the oldest were 74 years of age, 250 2—6—2 and 0—10—0 engines dating from 1910, 300 2—8—2 and 0—8—0 from 1920, and 200 2—8—2, 4—8—4, 0—10—0, and 0—8—0, built from 1930 onwards. This great diversity of the locomotive stud and its unequal age was rectified by a programme of rapid depreciation so that locomotives could be withdrawn without too much delay. This programme included all those locomotives which were either insufficiently powerful for current needs

or which were so old that the cost of maintenance had become pro-
hibitive. It was not necessary to replace all locomotives withdrawn
because, owing to the progress in electrifying the French railways, fewer
steam locomotives were required than before the war. By 1950, for
instance, when the Paris-Lyon electrification had been completed, the
number of steam locomotives had been reduced by over 1,600. The
principal classes withdrawn were the old unrebuilt Pacifics and 4—6—0s
of the PO, Etat, Nord, and PLM, and goods or mixed traffic engines of
2—10—0, 4—8—0, 2—8—0, and 4—8—0T, belonging to the PO,
PLM, Est, and Midi. The years of construction of these various classes
ranged from 1897 to 1913. However, in contrast to the withdrawal of
comparatively recent locomotives some of a very old class were retained,
the 0—6—0 C class built for the Ouest Railway in 1867; of 179 engines
only 29 were withdrawn in 1945. These sturdy little two-cylinder simple
expansion locomotives only weighed about 40 tons and could be used
on routes of the lightest construction. With outside cylinders, a tall
chimney, and a massive dome, they were a picturesque reminder of
earlier days and could be seen on all sorts of duties from rural passenger
to local goods.

The requirement plan for steam locomotives was worked out in the
light of the traffic envisaged during the ten-year period 1945–56,
taking into account locomotives rendered surplus by the Paris-Lyon
electrification. It was appreciated that it must be flexible to allow for
modification to meet the actual as opposed to the anticipated traffic
evolution and the possible spread of diesel and electric traction. It was
decided that new construction must have priority, and that, even if
traffic increased to the extent that more engines were required than had
been planned for, the additional number needed would be met by
accelerating new construction and not by slowing down the depreciation
of old locomotives; for it was in the renovation of the locomotives stud
that significant economies would be achieved.

It was an important aspect of the cost of traction that the costs of
annual maintenance increased with the age of the engines, and a time
came when their retention was more expensive than building new ones.
The age when this occurred had been the study of an American engineer
who had conceived the idea of an economic life of a locomotive, corresponding to the time at the end of which the increase in maintenance
costs became equal to the decrease in the costs of depreciation. He
worked this out as between 15 and 20 years. Rather curiously this
upper limit of 20 years was the period at the end of which locomotives
in France became inadequate for the service for which they had been
intended. Thus the Crampton of 1850 was outmoded in 1870; the
compound 4—4—0 of 1890 could not meet the requirements of 1910;

and the Pacific of 1910, with its maximum power of 2,000hp, was barely up to its task in 1930. These last engines, in fact, were only retained in service by their extensive rebuilding on Chapelon lines.

The American argument was, it is true, somewhat misleading, because it was the American practice to send a boiler back to the engine from which it was removed, even if this entailed welding a new barrel on to an old firebox, or vice versa. The general practice in France and Great Britain was to treat the engine and the boiler separately and on the British LMS Railway the locomotive building programme was based on an average of three new boilers for each engine during its working life. The American figure was based, therefore, on the life of a boiler rather than that of a locomotive. Thus, whilst from an economic as well as a technical point of view there appears to be little value in retaining an engine much beyond its economic life, French experience fixed an age of 40 years as the limit beyond which it was not worth while keeping an engine because the annual cost of running it became considerably greater than the running costs of a new locomotive.

With all these considerations in mind, it was decided in 1945 that, if during the succeeding ten years only sufficient engines were built to meet the traffic needs of the twelve months preceeding hostilities, the number required would be between 2,000 and 3,000, depending on whether or not the engines removed to Germany were returned. Even on this modest forecast, therefore, from 200 to 300 engines would have to be ordered every year for the next ten years.

Under the conditions of 1945 and the immediately following years, and having regard to the stated passenger train policy, it was apparent that new express locomotives were not immediately required. For the time being it was intended to run few and heavy passenger trains at moderate speeds (650–700 tons by steam traction and 850 tons by electric, both at 40–47mph) so as to keep within the capacity of the existing engines—the steam Pacific and the 2—D—2 electric locomotives. These same engines would suffice too, at any rate during the first post-war stage, for the traction of the light fast services, known as "Flag Trains", which were intended to provide at least a few creditable performances over the principal main lines.

The Pacifics to which Chapelon referred were, of course, the various rebuilt Pacifics of the PO and PLM, Etat, and Nord which have been described in previous chapters. PLM Pacifics, as they became displaced by electrification, were drafted to the Nord and Est Regions on which Chapelon-type PO Pacifics were already running. The comparison between the two types was interesting. As one would expect, the PO type engines were more robust than the PLM Pacifics, for the construction of the former followed the practice of the Société Alsacienne (who were responsible for the detailed design) and had benefited as well from the various reinforcements to the chassis during rebuilding at Tours from 1929 onwards—reinforcements which had been incorporated in the 28 locomotives built new for the Nord in 1937. The PO longitudinal frame members were 1·26in thick as compared with the 1·1in of the PLM, and the PO members were also cross-braced. This cross-bracing was particularly strong near the outside high pressure cylinders which, following the de Glehn arrangement, were immediately in front of the leading coupled wheels. On the PLM engines, on the other hand, the four cylinders were mounted in line across the frames between the leading and trailing bogie wheels, and the chassis was more liable to flexing as it was less rigidly cross-braced. This type of construction was less suitable for high power outputs than that of the PO engines; and it was for this reason, amongst others, that the PO Pacifics were selected for the pantograph tests described in Chapter 4. The boilers of the two types differed; that of the PO having a Belpaire firebox with trapezoidal grate and Nicholson syphon, whilst the PLM had a round top firebox with an essentially square grate. The PLM engine had conventional Walschaerts valve gear with piston valves, and steam passages to the low pressure cylinders which had been enlarged from the original PLM design—though they were not as large as those of the rebuilt PO engine. The PO had Lentz oscillating cam poppet valves driven by the original Walschaerts gear, with steam passages that were virtually doubled in section. The PO engine had independent HP and LP valve gear, whilst the PLM used a derived motion. In the PLM engine the HP cylinders normally developed about two-thirds of the total power, whereas in the PO engine power output was equally divided between HP and LP cylinders.

As regards new construction, it was decided that existing designs should be developed as described in the following paragraphs.

Class 150.P

In 1911 the Nord produced a very good four-cylinder compound 2—8—0 locomotive, with HP cylinders outside the frames and LP inside. Engines of this class, 4061–4340, were noteworthy for having steam passages of relatively large section. As a result they could run freely and were occasionally put on to the haulage of express trains, which they could haul at 65mph in spite of their small wheels. Sometimes they worked Chantilly race trains and on these could reach a speed of 72mph down the 1 in 250 gradients of Orry-la-Ville and St. Denis.

The following year the Nord put into service the first two engines of their new 5.0001 class 2—10—0s which were derived from the 4061 class 2—8—0s; differing from them only in a lengthening of the chassis and boiler and an increase in the volume of the cylinders. The Belpaire firebox with narrow grate remained the same. One of these first two engines was built as a four-cylinder simple expansion engine; but it did not compare well with its compound sister and was itself rebuilt as a compound. All the other engines of the class were compounds from the start. The last batch of the class went into service in 1930 and were fitted with ACFI feed water heaters. These engines, which eventually numbered 84, were rebuilt in succession by changing their cylinders and improving their steam circuit. They could haul trains up to 2,000 tons in weight, and though some were used on the Paris-Lens coal trains, most worked over the Valenciennes Hirson line, pulling trains of 1,300 tons over its 1 in 100 gradients.

In 1933 the Nord built 30 2—10—0 of class 5.1200,[1] designed by de Caso, which were a development of the previous engines and had many similarities with the 3.1250 class Pacifics. They had the same boiler but with 256lbs per sq in pressure instead of 242 and had a larger superheater and larger and particularly well-designed steam passages. In the design of the 5.1200 class it was clear that de Caso had been influenced by Chapelon's methods. They had an ACFI feed water heater and smoke deflectors, and ten of them were supplied for trial with a mechanical stoker. In continuous running on the level they could develop 2,200dbhp at cut-offs of 50 per cent HP and 60 per cent LP running at 56·2mph, and on trials they exceeded a speed of 75mph. Their performance in service was outstanding, with the result that the SNCF continued their construction, building 115 between 1939 and 1949. All of the engines built for the SNCF had a mechanical stoker, together with a steel firebox and Nicholson syphon. They were all used on the Nord Region, and it was in the light of the purely Nord requirement that the selection of such a good Nord design was inevitable.

Class 141.P[2]

The 2—8—2 type of engine appeared first in France on the PLM in 1914 in the shape of a four-cylinder superheated compound, and was subsequently built in considerable numbers on that railway. The first of the class, No. 1.001 (later No. 141.A.1), was shown at the Lyon Exhibition of 1914. During the war some more of these engines were built by the American Locomotive Company for the PLM (Class 141.B) and also for the Nord. These were followed by Classes 141.C and 141.D, built form 1919 to 1934, with only slight differences between them. In 1937 one of these engines, No. 141.C.623, was modified in a similar way to the PLM 231.G class Pacifics. The steam passages of the

1. Appendix B.26   2. Appendix B.27

LP cylinders were enlarged and the trefoil exhaust was replaced by a double exhaust with cross-bars. Following this a less extensive modification was made by the Est, on which railway the engine was in service, to No. 141.C.7. The superheat was increased by substituting Houlet elements for Schmidt, and LP piston valves with double admission and double exhaust were fitted. The cylinders remained unaltered. The Sud-Est Region then, in 1940, began rebuilding a number of engines with similar valves and with the exhaust fitted to No. 141.C.623 (renumbered 141.E.623). Eventually there were 344 rebuilt engines, of which only 23 were given new LP cylinders like No. 141.E.623. Of these latter, No. 141.E.11 was tested on the Vitry bank and developed at 43·75mph a maximum of 2,050hp at the wheel rims, whilst an unmodified engine could only manage 1,870 and required 9·3 per cent more water to do it.

But No. 141.C.7, with its large increase in superheat, was able to develop a maximum horse power of 2,400 with an economy in water of 13·2 per cent compared with an engine in the original condition; and this was accomplished with a six-jet trefoil exhaust which was little superior to that fitted to it when built. This test showed the great effect of increasing the superheat, particularly when an engine was working at maximum power; and it confirmed the results obtained with the rebuilt PO Pacifics, indicating that to obtain the maximum advantage of an increase in the cross-sectional area of the LP cylinder group steam passages there must be a substantial increase in the degree of superheat.

In 1941 the SNCF started work on a batch of 358 Mikado type locomotives for mixed traffic working (of which 318 were actually built —the remaining 40 being cancelled in favour of 35 4—8—2 locomotives). These engines were derived from the PLM 141.C class, but Chapelon incorporated in the new engines the principles and methods which had proved so successful in his Pacifics and 4—8—0s. The general arrangement of the 141.C class was retained, in so far as it concerned the overall dimensions of the boiler and the dispositions of the wheels and mechanism. The boiler pressure was raised from 232lb per sq in to 290. The object of this was to allow of a reduction of the cylinder diameters so that the low pressure cylinders could be placed inside the frames (instead of outside as in the 141.Cs). At the same time the axis of the boiler was raised about 4 inches above rail level. These measures allowed the provision of a much better steam circuit and better connections to the blastpipe. Of the first 50 engines, half were given the PLM variable double exhaust with cross bars and half the double Kylchap. In comparative working it was found that the Kylchap pattern provided a more uniform draught with significantly lower maintenance costs. The double Kylchap exhaust was therefore fitted to all of the new engines, and the operating division of the Sud-Est Region asked that the PLM exhaust fitted to the 25 of the first batch (which had been sent to them) should be replaced by the Kylchap. However, although designs were prepared they were not put into effect.

The high pressure cylinders had lightened cylindrical piston valves, whilst those for the low pressure cylinders were the Willoteaux double admission and double exhaust type. One set of Walschaerts gear operated both HP and LP valves on the same side and these were fixed at the same cut-off. Provision was made for using simple expansion working on starting. A mechanical stoker was fitted and also an ACFI feed water heater.

The new engines had plate frames, as in the 141.C class, but they were thicker (35mm instead of 28mm) and strongly stayed, particularly in line with the driving axles. As in the Nord 5.1200 class, the frames were interrupted in line with the cylinder block which was of cast steel.

The simple leading bissel truck was replaced by a bissel bogie of the Italian Zara type (incorporating the carrying and leading coupled wheels), which gave the engine much better riding in the passage of sharp curves, such as those encountered in the Massif Central.

The new engines were designated class 141.P and their success in traffic was immediate. Not only were they extremely powerful, but their stability was so good that they could run easily at speeds of from 72 to 78mph and they were very economical in their consumption of coal and water. In the course of trials with brake locomotives No. 141.P.75, with a Kylchap exhaust, developed continuously the following maximum horsepowers at the tender draw bar:

2,142 at 25mph with 72 per cent cut-off
2,970 at 37·5mph with 72 per cent cut-off
3,330 at 50mph with 55 per cent cut-off
3,223 at 62·5mph with 52 per cent cut-off

In continuous working therefore it was possible to obtain (and with both pressure and water constant in the boiler) the remarkable figure of 780hp per sq m of the grate area (total 4·28sq m) at 58mph; a value little inferior to the 800hp of No. 242.A.1 (described later). But in mentioning these high figures in normal working, one must recall the truly exceptional effort of 4—8—0 No. 4701 recorded in Chapter 3 when, in a notable feat of hand-firing by Fireman Marty, 820hp per sq m of grate area was developed continuously at 62·5mph.

With their 5ft 5in coupled wheels, great power, speed, stability, adhesion, and economy of working, the 141.Ps were probably the finest mixed traffic class of steam locomotives ever built. To-day, 30 years after they were first designed, it is perhaps interesting to consider what diesel-hauled traffic in the Great Britain of 1971 they could *not* have worked.

Class 151.TQ

In 1928 the firm of Corpet, Louvet, et Cie. built some two-cylinder simple expansion engines for the Ceinture Railway, which was mostly concerned with the transfer of traffic round Paris between the great railway companies. They had Schmidt superheaters, Kylchap exhausts, and ACFI feed water heaters. In 1941 the SNCF ordered 30 more engines from the same firm to meet a requirement from the Nord Region which had become responsible for the lines of the old Ceinture. Except for a few details, these engines, class 151.TQ, were identical with their predecessors.

Class 050.TQ

Between 1908 and 1914 the Midi Railway had constructed for them 47 0—10—0 tank engines of the 5000 class for the haulage of the heaviest goods trains on steeply graded lines, particularly on that between Neussargues and Béziers, running north and south through the very middle of the Massif Central. The idea of these engines was conceived from the presence of a Prussian State Railways T.16 class two-cylinder simple expansion 0—10—0 tank engine at the Milan Exhibition of 1907 and the obvious advantages conferred by its total adhesion.

At that time goods trains on the Neussargues-Béziers line were worked by four-cylinder compound 2—8—0 locomotives of the 4000 class, built from 1901 to 1907 (and the first of this wheel arrangement in France). But the great effort demanded every day from even these relatively powerful engines in heavy haulage over such formidable gradients entailed considerable maintenance both of mechanism and boiler. (The latter had the high pressure for those days of 215lbs per sq in).

At the request of the Midi the German builders, in conjunction with the Prussian State Railways, organised a series of trials in June 1907 with a T.16 locomotive on a line with gradients similar to those between Neussargues and Béziers. As a result of these trials the Midi fixed the specifications for the 5000 class, which were similar to those of the T.16, except in a number of minor details, but with increased dimensions of grate and cylinders to allow the working of trains as heavy as those hauled by the T.16s but with shorter cut-offs.

On trial the Midi engines were very successful and showed an economy of 8 per cent in coal and 15·7 per cent in water over the 4000 class. They therefore operated all freight traffic on the Neussargues-Béziers line until electrification in 1932. From 1930 some of the engines were fitted with the Kylchap 1K/1C exhaust with lengthened smokebox and large chimney. More were so fitted after the amalgamation of the PO and the Midi, though a number of engines retained their original exhausts.

In 1908, in the meantime, the PO, impressed with these locomotives, ordered 25 of similar design though with minor differences (their class 5500) for use on their own heavily graded lines running eastward into the Massif Central and also for shunting at various important marshalling yards.

Both Midi and PO engines were two-cylinder simple expansion, superheated, and with a boiler pressure of 172lb per sq in. The 2nd and 4th axles were fixed, but the others had some lateral play to facilitate passage over sharp curves. The cylinders drove on the 4th axle, which entailed exceptionally long piston rods.

In 1948 the SNCF put into service the first of 35 0—10—0 tank engines which were nearly identical with the Midi type, but with bigger bunkers, Kylchap exhaust, and other modifications, and designated them 050.TQ. This was a very interesting retention of a remarkably successful class over 40 years after the first of the original engines had been built for the Prussian State Railways. What made it even more interesting was that these new locomotives were not required for the Sud-Ouest Region but for the Nord. The old Midi and PO engines remained on the Sud-Ouest and became classes 050.TB and 050.TA respectively.

7
241.P and 141.R

THE LAST chapter dealt with locomotives which had been designed either before or during the war and which were selected by the SNCF for further construction. But this programme did not go far to meet the 2,000 to 3,000 locomotives which M. Chapelon said would be needed. Large numbers of powerful and reliable general-purpose locomotives were an immediate necessity to operate all sorts of services until the French railways could be restored to normal conditions. But in addition to this, the Sud-Est Region found that it had not sufficient powerful express locomotives to work trains between Laroche and Dijon, pending the completion of the electrification of the line from Paris to Dijon. This latter problem will be considered first.

Class 241.P
The Sud-Est stated a specific requirement for 35 4—8—2 locomotives of a class similar to No. 241.C.1 which had been designed in 1931. In M. Chapelon's opinion this was a bad choice. There were two alternatives: the 240.P class 4—8—0 locomotives and Chapelon's prototype 4—8—4, No. 242.A.1, which was already displaying its great power and efficiency under test. It was the success of No. 240.705 on the PLM main line in comparison with No. 241.C.1 which had resulted in the order for the 240.Ps. This engine's performance on a 672-ton train running to the 'Cote d'Azur' timings is recorded in Chapter 3. No. 241.C.1 was tried on the same test train, made rather slower running, and had to stop owing to the heating of a HP axle box. This had happened before in 1932 at the start of the trials on the Nord, and it occurred this time in the presence of the Director of the Sud-Est Region during a meeting between Laroche and Dijon, a little before the decision to build the 241.P class was taken. In a whole series of tests with heavy loads between Laroche and Dijon the 4—8—0 had consumed 11 per cent less water for equal work in hp hours than the 4—8—2. But the 240.P was an even better engine than the 240.700, and this makes the preference for the 241.C type even more inexplicable. A better proposition than either would have been a class of 4—8—4 locomotives similar to No. 242.A.1 which, like No. 241.C.1, was a prototype. However, the then Director of Rolling Stock and Motive

68

Power on the SNCF decided that the need for heavy express engines was so urgent that the completion of 242.A.1's trials could not be awaited; particularly as the post-war shortage of metals would entail a delay in their provision. These arguments were difficult to follow because they applied equally to No. 241.C.1, and if engines were wanted quickly there were the 240.Ps for which no new design would be required. However, the decision was given in favour of the PLM engine and Chapelon was faced with the task of turning a mediocre locomotive into a good one without it entailing any major new design.

That improvements were necessary was apparent from the tests on the Nord described in Chapter 2, when the Nord authorities had no hesitation in preferring a Chapelon Pacific to the PLM Mountain.

The Mountain type of locomotive was introduced into France in 1925 by both the PLM and the Est Railways. The Est engine had 6ft 4¾in coupled wheels and was intended for express passenger work.[1] The PLM engine, with smaller coupled wheels of 5ft 10¾in diameter, was intended specifically to haul heavy express trains over the steeply graded lines between Laroche and Dijon.[2] The Est engine was a four-cylinder compound of the Du Bousquet de Glehn type, whilst the PLM engine, No. 241.A.1, was also a four-cylinder compound but of the standard PLM pattern. The smokebox front of the latter was of a peculiar ovoid shape, intended to act as a smoke deflector and rather reminiscent of the PLM's wind-cutting locomotives.

From 1927 the PLM put into service a series of 145 locomotives identical with No. 241.A.1, the last of which was turned out in 1932. Later on some of them were modified in accordance with Chapelon principles with an improved steam circuit. New low pressure cylinders were provided with enlarged steam passages, a PLM double exhaust was fitted, and the ovoid smokebox front was replaced by wind deflector plates of the normal pattern. These engines were reclassified 241.D. A few of the 241.A class received only the comparatively minor modifications of Est pattern low pressure valves with double admission and double exhaust.

No. 241.C.1[3] was built in 1931, before all the 241.A class engines had been finished, but it embodied lessons learned from the latter in traffic. The diameter of the coupled wheels was increased to 6ft 6¾in, the boiler pressure was raised from 232lbs per sq in to 292lbs, the outside low pressure cylinders drove the second coupled axle instead of the first, and the inside high pressure cylinders drove the third instead of the second.

The success of Chapelon's Pacifics on the PO came as a shock to the PLM, particularly as No. 241.C.1 on trials with brake locomotives had

1. Appendix B.16   2. Appendix B.18   3. Appendix B.17

only developed 1,840hp at the drawbar in continuous running in its original form, whilst the Chapelon Pacifics were developing much more. As a result some modifications were made to No. 241.C.1, the engine being fitted with a PLM designed variable double exhaust with petticoat and cross-bars, together with smoke deflector plates. This effected some improvement, for before the modification the engine produced 3,200ihp on test with brake locomotives and after it 3,500ihp. In 1941 a 241.A class locomotive was rebuilt to conform with the modified 241.C.1, though retaining its original boiler pressure, and was renumbered 241.E.27. In addition, and contrary to normal PLM practice, it incorporated a starting arrangement which allowed the high pressure cylinders to exhaust directly into the atmosphere.

The 241.P class engines,[4] like No. 241.C.1, were designed and constructed by the Creusot Company in consultation with the SNCF. Chapelon improved the steam circuit in the same fashion as he had adopted in the rebuilt Pacifics, providing new cylinders with an increase in the area of the steam passages. At maximum cut-off this increase amounted to 38 per cent at the admission to both high and low pressure cylinders and to 25 per cent and 18 per cent at their respective exhausts. The frames of 241.C.1 were well known to be too light; but there was no time to re-design them, so that frames only 1·1in thick had to be used. To strengthen them the chassis was reinforced slightly at the level of the driving axle boxes by cast-steel longitudinal cross members, but the maximum axle weight permitted did not allow of the full strengthening which Chapelon had pointed out was required, and to take the extra weight of which he would have preferred a 4—8—4 wheel arrangement instead of a 4—8—2.

At the request of the Director of the SNCF a great improvement was made in the appearance of the locomotives, particularly in the shape of smokebox, chimney, smoke deflectors, ACFI feed water heater, cab, etc.; presenting the same sort of outline as the Chapelon team had so successfully produced in the 141.Ps. As compared with No. 241.C.1, the modifications increased the weight of the engine by 5,320 tons.

The first of these new engines, designated class 241.P, were put into service in 1948 and the last in 1952. As stated in the last chapter, they replaced 40 of the 141.P class. They never ran on the line for which they had been requested, for electric trains were running between Paris and Dijon in 1951, a year before the last of the class had been completed, and the 240.P class 4—8—0s continued to work express trains between Paris and Dijon until the electric locomotives took over. The 241.P locomotives were all despatched instead to the Marseilles depot, and hauled heavy express trains, the "Mistral" in particular, between Lyon

4. Appendix B.28

(which the electric track reached in 1952) and Marseilles. They did not run between Marseilles and Nice, over which route as many trains as possible were worked by the oil-burning locomotives of the 141.R class. When the 241.Ps were displaced by the extension of electrification southwards from Lyon they were sent to the Nord, Est and Ouest Regions.

The 241.Ps were very fine looking engines and achieved some very satisfactory performances. Nevertheless, they cannot be said to have been a complete success. The draughtsmen working out the detailed plans for these locomotives were too restricted by the specifications to be able to do more than produce a good, but no by means outstanding, class of engines. The 241.Ps inherited many of the faults of the original 241.C design and in spite of their 54·3sq ft of grate area their performance never equalled that of the 240.P class with only 40sq ft. Under the most favourable circumstances they barely registered 3,000hp at the drawbar. The 241.P boiler and that of Chapelon's 4—8—4, No. 242.A.1, were very similar, but, as stated above, the weight permissible on a 4—8—2 did not allow of the frames being given adequate strength. There was also the greater tendency to flexing of double-cranked axles with consequent overheating of the driving axle boxes, from which the 241.Ps suffered. No. 242.A.1 was a three-cylinder compound with a much more rigid single cranked axle for the inside HP connecting rod.

But the 241.Ps have their niche in railway history, for they were the last of the great French four-cylinder compounds in regular service, and when they ended their days in 1970 they were probably the most powerful express steam locomotives running anywhere in the world. On May 21st 1970 there were three left at the Le Mans locomotive depot, Nos. 241.P.9, 241.P.16, and 241.P.17. They had all three been withdrawn from regular service, but 241.P.17 had been repainted for static exhibition and the other two were destined for museums. Their last active service had been on the express service between Le Mans and Nantes, and on this route they could run with trains of between 700 and 800 tons at average speeds of 62–56mph without exceeding the 74·6mph to which they were limited.

Class 141.R

In November 1944 a French mission went to the United States to arrange for the manufacture of a vast batch of locomotives to meet the immediate needs of the railways following the liberation of French territory. They wanted a powerful mixed traffic engine which, having regard to the postwar conditions, should be robust with more emphasis on easy maintenance and driving than on economy of operation. What the mission had in mind was a two-cylinder simple expansion version of their own highly successful 141.P class 2—8—2, and what they therefore took with them was a specification which, to ensure speed of construction, gave wide latitude to the incorporation of American standards and practices. This welding of American practice to French ideas was not of course new. In 1914 the PO designed a two-cylinder simple expansion 2—8—2 mixed traffic locomotive, of which they intended to have a class of 30. Owing to the outbreak of war only two were built. In 1916 a mission was despatched to the United States to order 150 locomotives, built according to American practice but adhering as far as possible to that of the PO. During the war the idea arose of a simple expansion Pacific common to all French railways; an idea which came to nothing, but in 1920 the PO ordered from the American Locomotive Company 50 simple expansion Pacifics which were delivered in 1921.

It is safe to say that if it had not been for the war no class of locomotive so foreign to French practice as the 141.Rs would have ever run in France. But equally they would never have run anywhere else, because, although embodying American construction methods and American detailed design, they were even more foreign to American practice than they were to French.

As a result of the visit an order for 700 2—8—2 locomotives with mechanical stokers was placed with the American firms of Baldwin, Alco, and Lima to a design prepared by the first; and a second order for 640 engines was submitted later. The total number received was only 1,323 because a ship carrying 17 of them foundered in an Atlantic gale.

There were a number of differences between various batches— differences in frames, axle bearings, wheels, fuel (i.e. coal or oil), exhaust, etc. The locomotives, designated 141.R, were built in both the United States and Canada and were delivered to the SNCF from 1945 to 1947. Like the 141.P class, they had 5ft 5in coupled wheels, but the boiler pressure was lower (220 instead of 292lbs per sq in) and the grate area larger (55·5sq ft instead of 47·1sq ft). A combustion chamber and two Nicholson thermic syphons were incorporated in the design, neither of which features figured in the earlier 141.P engines (though the final batch of these had Nicholson thermic syphons to help strengthen the brick arch). The first 700 engines had the standard American pattern exhaust together with self-cleaning smokebox, bar frames, and Timken roller bearings on the bissel carrying axles; the last of this order being delivered in April 1946. In the second order of 623 engines, all were equipped with the Kylchap exhaust instead of the American pattern. But there was much greater variety than amongst those of the first order; 604 engines were fitted for oil firing, 400 had Boxpok driving wheels with Timken roller bearings, 223 had Boxpok wheels and Timken roller bearings on all the coupled axles, and 199 had a mono-bloc chassis (the first appearance of this type of frame in Europe).

Very thorough trials were carried out with the 141.R class on both the Vitry bank and on the line with brake locomotives; and these trials were of great interest in comparing results between the different varieties and also between the 141.R and 141.P classes in general.

No. 141.R.469 of the first order, that is to say with American exhaust, developed continuously at the drawbar maximum powers of:

    2,197 at 25mph with 60 per cent cut-off,
    2,600 at 37·5mph with 55 per cent cut-off,
    2,633 at 50mph with 45 per cent cut-off, and
    2,509 at 62·5mph with 40 per cent cut-off.

No. 141.R.874 of the second order with Kylchap exhaust returned the following figures:

    2,269 at 25mph with 60 per cent cut-off,
    2,737 at 37·5mph with 55 per cent cut-off,
    2,929 at 50mph with 55 per cent cut-off, and
    2,700 at 62·5mph with 45 per cent cut-off.

In addition to its greater power output, No. 141.R.874 was more economical than 141.R.469 by 13 per cent in water and coal consumption. However, the 141.Rs of the second order were neither as economical nor as powerful as the 141.P class. For comparison the maximum powers developed continuously at the drawbar of the 141.P and two varieties of 141.R engines are set out below with the relative speed in miles per hour:

Speed	141.P	141.R (1st order)	141.R (2nd order)
25	2,142	2,197	2,269
37·5	2,970	2,600	2,737
50	3,330	2,633	2,928
62·5	3,223	2,509	2,700

The superiority of the 141.P in the higher speed range is most marked.

In 1945 the Ouest Region, wishing to improve its Mikados, designed an application to these engines of the modifications made to its Pacifics, following the principles adopted on the PO. A two-cylinder simple expansion 2—8—2, No. 141.E.113, was selected for conversion. It was provided with an improved steam circuit with wide steam passages, steam chests of large volume, modified cylinders with inlet ports increased by 50 per cent and exhaust ports by 20 per cent at all cut-offs, a Houlet superheater instead of the previous Schmidt pattern with a much increased degree of superheat, a Kylchap exhaust, and a reinforced chassis. At Chapelon's insistence, the exhaust ports were of progressively decreased section with the object of countering the violence of the exhaust, which had been accentuated by the wide steam passages, and which would otherwise have been detrimental to the fire. Comparative trials were carried out between the rebuilt engine and one of the same class, which also had a Kylchap exhaust but was otherwise unmodified, on express trains between Paris and Caen. With 608 tons behind the tender No. 141.E.113 climbed Bréval bank of 1 in 143 in the direction Caen-Paris at an average speed of 43mph, developing the equivalent of 1,865dbhp with 30 per cent cut-off; whilst No. 141.199 (unmodified) climbed the same gradient with 641 tons at 39·7mph, sustaining the equivalent of 1,678dbhp at 50 per cent cut-off. Doing its work on much smaller cut-offs, the rebuilt engine achieved economies of 23 per cent in water and 25 per cent in coal over the unrebuilt. On the Vitry bank No. 141.E.113, developing 2,032dbhp, showed an economy in water of 16·7 per cent over one of the 141.R engines of the second order producing the same power at the same speed. However in this trial No. 141.E.113 was at a considerable disadvantage because of its much smaller boiler. As a result of this trial Chapelon applied the same modifications as had been made to No. 141.E.113 to No. 141.R.672. Thus altered, the 141.R class engine consumed 15 per cent less coal and water per dbhp than other engines of its class on all types of trains. Chapelon accordingly effected similar modifications to another 100 141.R class coal fired engines and to a few of the oil fired ones. The Ouest Region wanted to modify another 30 2—8—2 engines in the same fashion as 141.E.113 but the SNCF would not sanction the request.

In general the 141.P and 141.R engines were neither allocated to the same types of trains nor used on the same routes. The 141.P class did an average of 85 per cent of their running on express passenger and fast freight trains, whilst the 141.Rs worked for only about 25 per cent of their mileage on such services. But these latter engines, unlike the beautifully riding 141.Ps, were very hard on the track and were therefore limited to a maximum speed of 62mph. They were used on all main lines on freight and express passenger services that did not need speeds exceeding that figure. Until the 241.P class 4—8—2s became available, they worked the heaviest express trains on the Ouest Region between Le Mans and Quimper, and on the Sud-Est they handled express trains from Vierzon to Clermont-Ferrand and Lyon over the Bourbonnais line. Along the Mediterranean coast, as mentioned earlier, they eventually took over the working of all traffic until electrification. In more recent days they have been working expresses between Amiens and Calais, and also Boulogne, when the diesel locomotives, which replaced the Pacifics, have broken down.

The vast number of 141.R class engines have given valuable service, and they were particularly useful during the last days of steam on the French railways when, as maintenance facilities decreased and common manning became more usual, their simplicity and reliability led to their being used on all types of trains until diesel and electric traction took over. In the difficult days after the war the 141.Rs were operating one-third of all train mileage and 49 per cent of the total ton-miles, and they have the final distinction (for they are still in service at the time of writing) of being the last steam locomotives in regular service in France.* Their thermal efficiency is low, but because their maintenance costs are also low and their percentage availability high, the total costs remain low provided that they can be kept heavily loaded.

At the end of May 1970 large numbers of 141.R class engines stood on the network of lines at the Le Mans locomotive depot. Many were obviously awaiting scrapping, but others were in working order and No. 141.R.898 in immaculate condition was just leaving the depot to take over a freight train. These engines were oil fired, but at about the same time coal-fired engines were working freight trains through Calais-Ville.

* But in May 1971 there was an Etat 140.C Class 2-8-0 in steam at Le Mans depot, which had been built by the North British Locomotive Company in 1917!

8

Locomotives of the War and Nord 232.R, S, U & 141.TC

APART from the locomotives discussed in the last two chapters, there were a number of foreign design running on French railways after the war which had been built by both sides for military purposes. These could only be regarded as temporary additions to the French locomotive stud because they could not be made to fit into any form of standardisation. There were a great many German 2—10—0 engines of three different classes, which were designated by the Germans as, respectively, 44, 50 and 52, and by the French as 150.X, 150.Z, and 150.Y.

Class 44 appeared first in 1926; three-cylinder simple expansion engines which became the standard for heavy freight and of which 1,755 were built up to 1944. Of these, French firms were forced to build 238, but they were able to delay work to such an extent that 226 were still under construction after the liberation of French territory, and these were taken over by the SNCF and used for hauling mineral trains on the Nord and Est Regions. In 1956, when owing to electrification they were no longer needed, 90 were sold to Turkey. On a trial at the Vitry bank a class 44 locomotive, working at 45 per cent cut-off, developed 2,500hp at the wheel rims and 2,950 in the cylinders at 37·5mph.

The 50 class were two-cylinder simple expansion engines which were built from 1938 as light 2—10—0s, with only 15 tons axle weight as compared with the 19·8 tons of class 44. A total of 3,146 of these engines were built up to 1944. By any standards this was an extremely large number; but it was easily surpassed by the 6,292 locomotives in class 52. However, this was really a wartime or 'Austerity' version of the 50 class; also a two-cylinder simple expansion 2—10—0 with 15 tons axle weight, but so designed as to cut down as far as possible the time spent in construction (which was reduced to 14 hours) and reduce to a minimum the amount of metal required (the tyres, for instance, were only 50mm thick). Construction of this class began in 1942 and continued till 1949. Many were forcibly built by firms in both France and other countries that came under German control during the war.

Two classes of engines were designated, respectively, 140.U and

140.W by the SNCF. The 140.W class consisted of British 'Austerity' two-cylinder simple expansion engines designed by R. A. Riddles of which a total of 935 were built in Great Britain (545 by the North British Locomotive Company and 390 by the Vulcan Foundry); the first being handed over to the Ministry of Supply on January 16th 1943. For ease of manufacture they had a parallel boiler and round top firebox, and, to economise in valuable metal, cast iron replaced steel castings for all except the driving wheel centres. Boiler pressure was 225lbs per sq in, the grate was 28·6sq ft, and the diameter of the coupled wheels was 4ft 8½in. Because of the simplicity of the design the production of the "Austerities" was rapid, and eventually seven were built each week. They were extremely successful engines. At the end of the war 373 were running on the SNCF. The 140.U class engines were the American-built "French Front" two-cylinder 2—8—0s, a Transatlantic version of the "Austerity" idea, and of unbelievable ugliness. The SNCF acquired 578 of these, of which 116 were oil fired (35 on the Est Region and 81 on the Sud-Est). One of the coal-fired engines was tried on the Vitry bank, but it was necessary to modify the exhaust before a normal output could be obtained.

In addition to these goods tender locomotives, there were a number of tank engines of two main types: German 0—10—0s, built by French firms, and American-built 0—6—0s.

It was decided that the three German classes of 2—10—0 tender engines would be retained by the SNCF for some time, because they were suited to current French requirements, but the British and American 2—8—0s would be withdrawn when they needed heavy repair.

As regards improvements to or rebuilding of the older French locomotives, the type of treatment required and the engines to which it should be applied were decided, subject to any alterations in the depreciation programme. The plans, in short, included improvement of steam circuits, improvements of exhaust, feed water heating, and the fitting of water purification devices. This last was met by the TIA system (the initials standing for Traitement Intégral Armand, the highly effective method invented by M. Armand). By this system a 'disencrustor', consisting of carbonate of soda, phosphate of soda, caustic soda, and tannin, was introduced into the feed water by a distributor. Armand had started working on this in 1940–41, basing his investigations on the physico-chemical action of tannin on a soda environment and, at the temperature of boilers, on the calcium encrusting salts. The particular importance of this equipment was that boiler repair constitutes the most expensive part of locomotive maintenance, and that the introduction of water purification on American railways had reduced this cost by from 50 to 65 per cent.

Some of the practical applications of these plans were as follows. On the Sud-Est Region 234 141.C class 2—8—2 locomotives were rebuilt to class 141.E, as described in Chapter 6. Of the PLM Pacifics which were still in their original condition, 190 were rebuilt to class 231.G (see Chapter 4) and 27 to class 231.H with the Superheater Company's 5P4 type superheater. Forty-seven of the 241.A class 4—8—2 locomotives were rebuilt as 241.D and one as 241.E (see Chapter 7); and 8 of the old class 2600 locomotives were rebuilt in accordance with the same principles.

On the Sud-Ouest, the old PO-Midi, it had been for some time the standard practice to fit the Houlet superheater, Willoteaux pattern valves, and the Kylchap exhaust. (The Houlet superheater had at first been fitted only to 10 of the 3500 class Pacifics, and next to all the rebuilt engines).

On the Ouest Region design work had been completed for a considerable modification of the earlier saturated compound Pacifics of the 231.011 class (later 231.B) of 1910, including poppet valves to the LP cylinders, long-travel piston valves for the HP cylinders, Houlet superheater, and double Kylchap exhaust; but this conversion was cancelled because of an amendment to the depreciation programme.

On the Nord mechanical stokers were fitted to all 5.1200 class 2—10—0 locomotives, the HP and LP cylinders of some of the earlier 5.001 class were replaced, and the 4061 class 2—8—0s were provided with ACFI feed water heaters.

On the Est ACFI feed water heaters were fitted to the class 150.E 2—10—0 heavy freight locomotive of 1926. The 48 4—8—2 locomotives of Est design which had been transferred from the Ouest were rebuilt in the same way as had by this time been carried out on all those originally belonging to the Est (see Chapter 4); and some of the 4—8—2s were supplied with coal pushers as had been fitted on the 240.700 class 4—8—0 engines of the PO.

Two of the brilliant 240.P class 4—8—0 locomotives were given new ALCO type bogies with SKF roller bearings which had been chosen for all future SNCF engines. These ALCO bogies replaced the existing *Alsacien* type on which there was insufficient space to fit the SKF bearings.

The last of eight 4—6—4 locomotives designed by M. de Caso for the Nord was completed in 1949. These were rather remarkable engines. In 1933-4, when Chapelon's Pacifics constituted the main element in the Nord express locomotive stud, that Company, true to its traditions, was looking ahead to its next advance in motive power. As a preliminary, tests were carried out which, in the opinion of the Nord, showed the necessity for a larger grate to meet the needs of the engines they envisaged. The Nord had always preferred a narrow grate, even if (as on the 5.1200 class for example) it provided a smaller area, because it made the task of keeping the fire in good condition easier. But a narrow grate would not have provided sufficient area for the proposed engines, and therefore the Nord engineers produced specifications for a boiler with a wider grate than normal that would be suitable for two new types of large engine—a 4—6—4 for ultra-fast trains and a 4—8—2 for heavy express trains.

The latter project was, after further consideration, abandoned, but the OCEM, of which de Caso was then head of the design department, was asked to plan a 4—6—4 locomotive capable of working 200-ton trains at 106mph. After discussion this requirement was modified. It was decided to seize the opportunity to compare compound and simple expansion locomotives, both incorporating Chapelon techniques; but they were to be much more of a general-purpose express passenger type. The maximum speed demanded was lowered to 99·5mph and the permissible axle load raised to 22 tons. The Belpaire firebox was a compromise which could be described as an enlarged narrow firebox, the grate being 9ft 10in long and 5ft 8in wide.

De Caso's design was accepted and in 1938 an order was placed with the Société Alsacienne for eight 4—6—4 express locomotives, of which four were to be four-cylinder compounds and four three-cylinder simples The war had started before the order was finished, and one of the simple expansion engines could not be completed. Three simple expansion engines, class 232.R,[1] were delivered between January and April 1940, and in the latter part of 1940, after Nord territory had been occupied by the Germans, the four class 232.S[1] compounds were received. The DEL (*Division des Etudes de Locomotives à Vapeur*, i.e. the SNCF Division for Steam Locomotive Studies) proposed that the unfinished engine should be purchased for completion with a turbine drive, in a similar fashion to Sir William Stanier's LMS Pacific. As this proposal was not followed up, M. de Caso proposed that the firm of Corpet-Louvet should be asked to complete it as a four-cylinder compound. This was done, and it was eventually delivered in 1949 as No. 232.U.1.[1]

The particular features of the 232.R and 232.S class engines were:
(a) a large boiler with a combustion chamber, a pressure of 292lbs per sq in, and a grate area of 55·7sq ft.;
(b) large cylinders with wide steam passages and rotary cam poppet valve gear;
(c) strong bar frames, driving axle boxes of large dimensions, and roller bearings for the carrying axles; and
(d) a mechanical stoker.

1. Appendix B.29

The 232.R and 232.S classes had a Schmidt type superheater, but No. 232.U.1 was fitted with the Houlet superheater. Much mention has been made in these pages of the Houlet superheater. In the Schmidt type, on which most others were based, saturated steam was carried from a superheater header in the smokebox through a number of small tubes, which were themselves inserted inside large flue tubes, back towards the firebox and then bent round inside the same large tubes to carry the now superheated steam back to the header. In the Schmidt superheater each superheater tube, or element, did this round journey twice, but in the almost equally popular Robinson pattern it only did it once. There were various modifications. The Duchatel and Mestre superheater embodied a rather different type of element; in the first pattern (the DM4) saturated steam travelled towards the firebox in four small flattened tubes and returned through one of larger diameter; whilst in the second and final pattern (the DM3) there were only three of the small tubes, with resulting increase in the section of the flue tube available for the hot gases and consequent greater efficiency. The Houlet superheater was tried first on the Est Railway and was adopted by André Chapelon for all the rebuilt PO Pacifics. Its principal feature was that the element was made up of concentric tubes which were united at the firebox end. The saturated steam flowed through the outer tube and returned, superheated, through the central one. Its advantages were a high thermal efficiency and little resistance to the passage of the steam.

On the 232.R simple expansion class all three cylinders drove on to the centre coupled axle; whereas on the 232.S compounds the two inside HP cylinders drove the first coupled axle and the two outside LP cylinders the centre axle. As compared with both these classes, M. de Caso had certain alterations made in No. 232.U.1. Instead of the Dabeg rotary cam poppet valve gear, which had not been very successful, this last of the 4—6—4s had piston valves with exceptionally long travel, particularly at short cut-offs, driven by Walschaerts valve gear, of which there was one set on each side for both HP and LP cylinders. For starting, live steam was admitted automatically to all four cylinders until the cut-off was reduced below 55 per cent, and it could also be admitted to the LP cylinders for 90 per cent of their stroke to provide sufficient tractive effort to start a 600-ton train on a 1 in 125 gradient. SKF roller bearings were fitted to all axles. All the eight engines were streamlined but No. 232.U.1 was by far the best looking, and had the casing cut away to allow access to the working parts. There were side deflector plates and also vertical screens on both sides of the double chimney on this engine to assist in lifting the smoke and steam.

They were all very powerful engines and achieved some notable performances. But due partly to the Dabeg gear the fuel consumption of the 232.S class compounds was higher than that of the Chapelon Pacifics on the Nord. On trials between Paris and Lille the PO Pacific achieved an economy of 10 per cent in coal per dbhp over the 232.S 4—6—4, which itself was more economical by 12 per cent than its 232.R simple expansion sister. Later the 232.S locomotives were fitted with the same Lentz oscillating cam poppet valve gear that Chapelon had used for the 4—8—0 PO rebuilds. It was the poor results obtained with the Dabeg gear and the superiority of the compounds over the simples that led to the last engine being built as a four-cylinder compound with piston valves and Walschaerts gear.

In service the engines, particularly the compounds, were very impressive. On October 24th 1941 No. 232.S.3 had the task of hauling a 710-ton train between Paris and Dijon. After a stop at Les Laumes it reached a speed of 62·5mph up the subsequent gradient 4·4 miles from the start, having covered this distance in 7mins 30secs.; and 9·4 miles from the start the speed had risen to 73·7mph, and the time taken from Les Laumes was 12 mins. The maximum dbhp was 3,100, equivalent to 3,500 on the level at a uniform speed. On the Nord on September 20th 1954 No. 232.S.4 developed an equivalent of 3,400dbhp whilst mounting the Survilliers gradient with a 585-ton train.

No. 232.U.1 was tried between Paris and Lille shortly after it had been put into service. On May 8th 1950 the engine ran from Paris to Lille and back with a train of 567 tons on an accelerated schedule. There were stops at Arras and Douai and many slacks, but deducting these the average running speed for the round trip was 71mph. On May 10th 1950 the same engine with a 615-ton train climbed a gradient of 1 in 120 at an average speed of 75mph, developing 2,820hp at the tender drawbar, corresponding to 3,265 on the level.

However, these great engines scarcely equalled the 240.P class 4—8—0s in performance, and they were notably inferior to 4—8—4 No. 242.A.1 (see Chapter 9), which had the same boiler pressure and a rather smaller grate area of 53·8sq ft instead of 55·7ft.

Although they were not included in the SNCF list for further construction, mention must be made of some other locomotives designed by de Caso because they were the last purely French steam engines in normal service and so their departure from the Paris scene at the end of 1970 was lamented by Chapelon. These were the 2—8—2 tank engines of class 4.1200 (latterly 141.TC) designed in 1931 for the Nord Railway and the most powerful of their type in France. They had a modified version of the excellent 3.1200 class Pacific boiler which Chapelon had chosen for his 4—8—0s, but in this case the grate was reduced in area to 33·4sq ft and the boiler barrel was slightly longer. The steam circuit was particularly well designed, and a distinctive feature was the Cossart poppet valve gear. The chassis was very strong and exceptionally rigid; consisting of plate frames 1·4in thick, strongly stayed and reinforced longitudinally. The axle weight of 21½ tons was heavy. They were limited to a maximum speed of 65·6mph, which was high, considering that the diameter of their coupled wheels was only 5ft 1in. On July 26th 1932 one of them actually pulled a 482-ton train over the 31 miles from Paris to Creil in 30 minutes, start to stop. On this run a gradient of 1 in 200, 5½ miles long, was climbed at a sustained speed of 68mph with the cut-off at 10 per cent, and Chantilly was passed at 70mph. The equivalent dbhp developed during this effort was 1,900–2,000. For use with reversible trains these engines were fitted with Aubert remote control apparatus and automatic coupling.

The 141.TCs were still working suburban trains out of Paris, Gare du Nord, throughout 1970, as they had done for the past 38 years. These trains latterly consisted of five of the latest all-steel coaches and they were operated 'push-pull' with the engine always facing away from Paris. When the engine was pushing the train (bunker first) the driver could alter the cut-off from the driving compartment at the end of the leading coach. He could also make partial adjustments to the regulator; final adjustments being left to the fireman, to avoid any slipping.

During their last years they were working the suburban service to Valmondois. However, electrification of the route was completed by the end of the year, and December 12th 1970 saw the last steam trains at the Gare du Nord.

9

The Greatest Steam Locomotive of all

In 1932 the Etat Railway asked the *Office Central d'Etudes de Materiel* for the design of a 4—8—2 express passenger locomotive. The OCEM accordingly produced plans for a three-cylinder simple expansion engine which was intended to achieve expansion ratios equal to those of Chapelon's highly efficient compound locomotives. The engine was built by the works of Fives-Lille in 1932 and launched with great publicity. It was specially displayed for admiration by railway officials and the general public at the Gare St. Lazare and in 1935 it was on view at the Brussels Exhibition. It had a boiler pressure of 292lbs per sq in, Renaud poppet valves, driving wheels 6ft 4¾in in diameter, a round-top firebox, a rectangular grate of 53·8sq ft, and a mechanical stoker which reduced the effective grate area to 47·3sq ft. A trefoil exhaust was fitted originally but this was later replaced by a single Kylchap exhaust with six lobes.

This engine, No. 241.101,[1] was perhaps the poorest investment in steam traction that the Etat ever made and no advertisement for the design ability of the OCEM. It failed to produce the expansion ratios expected, partly because of radiation losses, it was restricted in its maximum power output by the small cross-section of the Renaud poppet valves, and its bad riding caused much trouble to the permanent way and traction departments. Amidst some embarrassment it was soon withdrawn and quietly hidden away so that enquiries as to its whereabouts could be met by polite ignorance.

Ultimately its cylinders were accidentally damaged and the Ouest Region asked the Locomotive Study Division for advice. M. Chapelon seized the opportunity to submit a proposal to rebuild the engine as a three-cylinder compound, so that the potential power in its large dimensions could be used. However, the Directorate of Rolling Stock and Traction would not agree to the suggestion. Chapelon had to wait, therefore, until such a rebuilding could be justified as a prototype for the projected range of three-cylinder compound 4—8—4, 4—6—4, 2—10—4, and 2—8—4 locomotives for the SNCF. Official approval,

1. Appendix B.30

however, was received too late to do anything before the war broke out, and it was not till 1942 that conditions allowed work to start.

Chapelon's brilliance as a locomotive engineer has never been displayed more impressively than in this rebuilding; for the fairy wand which changed Cinderella into a Princess scarecely equalled the genius which transformed this slut amongst engines into the most outstanding steam locomotive that ever ran upon rails.

The frames of No. 241.101 were only 1·4in thick, and this was quite insufficient for the power that Chapelon intended the engine to develop, without strengthening the chassis. However, such strengthening on the existing wheel arrangement would entail raising the axle weight above the permitted maximum of 21 tons. He therefore decided to replace the trailing bissel axle by a two-axle bissel truck, thereby altering the wheel arrangement from 4—8—2 to 4—8—4. Chapelon would have liked a chassis of monobloc construction, such as he envisaged for the powerful SNCF locomotives of the future, but such a solution being impracticable, he decided to strengthen the chassis transversely by joining the frames with steel stays at convenient intervals along the length of the engine, and longitudinally by welding horizontal plates to the upper part of the frames. Although not an ideal arrangement it worked well and gave the additional strength required.

Of particular interest was the compound arrangement. All Chapelon's previous compound rebuilds had been four-cylinder engines. But two inside cylinders need two cranks on the driving axle. This inevitably detracts from the rigidity of the axle, leading to a tendency to flexing at high powers and consequent adverse effect on the seating of the axle boxes. Chapelon therefore decided to use three cylinders, compounded on the Smith-Sauvage system with one inside high pressure cylinder and two outside low pressure. This had the additional advantage that the crank axle webs could be increased in thickness to 7·1 inches as compared with the maximum of 4·1 inches which could be allowed in the 240.Ps. The outside cranks were at 90deg with each other and the inside crank was at 135deg with the other two. The inside HP cylinder drove the leading coupled axle and the outside LP cylinders the second. The ratio between HP and LP cylinders was 2·71. The LP cylinders were placed in line with the HP cylinder, between the bogie wheels. The HP cylinder had Trick valves with double admission and the LP cylinders Willoteaux valves with double admission and double exhaust. and there was independent Walschaerts valve gear to all cylinders with independent cut-off to HP and LP cylinders. (This last arrangement was adopted because this was a trial engine. Once the relationship between HP and LP cut-offs necessary to divide power between the two cylinder groups in the best proportion had been established, they could be permanently tied to that relationship in future production of similar engines.)

Naturally, as in all Chapelon designs, particular attention was paid to the steam circuit. Because of the very large dimensions of the boiler a double Kylchap exhaust would not have provided sufficient width of chimney, and the engine was therefore fitted with a triple Kylchap and chimney. The boiler was pressured at 292lbs per sq in and a Houlet superheater was of course fitted, as well as two Nicholson thermic syphons.

The problem of the riding of the engine had now to be tackled, particularly the entry into sharp curves. This was not a difficulty peculiar to No. 241.101; other engines with long rigid wheel bases had experienced trouble in entering curves of small radius and some of them had caused distortion of the track at high speed due to insufficient control of the leading bogie. Chapelon fitted the new engine with the ALCO type bogie with which he had equipped two of the 240.P locomotives, as described in the last chapter. This had a geared roller-centreing device in which the resistance was practically constant until there was a considerable displacement, when it began to decrease. The trailing truck, instead of the previous type with inclined plane control of the single axel bissel, was of the two-axle Delta pattern with rocker centreing. The front bogie had Timken roller bearings and the Delta truck had SKF. To counter 'chattering" of the axle boxes, which caused fatigue of the chassis, Franklin automatic wedges were fitted to reduce to a minimum the play between the axle boxes and their horn guides. This was the first time these wedges had been used in Europe, and they proved very satisfactory, for no shock or vibration was perceptible on the engine whatever the tractive effort and speed. Thanks to all these measures the locomotive rode excellently at all speeds at which it was tried, and which were raised as high as 93·7mph. The state of the track was checked after each trial run on a wide variety of routes and gave no cause for particular comment, and the engine had no difficulty in negotiating sharp curves in the depots.

When completed the locomotive weighed 148 tons, as compared with 128 before rebuilding; but the increase in power obtained was relatively very much greater, because, whilst the original locomotive could only develop 2,800hp in the cylinders, after its transformation it could manage 5,500!

Now numbered 242.A.1,[2] André Chapelon's masterpiece was built at the St. Chamond works of the *Forges et Aciéries de la Marine et d'Homecourt* and completed on May 18th 1946. When one studies the astonishing performances of this locomotive under test, it makes even more

2. Appendix B.30

surprising the decision to build the 241.P class; for No. 242.A.1 was Chapelon's next step in express locomotive design after the 240.Ps, whereas the 241.Ps were inferior to No. 242.A.1 in power output, and also to the 141.Ps and de Caso's 4—6—4s.

As regards performance; it is perhaps as well to remark here that perhaps overmuch attention has been paid to phenomenal speeds achieved on falling gradients with lightweight trains; conditions which call for relatively low tractive effort from the engine. Of greater importance and far more demanding on the quality of a locomotive are performances achieved with heavy loads or on a bank, because it is much more difficult to sustain high speeds at long cut-offs on account of the throttling losses which accompany heavy outputs of steam. It is by these standards that the qualities of Chapelon's locomotives have been assessed in these pages, and it is by the same standards that the remarkable capacity of No. 242.A.1 can be demonstrated.

During trials of No. 242.A.1 carried out on the Vitry bank and on the line with brake locomotives, it was found possible, for the first time in Europe, to sustain in continuous working (with pressure and water constant in the boiler) 4,000hp at the tender drawbar, or 800hp per square metre of grate area, corresponding to more than 5,000hp in the cylinders; and this was achieved at speeds of 50mph (cut-offs 80 per cent HP and 50 per cent LP) and 62·5mph (cut-offs 70 per cent HP and 45 per cent LP). At 75mph (cut-offs 60 per cent HP and 40 per cent LP) horse power at the drawbar was 3,800.

Fuel consumption figures were remarkably satisfactory. In water a record in economy was recorded with 13·64lbs (cold) per hp/hr at the tender drawbar for a total power output of 2,800hp at 37·5mph, and consumption did not rise above 13·86lbs for 3,500dbhp at 50mph, or 14·3 for a ceiling of 4,000dbhp at 62·4mph. Of coal the engine burnt 1·87lbs per hp/hr at 37·5mph for a total of 2,200dbhp, 2lbs at 50mph for 2,600dbhp, and 2·64lbs at 75mph for 2,700dbhp. At the power ceiling of 4,000dbhp the respective coal figures were 2·5lbs at 50mph and 2·64 at 62·5mph. The steaming rate of the boiler was 52,240lbs of cold water per hour, which worked out at more than 1,000ihp per square metre of grate area. On these figures the three-cylinder compound showed itself to be as economical, if not more, than the best French four-cylinder compound locomotives. It is perhaps interesting to compare some pre-war British figures relating to the running of the LMS *Coronation Scot* hauled by one of Stanier's streamlined Pacifics,[3] and quoted by O. S. Nock in his *The British Steam Locomotive 1925–65*. At an average speed of 60mph with an average dbhp of 825, coal consumption was 3·03lbs per hp/hr and water 25lbs, and on a number of

3. Appendix B.31

test runs in February 1939 by No. 6234 the maximum recorded dbhp was 2,511.

From the moment that No. 242.A.1 was put into service it showed that with the three-cylinder compound arrangement, powers of 4,000 to 4,200dbhp at the drawbar were easily obtainable; and the high steaming rates at all speeds showed that the new problem of regrouping the steam jets and dividing them into the triple Kylchap exhaust had been solved. In addition, because No. 242.A.1 was able to develop 2,000–2,500hp in its HP cylinder, it was apparent, as Chapelon had envisaged, that in the powerful locomotives planned for the future three cylinders could provide the 6,000ihp required.

In June 1946 No. 242.A.1 was put on to working trains over the heavily graded line running from St. Germain des Fossées to Roanne, then south to St. Etienne, north-east to the Rhône valley, and finally north to Lyon. It was, perhaps, appropriate that the first major trials of his great engine should be carried out close to the neighbourhood in which André Chapelon had spent his childhood and where his love of the steam locomotive had first been aroused. Trains of from 600 to 660 tons were worked over this line with considerable gains on the scheduled times. For example, on June 20th, with a train of 16 coaches weighing 664 tons, 47mins 20secs were regained between St. Germain des Fossées and Lyon. Drawbar horsepowers of 3,000 to 3,500 were often registered, equivalent to 3,500 to 4,000 on the level at uniform speed, and even higher figures were reached.

Contrary to current thought on the three-cylinder compound system, the engine never displayed any tendency to slip. Thus, starting from St. Chamond station, which is on a gradient of 1 in 71, was always effected smoothly and without assistance. The tractive effort at the tender drawbar often reached 25 tons (56,000lbs) at starting; a figure which represented the greatest coefficient of adhesion which it is possible to attain, that is, one-third of the adhesive weight on dry rails.

There was a very fine run on July 18th 1946. With a train weighing 621 tons, 3,400 gross dbhp was reached 3 miles after St. Germain des Fossées at 50mph up a gradient of 1 in 130, and 3,500 at 62·4mph at the summit of the 1 in 125 bank at kilo. post 368; figures equivalent to 3,950 and 4,100 respectively on the level. After the stop at Roanne, and having passed Coteau station about 2 miles farther on at 45mph, the speed increased progressively on a continuous climb of 1 in 83·3 and St. Cyr de Favières 6 miles from Roanne was passed at 53mph with the train still accelerating. The 7·2 mile climb from St. Just sur Loire to St. Etienne on a gradient of 1 in 83·3 was started at 53mph, with the engine developing 2,400 gross dbhp, and was climbed at a practically constant speed; at Villars (5 miles from St. Just) the speed was 52mph and the gross dbhp 3,200, and La Terasse (2 miles beyond Villars) was passed at 51mph for a gross dbhp of 2,950, before the slack to 43·7mph at Etivaliere junction, where Chapelon's boyhood line joined from Le Puy. During this run the level of the water in the boiler was maintained with the greatest ease.

In July 1946 No. 242.A.1 was switched to the haulage of heavy express trains on the Paris-Dijon main line of the old PLM. On July 24th the engine had a train of 16 coaches weighing 702 tons, and with this its running was outstanding. At kilo. post 84, 5 miles beyond Montereau, on a climb of 1 in 100 it was developing 3,200 gross dbhp at 75mph, and passing Tonerre (beyond kilo. post 195) at the same speed and up a slight gradient of 1 in 909 the horsepower rose to 3,300. Up Blaisy bank of an average of 1 in 188 with a maximum of 1 in 125 (where 4—8—0 No. 240.P.5 had staged its phenomenal effort) the 4—8—4 averaged 69mph from kilo. post 283 to the summit at kilo. post 287 (2½ miles), developing a gross dbhp of 3,440, equivalent to 4,125 at uniform speed on the level. Assuming that the resistance was the same as for a PO rebuilt Pacific, the indicated horsepower would have been 5,155.

No. 242.A.1 belonged, of course to the Ouest Region and during 1947 the engine was being tried extensively between Paris and Caen. This is a difficult route with banks of 1 in 125 and 1 in 100 and for which the original No. 241.101 had been specifically ordered. The 4—8—4 immediately displayed its ability to master the traffic which had been beyond the capacity of the 4—8—2. On the several test runs that were made there were gains over schedule of no less than 40 minutes. On a down train on March 26th, loaded to 658 tons, the Bréval bank of 1 in 111 was climbed with a speed starting at 25mph and increasing to 57·5mph; the dbhp developed was 3,100, equivalent to 3,800 on the level. On the same train on April 22nd but with 775 tons behind the tender, the climb of 1 in 167 between La Bonneville and Romilly produced sustained gross drawbar horsepowers of from 3,000 to 3,400. The 8-mile bank at 1 in 125 from Bernay to St. Mards was surmounted at speeds of 50 to 53mph with gross dbhps of 3,300 and 3,500.

On the corresponding up train on April 23rd a particularly notable performance was the run by No. 242.A.1 up the Lisieux bank. The bank starts at about 2½ miles from Lisieux and is over 8 miles long with a gradient of 1 in 125. In spite of a strong side wind blowing at 25mph the speed with which the engine lifted its heavy train up the bank was astounding. An average tractive effort of 10 tons was maintained throughout, and the speed, which was already 55mph 2½ miles from Lisieux and up a gradient of 1 in 370, was maintained at between 56·2 and 59·4mph during the whole of the climb with a tendency to accelerate. The gross horsepower developed at the drawbar reached maxima of between 3,500 and 3,750; this last, at the speed of 56·2mph, was equivalent to *4,300* on the level. During the rest of the run the speed was maintained practically constant between 62·5 and 68·7mph whatever the gradient. Thus the Bréval bank of 1 in 143 was climbed at 62·5–66mph, the gross dbhp varying between 3,000 and 3,600— the latter figure being equivalent to 4,100 on the level.

In October 1948 No. 242.A.1 was back on the Paris-Dijon main line for more trials. During the course of these some most interesting indicator diagrams were made on this engine. These showed the great power developed in the cylinder and its division between the HP and LP cylinder groups; and it showed, too, a great design achievement in that each of the three cylinders produced nearly the same amount of work. It will suffice to give two examples:

(a) Cut-off 75HP/50LP; speed 62·5mph; boiler pressure 290lbs per sq in.; pressure in the intermediate receiver 145lbs per sq in.—

Power in HP cylinder	1,870hp
Power in LP cylinders	3,550hp
Total	5,420hp
Power per cylinder HP	1,870hp
Power per cylinder LP	1,775hp

(b) Cut-off 60HP/40LP; speed 74mph; boiler pressure 290lbs per sq in.; pressure in the intermediate receiver 138lbs per sq in—

Power in HP cylinder	1,920hp
Power in LP cylinders	3,580hp
Total	5,500hp
Power per cylinder HP	1,920hp
Power per cylinder LP	1,790hp

No. 242.A.1 was, of course, the most powerful express locomotive built to Chapelon designs; but what is of particular interest, is that if it is compared with much larger American locomotives, it becomes apparent that in the Chapelon technique power was no longer related directly to dimensions. He had, for instance, designed a Pacific which was more powerful than a much larger Mountain, and a 4—8—0 with narrow firebox having only 40sq ft of grate area that easily outclassed an unmodified 4—8—2 with a grate of 53·8sq ft.

On October 21st 1948, running north from Dijon with 16 coaches weighing 748 tons, No. 242.A.1 encountered a permanent way slack in Plombiéres station (3 miles from Dijon). The engine then accelerated up the 1 in 125 gradient towards Blaisy to 69mph. The gross power developed at the tender drawbar rose rapidly to 2,500hp, and then upwards to stabilise at 3,400hp with a peak of 3,600. From kilo. post 301 to kilo. post 292·8 (at the entrance to Blaisy tunnel) the average speed over this 5-mile stretch was 58mph with a drawbar tractive effort of 21,120lbs, corresponding to 3,305dbhp, or 3,553 on the level. Between kilo. posts 292 and 293 the maximum power of 4,150dbhp was reached at 63mph with a tractive effort of 20,284lbs. Similar performances were recorded on four successive trains with loads ranging up to 861 tons.

A week earlier, on October 14th, with a down train of 16 coaches weighing 861 tons, up a gradient of 1 in 143 between Laroche and Brienon, 68·7mph was reached in 7mins 31secs in $4\frac{1}{2}$ miles. The gross dbhp was 2,915; the equivalent of 3,215 on the level. On the section Montbard-Blaisy (29 miles) the power output continued to rise up to 3,700hp. From Les Laumes at kilo. post 284 (8 miles from Montbard) for 17 miles the average gross tractive effort was 16,380lbs at 65·3mph, corresponding to 3,060dbhp, or the equivalent to 3,440 on the level. Over the last 3 miles from kilo. post 279 to kilo. post 284 the gross tractive effort reached was 19,910lbs at an average speed of 65·4mph, representing an output of 3,500hp, or 3958dbhp on the level at uniform speed. The maximum was 3,600 gross hp at 65·6mph, equivalent to 4,280dbhp on the level.

Performances of the same order were reproduced on four occasions. At the end of October, with 16 coaches weighing 743 tons, No. 242.A.1 passed Laumes at 63mph (the maximum allowed by a speed restriction); at Thénissay, 9 miles farther on up the Blaisy bank, the speed was 75mph, and at kilo post. 285, after another 9 miles, it was 70mph. Except for a drastic slowing to 19mph a little before Blaisy, the $19\frac{1}{2}$ miles from Les Laumes to the summit would have been covered in 16mins 20secs. Over a distance of 17·6 miles the average tractive effort was 17,116lbs, corresponding to 3,175dbhp, of which the equivalent on the level would have been 3,510. Over the $2\frac{1}{2}$ miles from kilo. post 281 to kilo. post 285 on the 1 in 125 gradient, the average tractive effort was 18,062lbs at an average speed on 71·4mph, representing a gross dbhp of 3,480 and a net equivalent power of the level at a uniform speed of 4,030dbhp. At kilo. post 283 the tractive effort reached 18,304-lbs at 72·4mph, or a gross dbhp of 3,750 and net power of 4,130.

In the winter of 1949–50 No. 242.A.1 was doing test running on the Nord Region. During December and January it was working trains in the ordinary service but with specially increased loads of between 700 and 850 tons. Extra steam was of course needed to heat these trains, so that the demand on the engine was considerably heavier than if the trials had been carried out during the summer months.

With 693 tons the engine ran from Paris to Lille in (excluding stops) 2hrs 20mins at an average speed of 67mph. The first 71 miles were covered in one hour and Arras (120 miles) reached in 1hr 42mins, or

1hr 36mins if slacks are excluded. Up the Gannes bank, kilo. post 80 (at the beginning of the 1 in 250 gradient) was passed at 77·5mph, and at kilo. post 86·5, the summit of the bank, the speed was 75·7mph.

On December 19th, at the head of a Paris-Calais train weighing 692 tons, the engine ran from the Gare du Nord to Creil, 31 miles, start to stop, in 28mins 53sec. On the 10-mile climb of the 1 in 200 Survilliers bank (from kilo. post 11 to kilo. post 27) the speed rose from 70mph to 76mph. At the average speed of 74·3mph the power developed at the drawbar was equivalent to 3,610hp on the level.

A short time later with a heavier up train of 780 tons the start-to-stop time from Creil to Paris was 31 minutes and the summit of the 1 in 200 Survilliers bank, 14 miles from the start, was reached in 14mins 16secs. Between kilo. posts 43 and 27 on the climb the average speed was 70·3mph, and the equivalent dbhp over this distance of 10 miles was 3,820.

On December 22nd the engine had a very heavy train of 832 tons to haul from Calais Maritime to Paris. Up Gannes bank the average speed over the 7½ miles between kilo. posts 100 and 88 was 75mph. The tractive effort exerted over this distance was 6¾ tons and the equivalent dbhp was 3,228.

The peak effort was on December 28th with a train between Jeumont and Paris loaded to 854 tons, with stops at Creil and Chantilly, the latter being about one-third of the distance up the Survilliers bank. The power developed at the tender drawbar at kilo. post 43, just over two miles beyond Chantilly, was the equivalent at a uniform speed on the level of 4,290 at which moment the train was travelling at 61mph. On the short piece of level at kilo. post 27·7, the summit of the bank, the speed was 66·2mph and the equivalent dbhp 4,100.

In the course of these trials the tractive effort at the tender drawbar reached 27 tons without any slipping.

The remarkable feature of the outstanding performances recorded on these trials, carried out under such widely different conditions, was that they were obtained with a engine having a boiler pressure of 292lbs per sq in, 400deg of superheat, a grate less than 55sq ft in area, and an axle weight of no more than 21 tons on each of the four coupled axles. But because none of these figures were abnormal in current locomotive design the achievements of No. 242.A.1 showed that the possibilities of further locomotive development were far from exhausted, quite apart from any thermic or thermo-dynamic progress which might occur in the future. It was apparent, indeed, that there was still enormous potential in the so simple plan of the classic steam locomotive, as it had been fashioned by Stephenson, Hackworth and Seguin; and that it was capable of competing with any other type of locomotive in both power and speed. This comparison refers, of course, to the 1950s; and any competitive assessment in the 1970s would have to take account of another 20 years of Chapelon-type development of steam locomotives.

On September 12th 1952 a demonstration run was arranged for a South American railway delegation which was visiting France. No. 242.A.1 headed a train of 20 coaches weighing 810 tons, and was booked to work this over the 131·1 miles from Paris to Le Mans at the schedule allowed for the fastest electrically hauled trains, which were limited to 640 tons. The engine, in fact, improved on this schedule by 6 minutes, taking 1hr 49min, with an overall average of speed 72·2mph. Further, this improvement on the schedule was in spite of a special stop of 10 minutes at Chartres to take water.

There was an amusing sequel to this brilliant run. At the time the electrical engineers were designing the locomotives intended to work express trains over the Paris-Lyon line which was in course of electrification. The designs were for a locomotive slightly more powerful than the 2—D—2 type which had been so successful on the PO electrified routes. But when the result of this run and others became known the designs were changed very hurriedly and the 2D2.9101 class resulted with the horsepower increased by 1,000 to 4,900.

Another interesting result of this demonstration run was that the Brazilian members of the delegation, who had originally intended to order 100 diesel-electric locomotives, decided to order steam locomotives instead; and after Chapelon had led two GELSA-inspired missions to South America, the Argentine Railways became interested in the modifications proposed to them, and benefited from the consequent rebuilding of the 11C class 4—8—0 locomotives of the General Roca Railway (see Chapter 13).

IO

Lesser Locomotives

As FAR AS could be seen at the time, the locomotive programme outlined in the previous chapters would meet the demands of immediate post-war traffic. But there were vivid memories of the crisis in transport that had occurred after the First World War and a feeling that, if traffic growth had been underestimated, the same thing could occur again. If that should happen it would be necessary to ask industry to supply a great number of locomotives quickly. It was necessary, therefore, to plan locomotives the construction of which would need the minimum amount of work and the minimum of material (which was very scarce in the period following the end of hostilities). On account, too, of conditions and maintenance on the railways, the engines would have to be as simple as possible but at the same time incorporate the essential features to make them both reliable and economical. They would have to have the greatest possible number of parts in common, such as wheels, coupling rods, axles, etc.; and they would have boilers with deep and narrow fireboxes of a type which had given good results, both in efficiency and reliability, on the 240.P class locomotives. The pressure would be about 225lbs per sq in and the superheat temperature about 350deg. C to give high efficiency without making the engines liable to excessive maintenance.

Because the power required would be relatively low, the need for simplicity could best be met by two-cylinder simple expansion locomotives, having piston valves with a long travel, steam chests of large volume, and the same type of exhaust ports as had been fitted to the rebuilt 2—8—2 locomotive No. 141.E.113 of the Ouest. To defer the moment at which pounding starts, the driving and coupled wheels would be furnished with Franklin automatic wedges. With coupled wheels of 5ft 6in, they would be suitable for mixed traffic and for speeds up to 70mph.

It was decided that three types were needed, a 2—10—0, a 2—8—0, and a 2—6—0. Reference to Chapelon's outline diagrams shows that they would all have a distinct family resemblance; in fact their outward appearance, except for length and number of coupled wheels, would have been identical. The axle weight of the 2—10—0 was limited to 17 tons so that it could run on a very high percentage of SNCF routes, and with its great adhesion of 85 tons, it would be able to haul goods trains and heavy passenger trains over secondary routes with difficult gradients. It is rather interesting to compare this engine with the 2—10—0 which R. A. Riddles designed for British Railways. This too was a two-cylinder simple expansion locomotive with an axle weight of 17 tons, but with a wide firebox because Riddles wanted to ensure good steaming with the poor coal which seemed likely to be supplied to the railways. The British engine had wheels of only 5ft diameter, but in spite of this it could, and did, run at 90mph with express passenger trains. And this ability to run at high speeds with small wheels was itself an endorsement of the Chapelon principles which were incorporated in all the Riddles engines.

The Chapelon 2—8—0 would replace the many existing engines with three or four coupled axles which were either insufficiently power-ful or were incurring high maintenance costs, even though of com-paratively recent construction. One example of these was the 140.J class of 2—8—0 locomotives of which 170 had been built for the PLM between 1923 and 1925, but which were not included in the deprecia-tion programme. Riddles had not felt the need for such an engine because of the large numbers available of his own "Austerity" design 2—8—0 and the modern engines of this type which had been built by the LMS and LNE Railways.

Chapelon's 2—6—0 design was intended to replace six-coupled engines which were no longer up to the service required of them; and in this he was following the example of the Belgian State Railways which had built new 2—6—0s for a similar reason. The inadequacy of some of the old French six-coupled freight engines still in general service was shown by trials which took place between an old 0—6—0 of the Ouest, built in 1867, and a simple-expansion 2—6—0 of the Est, of a class rebuilt from the old Bourbonnais 0—6—0s of 1859–84 and superheated. With the latter, far better services could be ensured on secondary lines together with considerable economies in coal and water. The average power developed at the drawbar of 0—6—0 No. 030.C.795 of the Ouest varied between 80 and 200hp, whilst 2—6—0 No. 130.B.433 of the Est developed between 190 and 400hp, with economies over the former of about 30 per cent. Riddles also wanted 2—6—0 engines to replace the old smaller-powered locomotives and chose two-cylinders and narrow fireboxes, but to meet British route requirements he had three different classes with axle loads of, respec-tively, 16¾ tons, 16 tons, and 13 tons.

Unhappily the Chapelon designs were never built, because the next engine to be described will show what remarkable simple expansion engines they would probably have been.

The 140.J class of the PLM were mentioned above. The rebuilding of one of these in 1953 was André Chapelon's last major work for the SNCF, and one which proved valuable for the information gained.

The 140.J class had been designed by the OCEM for the PLM in 1923, but, whilst with their moderate axle load they have been used for general freight duties all over the system, they were on the whole poorly designed engines and had given much trouble.

Chapelon's initial aim was to stop the lineside fires that were constantly being caused by these engines. Owing to the very narrow chimney there was such a fierce blast that it pulled out the fire and hurled large incandescent cinders to a great distance. Because of the extensive damage caused by these fires the 140.Js had to be limited to their power output, which in turn limited the speed at which they could operate and the loads which they could haul.

Chapelon began by widening the chimney and replacing the PLM trefoil exhaust by a cross-bar placed at the exit of the blastpipe, at the same time lowering the latter to a more suitable position. He also replaced the valve sleeves by others with exhaust ports of decreasing section, of the same types as he had fitted to No. 141.E.113, to diminish the violence of the exhaust.

These measures certainly improved matters; the fire was pulled out to a much lesser extent and the engine could consequently be extended further. Nevertheless the ejection of cinders had not been sufficiently arrested, and to stop the large cinders, which travelled through the tubes at great speed, from being thrown straight out of the chimney, a metal plate was installed in the smokebox in such a way that the cinders, striking against it, were broken into pieces too small to start fires. The trouble was now completely cured and the engine could operate safely at its full power; at the same time the condition of the fire was improved and the steaming was excellent.

However, there was still much room for improvement in the exhaust. a Kylälä nozzle was therefore placed between the blastpipe and the chimney and the crossbar was replaced by the radial wedge-shaped inserts of the classic Kylchap which were more suited to the Kylälä fitting. This resulted in a most spectacular improvement of the exhaust and confirmed, as had been established on PO Pacific No. 4597 28 years before (see Chapter 2), that the Kylälä nozzle was a most excellent mixer and that it had been well worth while preserving it as part of the Kylchap exhaust system.

Steps were now taken to improve the steam distribution. The size of the ports was increased as far as possible whilst still, of course, retaining their form and progressive section. The maximum cut-off was reduced from 86 per cent to 76·2 per cent and improvements were made in the valve travel. But when the engine was tried with these new modifications its performance caused consternation amongst the observers; for power was decreased, consumption per hp/hr was increased, and the exhaust beats had become more violent. However, when the valves were inspected it was found that the workshops had made a mistake and had put the valve sleeves on the wrong way round so that the inlet and exhaust ports were inverted. This amply explained the poor performance and the mishap served to demonstrate once more the adverse effect of throttling at the admission on the efficiency of an engine and the importance of the progressive exhaust ports in softening the violence of the steam emission. Once it had been put into proper order, the engine showed, by comparison with an unaltered engine of the 140.J class, an economy of fuel at the tender drawbar of 10 per cent at low speeds and 20 per cent at greater.

Another very important point that these trials brought out was the necessity of having a really rigid chassis. On this engine it was noticed that each time that the cylinders drove the wheels round, the boiler was displaced by a few inches in relation to the chassis; a displacement which was very noticeable below the cab and which caused the breakage of pipes and boiler supports. In fact, this same torsion or distortion of the chassis had already been observed on other classes of engines. Chapelon instituted research on a rough model of the engine, and after much laborious work it was found that the movement took place in different directions according to the position of the cranks and was due to stresses in the mechanism which caused unequal bending in the top and bottom parts of the plate frames in relation to the driving axles. The remedy adopted was first to equalise the moments of inertia in the two parts of the frames in relation to the axis of the driving axles and then to strengthen the other weak points.

The locomotive, No. 140.J.153, thus thoroughly modified and provided with Franklin automatic wedges to counter the rattling of the axle boxes which was common on simple expansion engines, could run very comfortably, with its 5ft 6in wheels, at 68mph, though the unmodified engines were restricted to a maximum of 53mph, and even at that speed they produced quite unacceptable vibrations.

Much more to the credit of the rebuilt engine, however, was a comparison with the 141.R class locomotives. Running at a normal speed, with fuel weighed and work assessed in the dynamometer car, No. 140.J.153 showed itself capable of operating the same service as the 141.R with an economy at the drawbar of 30 per cent in fuel per hp/hr (though with the more economical hand, instead of 'stoker' firing), in spite of having a grate area of only 30·3sq ft as compared with 55·5sq ft of the 141.R class.

It is difficult, really, to appreciate the triumph of this remarkable achievement. An engine, built in the early 1920's' barely adequate for the work for which it was designed, was transformed into one which, weighing only 71 tons, was able to perform the same work, but more economically, as an engine weighing 115½ tons built 20 years later. It re-emphasised the point already made by Chapelon that the conventional steam locomotive had enormous potentialities for future development. Unfortunately, at the time that this memorable transformation was completed the abolition of steam on the SNCF had already been decided and Chapelon himself was on the verge of retirement.

II

Steam Locomotives That Never Were

In his address to the AFAC, Chapelon followed his description of the projected two-cylinder simple expansion engines with a discussion on the merits of diesel and electric traction as compared with steam. However, in the light of subsequent events, it would probably be better to deal first with his plans for a modern steam fleet for French railways in order that the decisions in favour of the rival forms of motive power can be assessed against the proper background.

As one would expect, after the outstanding success of his rebuilt locomotives, the types of locomotives which should be designed new to meet the needs of the future had been in Chapelon's mind for many years before the outbreak of World War II. In 1936 he produced recommendations as to the new steam locomotives which should be constructed for the PO-Midi. At that time electrification of the PO main lines had been either completed or approved to connect Paris through Orleans to on the one hand Bordeaux and on the other Brive, and the Midi had electrified the line from Bordeaux to the Spanish frontier and many other sections of its system. Whilst most of the route mileage of the amalgamated companies remained steam operated, there were obvious difficulties in obtaining approval for a large programme of steam construction; particularly when it is remembered that it was the reluctance of the PO to buy new express engines, owing to impending electrification, that led to Chapelon's remarkable rebuilding. Nevertheless, it was likely that large sections of the railway would remain unelectrified and it seemed to Chapelon that replacement of many of the older locomotives was both economically justified and indeed urgent if steam worked trains were to equal the electric in speed and weight. At this period diesel traction was not in the field as another alternative.

Chapelon's designs assumed that permitted axle loads would be raised to 22 tons on all main lines and to 29 tons on those carrying the heaviest and fastest traffic. This would entail, of course, much expense on existing track and structures, but he felt that the results would be of great future benefit. The value of high axle weights was evident in the United States where, for instance, six-coupled engines could be used of weights which in Europe would necessitate eight coupled wheels.

Chapelon planned that all engines should have certain features in common. Those of moderate power would be four-cylinder compounds and very high powered locomotives would be six-cylinder compounds with two HP and four LP cylinders in the same fashion as 2—12—0 No. 160.A.1, which he was then designing. Lentz poppet valves would be used with oscillating cams driven by Walschaerts valve gear. The superheater would be the Houlet type, the boiler pressure would be from 280 to 310lbs per sq in, according to usage and type, the boiler would be supplied by both feed water heater pumps and by injectors, there would be a Belpaire firebox with wide rectangular grate and Nicholson thermic syphon, and there would be an intermediate tube plate. Double Kylchap exhaust would be of course incorporated in all the engines.

In 1936 Chapelon thought that six types of engines were required to meet those traffic needs which were beyond the capacity of the existing engines. Two types of heavy express passenger locomotives were needed; one a 4—8—4 for the ordinary service and the other a 4—6—4 for the high speed crack expresses—both developing 6,000ihp. For light very high-speed inter-city services a 4—6—0 locomotive developing 3,600ihp was proposed. For heavy freight working there would be a 2—10—4 6,000ihp engine. The operation of fast and heavy suburban passenger trains would be undertaken by 4,500-ihp 2—10—2 tank engines. Finally there would be a 4—6—2 *fourgon* tank engine of 2,000ihp to operate light fast services over secondary routes. Diagrams of all these engines drawn by the late artist M. E. A. Schefer showed them emblazoned with the same PO-Midi monogram as had been used on the streamlined Chapelon Pacific No. 231.726.

The 4—8—4 and 4—6—4 express engines were of very similar design but had certain interesting differences. Both had the same boiler with a pressure of 310lbs per sq in, double Kylchap exhaust, and a grate area of 75·6sq ft; and both could be fitted for either coal firing with a mechanical stoker or oil firing. All four LP cylinders of the 4—8—4 were of the same dimensions, but on the 4—6—4 (as on No. 160.A.1) the HP and first stage LP cylinders had the same dimensions, whilst the second stage LP cylinders were larger. On both engines the HP cylinders drove the third coupled axle, the inside LP cylinders the leading coupled axle, and the outside LP cylinders the second coupled axle. On the 4—8—4 cut-offs could either be set to fixed relative positions in the HP and LP cylinders, or they could be moved independently in the HP and LP cylinder groups. On the 4—6—4 the classic du

Bousquet de Glehn arrangement was used. The 4—8—4 had driving wheels of 6ft 8in diameter, whilst those of the 4—6—4 were 7ft. The frames of the 4—8—4 were laminated and stayed whilst those of the 4—6—4 were of the American bar type. The 4—8—4 was to have a streamlined exterior similar to that of No. 321.726, but the streamlining for the 4—6—4 followed current American fashion. Weights of the two engines were very much the same, at 160 and 161 total and 88 and 87 adhesion for the 4—8—4 and 4—6—4 respectively, giving the latter an axle weight of 29 tons.

American 4—6—4 locomotives running at this time were of very similar weights to those of Chapelon's proposed type. Two examples of streamlined 4—6—4 were the New York Central J.1 class of 1932 and the New York-New Haven J.5 of 1937; of which the total and adhesive weights were respectively 160 and 85, and 166 and 89. The 4—6—4 had become a very popular type in the United States. The first had been built for the New York Central by the American Locomotive Company in 1927, and it was subsequently built continuously for many railways until 1948 as a high speed express passenger engine. In the USA it was considered that, as compared with a 4—6—2 of similar size, the 4—6—4 wheel arrangement allowed an increase of 12½ per cent in steam pressure, 13 per cent in heating surface, 20 per cent in grate area, and 28 per cent in the volume of the firebox. All the American engines were of course two-cylinder simple expansion and lacked the Chapelon-type steam circuit and exhaust. The proposed French engine would therefore be far in advance of current transatlantic practice.

Chapelon did not seek to emulate American 4—8—4 design. His own design had four coupled axles only to reduce the axle weight. The Americans introduced them to get bigger and more powerful engines. The 4—8—4 locomotives of 1935 for the Chesapeake and Ohio and the North Pacific Railroads had adhesive weights respectively of 124 and 127 tons and axle weights of 31 and 32 tons. (The task of the American locomotive designer was, it will be appreciated, greatly facilitated by a large loading gauge and high axle loadings.)

The 4—6—0 was intended to haul light trains at very high start-to-stop average speeds. An Atlantic would have done but a 4—6—0 was preferred on account of the extra adhesion. The engine was therefore a rather scaled-down version of a Chapelon 4—8—0 with a Belpaire boiler, a long narrow grate of 37·8sq ft area, a Houlet superheater, 310lbs per sq in boiler pressure, and a large-capacity smokebox with Kylchap double exhaust. The du Bousquet de Glehn four-cylinder compound arrangement was chosen; the outside HP cylinders driving the second coupled axle and the inside LP cylinders the leading coupled axle. The driving wheels had the large diameter of 7ft 3in. Like the large express engines, the 4—6—0 could be either oil or coal fired, the latter with a mechanical stoker. The total weight would be 98 tons with 66 tons adhesion. Both for publicity and because it was going to run fast the engine would be streamlined in the same style as No. 231.726. The weight of trains which the 4—6—0 would haul, according to route and service, would be between 200 and 400 tons—the more difficult the route the lighter the train. Overall average speeds would be 75–80mph, with the engine capable of sustaining a speed of 94mph and of reaching 125mph. Hauling a 400-ton train, speeds of 112·5mph should be possible on the level and 87·5 up a gradient of 1 in 200. With a 200-ton train the respective speeds should be 125mph and 110mph. (These figures relate to trains in which all the carriages, as well as the engine, were streamlined.) This 4—6—0 had the high axle weight of 22 tons, and much strengthening of track would therefore have been needed before it could have been used as intended. Otherwise no problems were anticipated because it incorporated the same features which had given such trouble-free running in the Chapelon Pacifics and 4—8—0s.

The 2—10—4 heavy freight locomotive was intended to have a boiler identical with that of the 4—8—4 and 4—6—4, but with increased superheat. It was to have driving wheels of the considerable diameter for its task of 5ft 9in. On the level it would be capable of hauling trains of 9,200 tons at 30mph and trains of 2,400 tons at 70mph. On gradients the engine could have managed 30mph with 2,850-ton trains up 1 in 200, 1,600 tons up 1 in 100, and 750 tons up 1 in 50. It could have run at 70mph up 1 in 200 with a 1,000-ton train, and with one of 900 tons up a 1 in 100 at 56mph, or at the same speed up 1 in 50 with one of 400 tons. With its large driving wehels, therefore, the engine was suitable for heavy mixed traffic working, fast goods, or heavy mineral. But larger wheels than normal for slow heavy trains were not necessarily a disadvantage because experience showed that an increase in wheel diameter resulted in a lesser resistance to movement. The inside HP cylinders drove the fourth coupled axle, the inside LP cylinders the second coupled axle, and the outside LP cylinders the third. The frames were of the American bar type. The total weight was 162 tons (emphasising its similarity to the two heavy express engines) and adhesion was 110 tons. In outside appearance this locomotive would have been very similar to No. 160.A.1.

The most important feature of the 2—10—2 four-cylinder compound suburban tank engine would have been its rapid acceleration, so important to the working of a heavy suburban train service, particularly having regard to the performance of competing electric traction.

Chapelon's engine was intended to reach 75mph from a standing start on the level with a 300-ton train in two minutes, and the same speed with a 600-ton train in four minutes. The weight would have been 142 tons of which 110 tons would have been adhesive. The driving wheel diameter was 5ft 9in. The firebox could have been coal-fired either by hand or mechanical stoker, or oil-fired. The grate would have had an area of 48·6sq ft and have been of the trapezoidal shape introduced on the PO Pacifics of 1907. The inside HP cylinders drove the third coupled axle and the outside LP cylinders the second coupled axle. (This, it will be noted, was the reverse of the normal du Bousquet de Glehn arrangement.)

The 4—6—2 *fourgon* tank engine was an ingenious idea to lighten the weight of trains and to dispense with a fireman on the engine. Unless there is special baggage accommodation in one or more of the passenger coaches, French trains incorporate a baggage wagon, or *fourgon*, which is normally marshalled next to the locomotive. Because on light trains the *fourgon* represented a large proportion of the total load, the Etat Railway in 1885 conceived the idea of combining it with the engine tender. The PO resurrected this idea in 1928 and it was decided to convert two old locomotives as a trial. Those selected belonged to the very successful 265 class of 2—4—2 express passenger engines designed by M. Victor Forquenot in 1876. Two engines, Nos. 366 and 382, were rebuilt in Perigueux works with new boilers, trefoil exhaust, and water tanks on either side of the boiler. The four-wheel tender was converted so that about the first third of its length was a coal bunker and the remaining two-thirds became a baggage wagon. The experiment was not repeated, probably because it was found cheaper and simpler to reconstruct a passenger coach with a baggage compartment. However, putting side tanks on to the engine did increase its low adhesion whilst they were full.

Chapelon was on the PO of courses when these locomotives were rebuilt and the experiment gave him the idea of the 4—6—2 *fourgon* tank engine. In Chapelon's locomotive, the main frames carried the whole unit, including the *fourgon* compartment, behind the coal bunker. The object was to economise in the weight and length of the train and the ultimate aim was to retain for steam traction the services which were being increasingly operated by diesel and petrol-driven rail-cars. Chapelon's engine would have the advantage of being able to deal with increases of weight to the train, by the addition of extra coaches. It was their inability to do this which had been the primary reason for the failure of the British steam 'rail-motors'. The axle weight being only 16 tons, the engine would be able to operate over all the PO-Midi routes and could therefore work all light fast or stopping services that could be envisaged. To facilitate running over the more sharply curved of these routes some play was allowed in the second coupled axle. The engine would be oil-fired so that only one man would be needed on the footplate, because the guard, who would travel in the *fourgon* compartment, could stop the train if the driver became indisposed. The boiler pressure was 280lbs per sq in and there were a Houlet superheater, a Kylchap simple exhaust, and exhaust steam injector, and a grate area of 21·6sq ft. The four cylinders were all outside the frames but mounted side by side on each side of the engine; the LP cylinders being mounted on the inner position next to the frames with the HP cylinders outside them. The LP cylinders drove the leading coupled axle and the HP the centre axle. Poppet valves were fitted.

The following speeds and loads on different gradients show the power and flexibility of the engine:

Speed	Load in tons—Level	1/200	1/100	1/66	1/40
37·5			410	275	155
50		450	275	182	92
62·5		600	310	190	122
75		430	220	135	

This was the one project which was sufficiently advanced when the SNCF was formed to have been allotted a serial number, 231.1001 (though this number bore no relation to the number of these locomotives it was intended to build).

The re-organisation of the railways stopped all these PO-Midi projects, but Chapelon took the plans with him to the SNCF and in 1939 he had started work on them again with a view to their application to all the French nationalised railway system. At the time when war broke out in the same year, the idea of ordering a class of locomotives from the U.S.A., similar in type and capacity to the 141.P but of American detail design, was already being considered; an idea which eventually resulted in the 141.R 2—8—2s. Chapelon in the meantime, had completed designs for a 2—8—4 with 65sq ft grate, 5ft 9in coupled wheels, and cast steel frame bed. But instead of the six cylinders for new big engines which Chapelon had selected for his 1936 projects, he now chose a three-cylinder compound for the reasons given in Chapter 9. But before completing development it was decided to carry out the re-building which resulted in No. 242.A.1. This 2—8—4 would have been a logical development from the 141.P.

But the 2—8—4 was only the first of Chapelon's new designs, and he was engaged on the others, which were broadly similar to his 1936 projects. His plans were finally formulated in 1945 and they envisaged a stud of locomotives which would meet not only immediate needs but those of the distant future.

A locomotive was required for the haulage of very high speed light luxury trains which would be steam-hauled, at least on the Paris-Strasbourg and Paris-Marseilles main miles. This was the type of service for which Chapelon had intended his projected PO-Midi 4—6—0 and the new design was very similar. It was again a stream-lined four-cylinder du Bousquet de Glehn compound but with the HP and LP cut-offs set to fixed relative positions, instead of it being possible to move them independently. Experience with the PO rebuilt Pacifics showed that, with adequate clearance volumes and steam passages, an engine could run freely with equal HP and LP cut-offs. This had led to the simplified mechanism of the 141.Ps, in which the relative LP/HP volumes remained effectively the same. Poppet valves would be used and with wheels of 7ft 3in diameter it should be possible to exceed 125mph.

For services on secondary lines the *fourgon* tank engine project was retained, but as a 4—6—4 instead of a 4—6—2, because the Operating Division wanted this engine to run longer journeys than originally envisaged, and it was therefore necessary to increase the capacity of the water tank and to add an extra axle to carry the additional weight. Construction of these engines was actually started, but the diesel propagandists had persuaded authority that with diesel traction would dawn the golden era for secondary lines; and so a fascinating adventure in steam propulsion never materialised.

The above two projects were to meet rather specialised needs. For the general-purpose running of the railway Chapelon had designed a family of very powerful locomotives. Based on the experience of the past in the growth of the power demanded, he came to the conclusion that at least 6,000 cylinder horsepower would be necessary if locomotives were to ensure the operation of services during the period 1950–1970. (This was a remarkable accurate forecast, as the power required to operate British services at the close of this period will confirm; and far more accurate than that made by British Railways when the decision was taken to purchase diesel locomotives.)

To obtain the greatest possible economy in manufacture and operation, parts were standardised as far as possible; the engines were arranged for ease of maintenance; and in weights, construction detail, etc., the greatest possible utilisation of the locomotives was a major factor in design.

During the years immediately prior to 1945 the Americans had obtained remarkable results in the above aspects of steam locomotive economy. For this reason in the new types which Chapelon had designed he had incorporated those features of American practice which would lessen the cost of construction and maintenance, but which would not imperil the thermo-dynamic superiority and consequent efficiency in operation of French engines, together with their capacity to develop great power despite a low axle weight and limited loading gauge. A single type of construction had been adopted with variations to suit each of the principal locomotive types of passenger, mixed traffic, and goods. There were four of the 'family' types: a 4—8—4 to work heavy expresses, a 4—6—4 (streamlined) for high-speed expresses over the principal main routes, a 2—8—4 for mixed traffic, and a 2—10—4 for goods. All these would have had the same boiler (though with some variations in length), the triple Kylchap exhaust, the same cylinder arrangement and mechanism, the same axles and axle boxes, and the same bissel trucks or bogies. The accessories would be identical—for example, feed-water heaters, air pumps, injectors, and cocks. On stepping on to the footplate of one of these engines there would be nothing to show the observer which one of them he had in fact mounted.

As compared with the 1936 projects the new designs were three-three-cylinder, instead of six-cylinder, compounds. New techniques had shown that a maximum cylinder horsepower was possible in a three-cylinder compound with a pressure of 320lbs per sq in without too little loss of efficiency from insufficient volume of the LP cylinders. An additional advantage of using three cylinders was that the same mechanism could be used on all four types.

It will be noted that the suburban tank engine had been dropped from the list as compared with the PO-Midi projects. However, in the light of suburban electrification, the excellent Nord 2—8—2 tank engines, and the 2—10—2 tank engines ordered for the Ceinture lines, no further large tank locomotives were needed. The 2—8—4 mixed traffic locomotive was an addition to the original PO-Midi list, and in consequence of its inclusion the driving wheels of the 2—10—4 goods engine were reduced in diameter to 5ft 5in.

It having been decided to standardise parts and fittings, a certain number of construction practices which had proved their worth, which were suited to general duty-locomotives, and which would stand up to intensive service with the minimum of maintenance costs, were selected for incorporation in the designs of the four large locomotives. They included the following:

(a)   Roller bearing axle boxes to facilitate lubrication and stop the heating which was the cause of numerous and lengthy breakdowns;
(b)   A monobloc chassis instead of assemblies which could dislocate in service and have to be dismantled at considerable cost;

(c)   Axle boxes with controlled lateral displacement to give easy transit over points and sharp curves, without the premature tyre wear entailed in using thin flanges;

(d)   Automatic wedges to limit the longitudinal play of axle boxes in their guides, and thus prevent shocks which shake the engine;

(e)   Wheels with enlarged spokes and tyres with increased thickness, both to ensure a better grip on the rim, and the latter also to lengthen the distance run between tyre renewals.

In addition to the above, the increase of the permitted axle weight from 20 to 23 tons would allow of increased dimensions to enable the parts concerned to stand up to the greater power outputs and consequent stresses.

All the four engines would have a grate area of 65sq ft (less than that of the PO-Midi projects), a boiler pressure of 310lbs per sq in and 425deg C of superheat and would form a very powerful and highly efficient group. An interesting point which arose from these designs was that, having the same cylinders and mechanism and steam passages of suitable size, the tractive effort obtained at a given speed was practically the same from all of them, irrespective as to whether an engine had large or small wheels. The greater haulage obtained from a small-wheeled engine is balanced by its greater resistance to movement; and therefore the main consideration in selecting the diameter of the wheels for any particular engine is the number of revolutions per minute to which their mechanical strength makes it advisable to restrict them. Thus the 4—8—4 express locomotive, with 7ft coupled wheels and an axle load of 23 tons, could have pulled loads of up to 950 tons at 75mph up a gradient of 1 in 200, with a maximum speed of 87·5mph. The 4—6—4, with 7ft 3in coupled wheels and an axle load of from 23 to 25 tons was intended to haul heavy trains of perhaps 650 tons on very high speed services at 87·5mph up 1 in 200 gradients and to have a maximum speed of 125mph (It will be noted that the 29-ton axle load of the PO-Midi project had had to be dropped and the 4—6—4 was consequently a rather smaller engine). The 2—8—4, with driving wheels of 5ft 9in diameter and 20 to 23 tons axle load, for mixed traffic service could pull up to 1,200 tons at 56mph up 1 in 200 gradients and would have had a maximum speed of 70mph. Finally the 2—10—4 heavy goods locomotive, with 5ft 5in wheels and an axle load of 20 tons, could have hauled 2,000 ton freight trains at 43mph up 1 in 200 and been able to run at 68·7mph.

The first 2—10—4 locomotive[1] had actually been ordered and the first cylinders had been cast at St. Chamond, when the whole project

1. Appendix B.32

was cancelled. This was in 1946 when a shortage of coking coal in France resulted in a Government direction to the SNCF to reduce their demands for coal in order that the needs of the steel industry might be met. The SNCF accordingly halted all plans for new construction of steam locomotives, although Chapleon's projected big engines were 'stoker' fitted, using non-coking coal which was useless for the steel industry and of which France had ample resources. At the same time electrification plans were expanded and accelerated. It is conceivable that this temporary shortage of coal was used as an excuse by certain persons in authority to halt Chapelon's plans, which if completed would certainly have given steam traction a fresh and lengthy lease of life and thrown doubts on the economic justification for main-line electrification or for the introduction of diesel traction on non-electrified routes. The cessation of work was expensive for the SNCF, because indemnities had to be paid to the firms which had begun construction of the 4—6—4 *fourgon* tank and 2—10—4 engines.

The decision was a great blow to André Chapelon who, at the very moment when his great 242.A.1 was making such a triumphant entry on the railway scene, saw the end of the dream, which had started so many years ago, of a fleet of great steam locomotives powerful and economical enough to challenge any other form of railway traction.

12

Electric and Diesel Traction

THE MAIN LINE electrification of the French railways really started after the First World War. Some lines had been electrified before it, but they were comparatively short lengths. In 1899 the 2½ mile line, mostly underground, which connected the Austerlitz and Orsay stations of the PO, in Paris was electrified at 650 volts on the third rail system. In 1904 the third rail was continued to Juvisy and in 1921 to Brétigny. In 1910 the PO considered the possibility of electrifying the main line between Paris and Orleans, which carried very heavy traffic; but as it appeared uncertain whether there would be an adequate financial benefit, the matter was dropped.

On the Midi a number of lines were electrified in the region of the Pyrenees at the instigation of the French Government. A metre gauge line was built from Villefranche Vernet les Bains to Bourg Madame under a Government direction that it was to be electrified. It was opened in 1911 with third rail supply at 850 volts and extended in 1928 to Tour de Carel. In 1907 and 1908 the Midi received from the Government sundry concessions for lines running across or into the Pyrenees on condition that they were electrified.

To decide the best system of electrification, and the most suitable equipment and locomotives, the Midi opened a test section in 1910 electrified at 12,000 volts 16½ cycle single phase alternating current. This proving satisfactory, it was adopted and by 1914 the 12¼ mile line from Lourdes to Pierrefitte was electrified on the same system. During the war more sections of line were electrified in this area, but owing to a shortage of equipment they were operated partially by steam, and the war soon brought all further electrification work to a halt.

During the war, however, a new factor arose which was eventually to accelerate the electrification of French railways. The collieries in the North of France were either badly damaged or in enemy hands and by 1916 it had become difficult to import coal from Great Britain or other countries owing to the German submarine campaign. The collieries in the Midi and the Massif Central could not meet demands because little of their coal was suitable for locomotives. To prevent any such situation arising again, it was decided by the Government (whilst the war was still in progress) that there should be a large programme for the partial electrification of the PO, Midi, and PLM Railways, in the territory of which there were abundant reserves of hydraulic energy; thereby cutting down considerably the railways' consumption of coal. No such potential water power was available to the Nord, Est, or Etat; but in any case, as regards the two former, there were strategic reasons for not converting them to a traction system which, it was considered, was so vulnerable to disruption by an enemy in time of war. In response to the Government's decision the three railways concerned acted immediately, and in 1917 they despatched a mission to the United States.

One is inclined to forget how recent main-line electrification is. It was not till after the end of the First World War that the major part of the Swiss railways were electrified, and this took place over a period of about ten years. Electric locomotives were, of course, running through the Simplon tunnel much earlier, in 1906, and the Loetschberg railway was electrified, with single phase etc, from its opening in 1910; but it was in the United States that the first really large railway electrification first took place, when in 1916 the Chicago, Milwaukee, St. Paul & Pacific Railroad completed 660 miles of electrified route at 3,000 volts d.c., operated by 1—Bo—Do+Do—Bo—1 3,180/4,020hp passenger and 2—Bo—Bo+Bo—Bo—2 3,000/3,440 freight locomotives. It was therefore an obvious choice for the French mission. The difficulties of the route made it an added attraction, for there were not only the heavy gradients through the Rocky and Bitter Root Mountains, but also the very severe conditions of the winter weather. The passenger locomotives were intended to haul 1,000-ton trains up gradients of 1 in 50 at 25mph and were very large and impressive-looking machines.

As a result of their inspection of the system, the French mission formed the opinion that overhead d.c. electrification would be the most suitable for their railways, but that they would prefer 1,500 volts rather than the 3,000 of the Milwaukee Road. The report was accepted by the Minister of Works, who directed a preliminary study, and thereafter inaugurated a large electrification programme covering some 5,300 miles of the PO, Midi and PLM for which the energy would be supplied by the central hydro-electric plants installed in the Alps, the Massif Central, and the Pyrenees. For their part of the programme the PO planned to equip progressively the heavily graded main line from Chateauroux to the junction with the Midi at Montauban, and then possibly all the lines to the east of this, running up the Massif Central. However, when the matter was examined in detail it was found that the heavily graded lines, though obviously the most technically suitable for electrification, were not so attractive financially because their traffic was light and it was the lines carrying heavy traffic that promised the most rapid return on capital invested.

In 1923 a project was completed for the electrification of the 127·5-mile main line of the Paris-Orléans Railway from Paris to Vierzon. This was carried out and opened officially on December 22nd 1926, though some trains continued to be worked by steam until the summer service of 1927. This electrification was proceeding when Chapelon joined the PO, and it was this and the planned extension of electrified routes which deterred the Company from purchasing new steam locomotives.

When the Paris-Vierzon section was opened the PO had 200 B-B type mixed traffic electric locomotives, with a speed limit of 56mph and 5 prototype express locomotives, supplied variously by Hungary, Switzerland, and the United States. This was all too small a stock to operate the express services and during the holiday season and on special fête days steam locomotives had to be used for some of the trains. The two Hungarian express locomotives were of the 2—D—2 type and had been built by the Budapest firm of Ganz & Co. They were most unsatisfactory in service, developing one or two faults, either mechanical or electrical, on an average of every 60 miles of running—an appalling record. On the other hand, they were powerful engines and could run well. The General Electric Co of the U.S.A. (which had supplied all the equipment for the Chicago, Milwaukee, St. Paul, and Pacific Railroad) provided the PO with a 2—C+C—2 locomotive, which was really two half locomotives, close-coupled. It was a most unstable machine and had to be modified in 1929. The Swiss firm of Brown Boveri and Winterthur jointly provided two 2—D—2 type locomotives which were very satisfactory, and by far the best of the prototype express locomotives.

There were four different classes of the mixed traffic B—B locomotives, but they all had the same basic features. They could pull on the level passenger trains of 650 tons at 40mph and goods trains of 1,100 tons at 25mph. Two of them coupled in multiple unit could tackle a maximum of 80 trucks weighing 2,000 tons. So far as they went they were satisfactory locomotives, but they were too slow for passenger work and too weak for goods. In fact the PO had electrified quite a lot of route without having the locomotives to operate the trains.

Over the period 1933–36 the PO acquired 35 more express locomotives, both to operate existing services and to meet the needs of new electrification between Vierzon and Brive and between Orleans and Tours. These new locomotives were of the same successful type which had been supplied by Brown Boveri and Winterthur and they were built by a group company comprising Fives-Lille, Electro-Mécanique, and Brown Boveri. They were designated the E.500 class, and, with a continuous rating of 3,200hp and an hourly rating of 3,700hp, they were powerful machines; but their output at the drawbar was less than that produced by Chapelon's 4—8—0 locomotives. Indeed, for heavy trains they were less powerful than the railway company would have liked because they had no reserves of power if the voltage dropped, and this could happen for a number of reasons. Between Vierzon and Brive the voltage was sometimes as low as 1,000, instead of the nominal 1,500. In addition, as the driving wheels were not coupled, the loco-motives tended to slip on greasy rails. The Company therefore ordered four prototypes of a new class of 2—D—2 locomotives with about 400 more horsepower and with anti-slipping devices. Of these, Nos. E.701–2 were built by the Oerlikon-Batignolles Group, E.703 by Alsthom, and E.704 by Schneider. They differed, as between the firms, in quite a number of respects. They were satisfactory locomotives, in that they slipped less than the E.500s and were reliable. But at high speed their drawbar horsepower was not much more than the E.500 class and their efficiency was a little lower. In addition, their crews did not like them because they were hard-riding and considerably inferior to the E.500s in their road-holding. In fact, when they entered a curve the first driving axle set up such lateral reaction that their speed had to be limited to 62·5mph whilst investigation was made into a suitable remedy. The same trouble was experienced with the produc-tion models of this class, Nos. E.705–720 and 5302–5306. (These last five locomotives were built in the 1940s and three were removed to Germany, where they were eventually found and returned to France.)

On the Midi there were ten 1,850hp 2—C—2 express locomotives of class 3101, of which the first two were put into service in 1923 and the remainder in 1927–8. Within their power limits they were successful, but they did lack power and they had a number of minor troubles. In 1932 24 2—D—2 locomotives of the much more powerful 3,900-hp 4800 class were built. They had adequate power for the services they were required to operate and were reliable, but they were very hard on the track and had to be limited to 62·5mph.

For mixed traffic and freight the Midi had B—B type locomotives which were generally similar to those of the PO, but they were divided into power groups, each of two classes: firstly, the 4500 class mixed traffic and 4000 class goods of 1,050hp; and secondly, the 4600 class mixed traffic and 4100/200 class goods of 1,580hp.

The most successful electric express passenger locomotives on the amalgamated PO-Midi were undoubtedly the E.500 class of the former Company. It was their successful operation which led to their being selected as the basis for the design of the new locomotives to be built for the Paris-Lyon electrification, and it was these latter locomotives that were hurriedly re-designed to give increased power as a result of the remarkable running of No. 242.A.1.

In discussing electric traction in general, Chapelon pointed out that in a country such as France, which produced only two-thirds of the fuel it consumed, the use of the 'white coal' was of primary importance. But of the 35 million tons of coal consumed every year about half were used in domestic fires and various industries, and it was here that the greatest value could be obtained by replacing coal with electricity, not only in cutting down consumption of the former, but also in increased comfort and hygiene. Compared to the above, the 11 million tons of coal required annually by the railways in 1945 represented a relatively small proportion of the whole. Further, of the coal imported only $3\frac{1}{2}$ million tons were for railway use, which was only about one-seventh of the coal purchased abroad. Most of it was anthracite for domestic consumption, which would still be imported whether the railways were electrified or not. In any case, the railways' $3\frac{1}{2}$ million tons was intended especially to improve the fuel provided for express locomotives, and it would not be needed in the future because of the increasing use of mechanical stokers, which needed an entirely different type of coal and one which could be provided by the French collieries.

In calculating the fuel that would be saved by electrification, the figures were too often based on the performance of comparatively old steam locomotives instead of what could be achieved with modern stock. For instance, it was generally assumed that in power 1 kw/hr of an electric locomotive equalled 2–3 kg of coal consumed by a steam locomotive, and that the latter would have an average monthly running of 5,000 miles on passenger service and 2,500 miles on goods service. Whereas with modern steam locomotives it could be shown (in 1946) that the 1 kw/hr equated to 1 kg of coal loaded on to the tender of a steam locomotive, and that the latter's running averages were 12,500 miles per month on passenger service and 6,250 on goods.

Diesel traction on main lines was considerably more recent than electric. By the early 1930s diesel shunters had made their appearance in large numbers and diesel-powered trains had been introduced, particularly in Germany and the U.S.A., on fast inter-city services operated by rail-cars with trailers or in multiple units. But the first successful running of main-line diesel locomotives was on American railways in 1935, when the Electro-Motive subsidiary of General Motors produced two locomotives which, coupled in multiple unit, developed 3,600 hp. The makers considered this figure to be equal to the cylinder horsepower of the average large American express steam locomotive. But this was a very dubious contention if related to the

Top: LNER 2-8-2 No 2001 'Cock o' the North' on a test run with three of the PO 4000 class 4-6-0's as brake locomotives.
[Sarkis K. Gulbenkian

Above: Streamlined Pacific No 231.726 at Paris Austerlitz station on exhibition during the Railway Congress at Paris in 1937. From left to right in the photograph are Marcel Bloch (E-in-C of Rolling Stock at the PO Works), Marius Grialou (Motive Power Inspector), who rendered exceptional service in arranging the trials of Chapelon's engines, and André Chapelon, Engineer of Rolling Stock.
[Chapelon collection

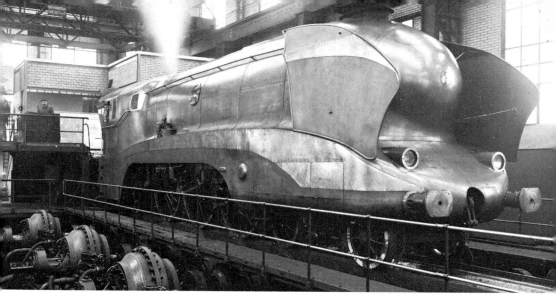

Top: No 231.726 on the Vitry test bank, where the engine sustained 3000hp at the wheel rims at 62.5mph continuously for two hours, whilst the water level and pressure in the boiler remained constant. Driver Maurice Gourault is in the cab and to the left is Fireman Léonce Miot.

[Chapelon collection

Above: Etat Pacific of the Ouest Region, No 231.D.686, rebuilt in accordance with Chapelon principles, at the Gare St. Lazare, Paris.

[Chapelon collection

Top: Etat Railway three-cylinder simple expansion 4-8-2 locomotive No 241.101, with Renaud poppet valves and 280lbs per sq in boiler pressure.

[Auclair

Above: Three-cylinder compound 4-8-4 locomotive No 242.A.1, rebuilt from 4-8-2 No 241.101 with Kylchap triple exhaust, Trick HP valves, and Willoteaux LP valves with double admission and double exhaust. Power as compared with the original Etat engine was doubled and No 242.A.1 could maintain 4000 horse power continuously at the tender drawbar between 44 and 62mph, and 3800 at 74mph.

[Sud-Est

Top: Andre Chapelon standing beside his 4-8-4 No 242.A.1 on its final exit from the Works of the Forges et Aciéries de la Marine et d'Homecourt at St. Chamond in June 1946.

[Chapelon collection

Above: No 242.A.1 climbing the 1 in 125 bank on leaving Lisieux with a train of 742 tons, during the trials on the Ouest Region on April 23, 1947.

[Schottli

Above right: No 242.A.1 at the Gare St. Lazare, Paris, after arriving with a trials train from Caen.

[Chapelon collection

Right: Scene inside the dynamometer car whilst No 242.A1.1 was passing the village of Verrey at 74mph and climbing the Blaisy bank (maximum 1 in 125). The figure of 3400dbhp registered on the dial is not corrected for gradient or acceleration. (The corrected figure would be considerably higher.)

[Dubruille

Top: 141.P class 2-8-2 locomotive,
No 141.P.171.

[Goston

Above: PLM 2-8-0 two-cylinder simple
expansion locomotive No 140.A.15, which
was subsequently re-numbered 140.J.15.
It was on one of this class, No. 140.J.143,
that Chapelon carried out the remarkable
rebuilding described in Chapter 10.
No photograph of 140.J.153 was taken,
but its appearance after rebuilding was
the same as 140.A1.15 except for the larger
chimney fitted with the Kylchap exhaust.

[PLM

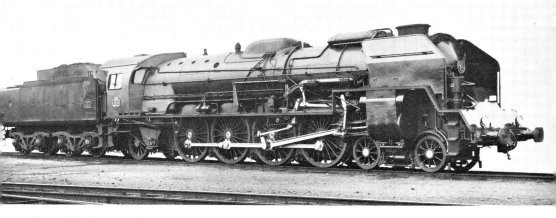

Top : 141.P class 2-8-2 locomotive No 141.P.305. The figure 1 on the buffer beam indicates that it belongs to the Est Region. (The other figures are: Nord 2, Ouest 3, Sud-Ouest 4, Sud-Est 5, and Mediterranee 6.)
[P. Ransome-Wallis

Above : 4-8-2 express locomotive No 241.P.1; the first of a class of 35 engines for the SNCF.
[SNCF

Top : 141.P class 2-8-2 No 141.P.138 at Bar-le-Duc on an Est Region Metz-Paris express in 1954.

[P. Ransome-Wallis

Above : A coal fired 141.R 2-8-2 of the first order at Calais in 1947; No 141.R.476.

[P. Ransome-Wallis

Top: Three-cylinder simple expansion 4-6-4 No 232.R.3 on an Amsterdam–Paris express.

[P. Ransome-Wallis

Above: Four-cylinder compound 4-6-4 locomotive No 232.U.1 at the Gare du Nord, Paris, with an express from Lille in 1961.

[P. Ransome-Wallis

Top: A 4-8-4 simple expansion locomotive with high superheat, wide section steam circuit, Kylchap double exhaust, 280lb per sq in boiler pressure, designed by Chapelon and built by GELSA for the Brazilian Railways; emerging from the Nantes Works of the Société des Batignolles.

[Chapelon collection

Above: The trials team in front of the Brazilian 2-8-4 locomotive during the trials on the Breton Railway. On the right of the group is Motive Power Inspector Deschamps (son of the head driver shown in an earlier photograph).

[Chapelon collection

Top right: Brake locomotive trials on the metre gauge Breton Railway of a 2-8-4 locomotive designed by Chapelon and built by the Creusot Company.

[Chapelon collection

Middle right: An 11.C class oil-fired 4-8-0 of the Argentine General Roca Railway, rebuilt under Chapelon's directions with improved steam circuit and incorporating the measures he introduced for simple expansion engines in Ouest Region 2-8-2 No 141.E.113 and included in the Brazilian locomotives. In addition, it had increased superheat and the RS burner (designed by Réné Segaud of the SNCF). At 40mph dbhp was increased from 1000 to 1400 with 28.5 per cent economy in fuel.

[Chapelon collection

Bottom right: Rebuilt PLM Pacific No 231.K.8 and 2-8-2 No 141.R.507 passing Pont de Briques on the Nord Region with a fast freight train in 1958.

[P. Ransome-Wallis

average *contemporary* large steam locomotives. In the first flush of enthusiasm at the performance of these diesel locomotives over a very lengthy trip, Electro-Motive calculated that they could haul a heavy train at a cost of from 40 to 60 per cent less than could have been done by a steam locomotive. A Chapelon 4—8—0 could, in fact, have done the same job at a cost which in the long term (including capital cost, depreciation, etc.) would have been cheaper. Where the diesel scored (and this probably confused the power comparison) was in its very high starting tractive effort which is an inherent feature of this type of machine. But as speed rose the tractive effort fell below that of a steam locomotive of equivalent power.

Following Electro-Motive's trial run, diesel locomotives were purchased from the company for the haulage of several American long distance high-speed passenger services; but it was 1939 before Electro-Motive succeeded in building a freight locomotive powerful enough to pull American freight trains. This was a lengthy four-unit locomotive developing 5,400 horsepower (or, less than Chapelon's projected 2—10—4 freight engine). Nevertheless, diesel salesmanship had started on the rapid conquest of the non-electrified railways of the world; a conquest which may well puzzle the railway historian of the future.

In his 1945 address Chapelon pointed out that this new form of traction required fuel of which all supplies had to be imported—a fuel moreover which was already scarce and liable to become more so on account of the enormous and rising consumption. A technical comparison between steam and diesel locomotives showed, as stated above, that if the latter had a clearly superior starting tractive effort, at speed the tractive effort was certainly inferior. Mr. Ralph P. Johnston, Chief Engineer of the Baldwin Locomotive Works (which built both types of locomotives) compared the performances of a steam and a diesel locomotive, both capable of developing about 3,600dbhp, in his book *The Steam Locomotive*. With a load of 640 tons, the steam locomotive took 4·9 minutes over a distance of 3·6 miles to reach a speed of 81mph; whilst the diesel needed 5·5 minutes and a distance of 4·7 miles. The diesel developed its maximum dbhp of about 3,400 at under 20mph, whereas the steam locomotive reached its maximum of about 3,800 at 50mph. M. Chapelon also quoted an article in the *Railway Age* comparing the 4—4—4—4 of the Pennsylvania Railroad and a 5,400hp triple-unit diesel electric locomotive. The Pennsylvania's great steam engine arose out of a proposal by the Baldwin Locomotive Works to the Baltimore & Ohio Railroad in 1932 to build an engine with a rigid wheel base and two groups of coupled wheels placed one behind the other and driven by separate pairs of outside cylinders. In 1935 Baldwins put the same proposal to the Florida East Coast and in 1936 to the New York-New Haven. All rejected the proposal on account of the excessive length of the rigid wheel base. George H. Emerson, Chief Mechanical Engineer of the Baltimore & Ohio, got over the difficulty by placing the cylinders of the second group of coupled wheels at the back under the firebox; but it was a solution which introduced a number of other difficulties that were only surmounted by using monobloc construction. This locomotive was built as a 4—4—4—4 in the Baltimore & Ohio Works and put into service on June 3rd 1937, named appropriately George H. Emerson. Chapelon rode on the footplate between Washington and Baltimore on October 31st 1938, when with 9 coaches weighing 810 tons the engine reached a speed of 82·5mph. But in spite of an impressive performance on trials, no more of the type were ever built.

In 1937 the Pennsylvania took up the idea, in its search for the best way of building very powerful locomotives, and decided on a 6—4—4—6 locomotive, with the cylinders placed in front of each group of coupled wheels. This locomotive, numbered 6100 of class S.1, was built at Juanita works in 1938–9 and was shown at the 1939—40 exhibition at New York. It was designed to haul passenger trains of 1,080 tons at 100mph, the anticipated drawbar horsepower being 4,500, from 6,000hp in the cylinders. On test the engine pulled a passenger train of 1,342 tons at 101mph and ran a distance of 140 miles at an overall average speed of 60mph pulling 65 goods wagons weighing 3,175 tons.

In practice, the dimensions of the boiler and cylinders of this great engine proved too great, particularly when related to its adhesive weight of 127·8 tons which was in fact less well used than in a locomotive with four normal axles. because the two groups could slip separately. In addition, the total weight of 482 tons and axle weight of 32 tons limited the availability of the engine, and finally it was withdrawn.

Nevertheless, the construction of this 6—4—4—6 led to the building of 52 4—4—4—4 locomotives, of which 27 were built by Baldwin in 1941 and 1946 and 25 in the Pennsylvania's own Works in 1946. These locomotives, designated class T.1, had the same general arrangements as the 6—4—4—6, but with considerable lightening of parts and much improvement in design. The grate area was reduced from 132sq ft to 92sq ft, the driving wheel diameter from 7ft to 6ft 8in, and piston valves were replaced by poppet valves with oscillating cams on the Franklin system. In the Pennsylvania tradition, the engine had a Belpaire boiler and there was a combustion chamber. Two chimneys were at first tried, then two of larger diameter, and finally a single oval chimney of the same diameter as the original double chimney. No difference was noted between these various arrangements and the last was retained as being the simplest.

Tested on the Altoona bank, after having run 120,000 miles in ordinary service, No. 6110 developed 6,755 cylinder horsepower and 5,930hp at the wheel rim at a speed of 100mph. On comparative tests against a 5,400hp triple-unit diesel electric locomotive, the 4—4—4—4, at 80mph, developed a tractive effort of 30,000lbs against the diesel's 19,800lbs, corresponding to respective dbhp of 6,500 and 4,350. During this test the steam locomotive hauled a 16-coach train of 880 tons at an average speed of 102·5mph for 7 miles near Fort Wayne. Later these engines showed themselves capable of hauling express passenger trains of 1,020 tons between Fort Wayne and Chicago at speeds of 102·5mph in normal service over a route with an average gradient of 1 in 3,330.

As regards maintenance costs, Ralph Johnston said that the question was still very controversial, but it should be approximately the same for both types of locomotives, and if one took account of all the running expenses one arrived at the conclusion that to pull trains of 450 tons at speeds of 100mph the expense per kilometre would be, in dollars, about 1·21 with steam traction and 1·55 with diesel traction, assuming an average of 600 miles daily running.

In 1946 comparative tests between diesel and steam traction were also carried out on the New York Central Railroad and were described by P. W. Kiefer in his book *A Practical Evaluation of Railroad Locomotive Power* published in 1947. He shows that the availability and monthly mileages for the steam locomotives tested reached 90 per cent of those for diesels, and this, as Chapelon pointed out, was far from the often cited ratios of three or even four steam locomotives being replaced by one diesel locomotive. These ratios, in fact, related to comparisons between modern diesel and obsolescent steam locomotives. Operating costs on these tests confirmed those arrived at by Johnston. They showed that for equivalent service the annual cost per mile was $1·22 for a 4—8—4 steam engine of 6,000 nominal hp, $1·11 for a twin-unit diesel electric locomotive of 4,000hp, $1·48 for a triple-unit diesel of 6,000hp and $1·15 for an electric locomotive of 5,000hp continuous rating (though the last figure did not include the quite considerable maintenance costs of the overhead contact system and the sub-stations).

The steam locomotives used for these tests were the Niagara class 4—8—4s which were put into service in 1945. These locomotives were designed jointly by the engineers of the New York Central and the American Locomotive Company and built by the latter. They had a grate of 102sq ft and were capable of sustaining 5,050dbhp continuously at 62mph. Outstanding as the performance of these powerful two-cylinder simple expansion engines was, Chapelon comments that the three-cylinder compound 4—8—4, No. 242.A.1, of the SNCF with a grate area of only 54sq ft (but having high superheat, a steam circuit of large cross-section, and triple Kylchap exhaust), developed 4,000dbhp continuously at the same speed. This worked out at 74dbhp per sq ft of grate area as compared with 49 for the Niagara, or 50 per cent better. Had the Niagara incorporated the basic design features of No. 242.1.A it should have been able to sustain continuously 7,500dbhp, and no less than five 2,000hp diesel units would have been needed to equal this.

If similar tests had been carried out in France, the cost difference in favour of the steam locomotive would have been more marked, having regard to the extra costs of purchase and maintenance. In fact, even in the U.S.A. it would appear that the cost difference in favour of the steam locomotive was unrealistically low, because lengthy experience on the Pennsylvania showed that costs increased twice as rapidly for diesel as for steam traction and reduced considerably the economic life of diesel locomotives.

The success of diesel traction did not depend only on the locomotive, as many railway admonistrations in different parts of the world have found out to their cost. A good operating and maintenance organisation and-well trained men in all grades were essential. Owing to the lack of these, in some countries the number of diesel locomotives out of service at depots, either for lack of spare parts or awaiting heavy overhaul has been up to 40 per cent of the entire stock. Good service with such a complex machine as a diesel locomotive is impossible without perfect maintenance carried out by highly skilled technicians, based on large and adequate workshops with a high standard of cleanliness. It was considerations such as these, Chapelon maintained, that emphasised the simplicities of steam traction, which depended only on the conscientious supervision of the condition of the engines, the meticulous execution of their comparatively simple maintenance, and the training of crews in their running.

Chapelon points to the frequent argument against the steam locomotive on the grounds of its poor thermal efficiency at the drawbar, and the commonly cited figures of 6 per cent for steam, 22 per cent for diesel, and 17 per cent for electricity. He comments that these differences are often nullified by the cost of the energy of the locomotive, which often varies in inverse ratio to thermal efficiency so that the eventual cost per hp/hr is very much the same for all three systems. In the light of this assessment, it would seem that, except where special circumstances favour another form of traction, an awful lot of money has been wasted in conversion from steam. Certainly few, if any, railways can say that they are better off in these days of diesel than they were in the days of steam.

13

Brazil and Argentina

IN 1948 André Chapelon, at Bulleid's invitation, paid a visit to Brighton Works, where the latter's controversial double-ended tank engine of the Leader class was under construction. The wheel arrangement, 0—6—0+0—6—0, consisted of two six-wheel bogies; and two separate groups of three simple expansion cylinders drove the centre axle of each bogie. The valve arrangement comprised a sleeve surrounding each cylinder in which were two rows of ports, one for admission and the other for exhaust, and which slid inside a liner. The coupling and mechanism of each of the cylinder groups were enclosed in a case where they were lubricated both by splash and by the circulation of oil. The valve gear was operated by chains (in the same way as in Bulleid's Pacifics) and chains were also provided to couple the three axles of each bogie. There was a driving cab at each end of the locomotive, with all controls duplicated, and there was central cab for the fireman.

Chapelon admired the details of construction, particularly the driving mechanism and the wide steam passages, but he thought that there were too many innovations in one locomotive. Nevertheless he considered it unfortunate that it was not possible to spend more time in overcoming the difficulties in order to get the engine into service. However, R. A. Riddles decided that further expense on such a complex machine which had no certain prospects of success was not justified.

In 1950 the SNCF acceded to a request from GELSA (*Groupement d.Exportation de Locomotives en Sud-Amérique*) that Chapelon should direct their design office in plans for 90 locomotives ordered by Brazil, 24 of which were to be of the 4—8—4 type and 66 of the 2—8—4.

The Brazilian railways at that time comprised about 24,000 miles of route of which about 20,500 miles were metre gauge and the remainder 5ft 3in and 2ft. There were a large number of different railway systems, of which about twelve had about 1,000 route miles or over. All these were under the authority of the *Departmento Nacional de Estrados de Ferre* (DNEF). Of all this mileage only about 580 was electrified, although Brazil had considerable hydraulic reserves. Practically all the traffic was steam operated at this time, although the coal available to the railways was of very poor quality.

On October 27th 1949 the DNEF gave their approval to a contract, which was signed on November 28th, for the supply by GELSA of the 90 steam locomotives, which were to be built by the following four companies: *Batignolles-Chatillon, Société Française de Construction Mécaniques, Société des Forges et Ateliers de Creusot*, and the *Compagnie de Fives-Lille*. These locomotives, of which the first was to be delivered within 18 months after the signing of the contract and the balance by the end of 28 months, were to meet two different requirements; one for a locomotive with an axle weight of 13 tons and a tractive effort at 85 per cent of 13 tons, and the other with an axle weight of 10 tons and a tractive effort of 10 tons.

In accordance with this requirement and to meet the wishes expressed by the DNEF, it was decided that the engines should be two-cylinder simple expansion, one a 4—8—4 with 5ft coupled wheels and the other a 2—8—4 with 4ft 2in coupled wheels.[1] Detailed design had to take account of the fuel which the engines were going to burn. The coal had a low calorific value and a high content of iron pyrites which caused much formation of clinker, and 25 of the 2—8—4 locomotives were to burn wood. Both had to negotiate curves of 264ft radius, the 4—8—4s at 50mph and the 2—8—4s 37·5mph. Chapelon decided that the 4—8—4s should have a grate area of 58sq ft, a pressure of 280lbs per sq in, a Kylchap double exhaust, and a mechanical stoker; whereas the 2—8—4s should have 43sq ft grate area, a lower pressure of 210lbs per sq in, a Kylchap single exhaust, and should be fired by hand. Tenders had to be of different sizes because of the length of turntables. Those of the 4—8—4 locomotives carried 18 tons of fuel, whilst the 2—8—4s had two different tender sizes, one carrying 12 tons and fitted to 16 engines, and the other with only 7 tons for the remaining 50 engines. Owing to the different systems on the various railways, a legacy from the old private companies, some of the engines had compressed air brakes and the others the vacuum type.

In his design of these engines, Chapelon aimed at economical operation combined with mechanical reliability. To this end, his plans profited by the latest information and experience, particularly as regards the proportions and arrangement of the boiler, the driving mechanism, the chassis, and the riding. At the same time the greatest possible standardisation was sought between the new engines and the principal existing Brazilian types, as regards parts and general arrangement, to facilitate both maintenance and the provision of spare parts. For this reason all the accessories, including the carrying axle boxes, were the same in both types of new locomotive, and the diameter of wheels and the axle dimensions conformed to those already in use on the DNEF. In addition, by adopting a pressure of 210lbs per sq in for the

1. Appendix B.31

2—8—4, instead of 280, it was possible to use cylinders of the same diameter on the two locomotives, as well as the same piston heads, the same piston rings, and all the other related components and fittings. The piston valve diameter was also the same, but the valve travel differed to take account of the different needs in steam distribution.

The firebox was the Belpaire type for both engines, but with a combustion chamber for the 4—8—4. The Belpaire firebox was preferred because of:

(a) its resistance to distortion, which was of particular importance when, as in these engines, Nicholson thermic syphons were used;

(b) its large evaporative area which allowed, with the minimum lowering of the water level, rapid acceleration and the use of the whole capacity of the boiler;

(c) the greater accuracy it allowed in calculating the staying required to obtain the necessary strength.

The distance between the ceiling of the firebox and the top of the boiler was so fixed as to avoid appreciable drops in the water level during hard pulling.

There were two Nicholson thermic syphons in the fireboxes, except in those of the wood-burning locomotive where the syphons would have been an encumbrance. The grates were, respectively, 8ft 10½in long and 6ft 7in wide in the 4—8—4 and 7ft long and 5ft 7in wide in the 2—8—4.

In January 1951 the first of each type was tested by brake locomotives on the metre-gauge Breton Railway of the SNCF, both with Brazilian coal of 4,800 calories and good-quality French coal of 7,800 calories. This gave Chapelon the opportunity to confirm in practice the theory that the general setting of the exhaust is suitable whatever the calorific power of the coal, as long as the formation of clinkers is not blocking the grate. Thus the 2—8—4 made a trip one way fired with French coal and then returned with Brazilian coal being used. There was no discernible difference in either water level or pressure between the two journeys. (The engine was, of course, equipped with the Kylchap exhaust.)

All the locomotives had been delivered by January 1953. The 4—8—4 engines were running on four of the Brazilian railways and the 2—8—4s on eleven. The mixed origin of the locomotives then running on the railways of Brazil is shown by the stock of one of them. This was the former British-leased Great Western of Brazil Railway, which, by some geographical miracle had become the Rede Ferroviara do Nordeste—almost a movement of Swindon to Darlington! This line, with its headquarters at Recife, had a variety of locomotives of many different types, of which the principal were 87 2—6—0s supplied by the U.S.A. in 1891–5 and Great Britain in 1904–14; 16 4—6—0s from the U.S.A. in 1921 and from Great Britain and Germany in 1927–9; and 14 4—8—0s from Great Britain over the period 1906–29. The total number of engines (of which there were none of more recent date than 1929) was 149, for a railway of 1,141 route miles.

In the spring of 1951 Chapelon led a French mission on the occasion of the entry into service of the new locomotives, which were arriving in Brazil from the various firms charged with their manufacture. During this mission Chapelon was asked to address meetings at Rio, Sao Paulo, and Porto Alegre on the improvements which could be made to the existing Brazilian steam locomotives. A tour by air between these various centres was ended by a journey in a special train pulled by one of Chapelon's new 2—8—4 engines over some 300 miles of the Viacao Ferrea do Rio Grande do Sul from Porto Alegre to Santa Maria. Whilst riding on the footplate Chapelon was impressed with excellent fashion in which the native firemen looked after the condition of the fire.

Chapelon thoroughly enjoyed his tour of Brazil. In the course of it he had been entertained by the Association of Brazilian Engineers at a banquet in Rio de Janeiro and he had the great pleasure of contemplating the Southern Cross and beautiful stars which are unknown in the Northern hemisphere. And his new engines, into which he had incorporated features from his two notable rebuilt simple expansion engines Nos. 141.E.113 and 140.J.153, were appreciated by the Brazilian railwaymen.

Chapelon's mission was continued into Argentina where, at Rio de la Plata, he received an even warmer welcome, notably from Ing. L. D. Porta, himself a brilliant steam locomotive engineer. Chapelon had further meetings in Buenos Aires where engineers crowded the rooms in which he spoke. From Buenos Aires he went to Cordoba where he was received by the Academy of Science. Here the Argentine railway engineers demonstrated to him one of their two-cylinder compound 4—8—0 tank engines, working on a steep gradient. He liked the good mechanical arrangement of the engine and admired the way in which the crew handled it. The long journey to and from Cordoba was very comfortable because the presidential coach had been placed at Chapelon's disposal for both the outward and return trips.

In July 1953 Chapelon retired from the French railway service and was appointed to the high distinction of Honorary Engineer-in-Chief of the SNCF. However, he was not retiring from locomotive work because GELSA appointed him their Consulting Engineer. In the same year they directed him to lead a mission to negotiate and sign with the Argentine authorities a contract for the rebuilding of some of their engines. On this occasion the Argentinian Ministry of Transport asked Chapelon to explain to an improvised meeting of Argentine transport engineers the details and of reasons for the modifications which he intended to introduce into the rebuilding of the engines. This exposition was given to about a hundred persons and was published by the Minister of Transport.

Before the French mission left Argentina the Minister of Transport organised, in honour of Chapelon and his team, a magnificent reception. There was a banquet which even by French standards was perfection in dishes and arrangement, and at which Chapelon sat on the right of the Minister. This was followed by a discussion of matters arising out of the visit and then there was a particularly brilliant evening party with country dances and pageants which interested and delighted the French visitors.

There was a remarkable programme of rebuilding on the railways of Argentina as a result of Chapelon's visit. This was carried out in accordance with the recommendations of André Chapelon and also of the Argentine engineers L. D. Porta (who had, indeed, started rebuilding engines on Chapelon lines even before the latters' visit) and J. Vittone, and it included modifying the draughting, improving the steam circuit, and, in the later engines, introducing the gas producer technique to combustion.

One very fine rebuilding under Chapelon's direction was that carried out in 1958 of a 11.C class three-cylinder simple expansion 4—8—0 locomotive of the 5ft 6in gauge General Roca Railway, one of a class of 75 built in England by Beyer-Peacock between 1924 and 1929. (Most of the General Roca consisted of the old British-owned Buenos Aires Great Southern Railway.) In spite of their wheel arrangement these were goods engines with 4ft 7½in coupled wheels, weighing 85·5 tons with 66·4 tons adhesive weight.

Chapelon regarded this rebuilding as comparatively simple, and for the driving mechanism and the exhaust he used the same techniques as in the rebuilding of 2—8—0 No. 140.J.153. Trials of the first rebuilt engine were carried out with brake locomotives under the direction of M. Réné Ségaud of the SNCF and were outstandingly successful. The engine sustained 1,400hp at the tender drawbar at 37·5mph as compared with the 1,000hp of her unrebuilt sisters and for the same consumption of fuel oil. (A Réné Ségaud RS burner was substituted for the American type with the object of getting better pulverisation and therefore more complete combustion in the firebox.) Not only was there an increase of 40 per cent in power and efficiency, but the total cost of the rebuilding was 15 per cent less than that of a general overhaul. The great success of the engine led to all the others in the class being rebuilt in a similar fashion.

The 11.C class 4—8—0s handled freight trains of 1,500 to 2,000 tons and, as rebuilt, they did the same job with the consumption of about 30 per cent less fuel than in their original condition. They eventually replaced the more modern and nominally more powerful 15.A and 15.B class 4—8—0s in the haulage of the 1,000-ton fast fruit trains over the 740 miles between the Rio Negre Valley and Buenos Aires.

Senor L. D. Porta presented a notable paper before the Manchester Centre of the Institution of Locomotive Engineers on March 7th 1969 on steam locomotive development in Argentina. Perhaps for steam locomotive enthusiasts the principal interest of this paper was that it showed that in 1969 Chapelon's revolutionary concept of the steam locomotive had not died with the change in France to other forms of traction, but that it was still being pursued on the railways of South America. At the start of his paper Porta generously acknowledged that the inspiration and starting of his work was an exhaustive study of the work of André Chapelon.

Porta rebuilt a four-cylinder compound 4—8—0 locomotive, and, he says, followed the principles closely that had been applied by Chapelon in the PO Railway rebuilt Pacifics. An interesting addition, however, was that he used a supplementary superheater between the HP exhaust and the LP admission in imitation of Chapelon's six-cylinder 2—12—0. After some troubles at the start, the engine was exceedingly successful and produced a maximum power output of 2,120dbhp, which was practically the same in proportion to their respective weights as that of the PO 4—8—0s. The engine, which was for the metre gauge, was completed in 1947, well before Chapelon's first visit to Argentina. Although the diameter of the coupled wheels was only 4ft 2in, the engine rode well, hauling 1,200-ton freight trains at 65mph and 2,000-ton trains at 50mph. Chapelon rode on the footplate of this engine during his first visit to Argentina and expressed his admiration of Porta's design. He says that it rode excellently and was exceptionally economical.

A number of suburban tank locomotives of the Roca Railway were rebuilt by Porta. The suburban services from Buenos Aires were operated by 30 2—6—2 tank engines built in 1916 and 60 2—6—4 tank engines built (25 by the Vulcan Locomotive Works) in 1925. During the period about 1950 there were labour difficulties which made it impossible to maintain the engines properly. The three-cylinder 2—6—4 tank engines, which after overhaul in the works could develop 900dbhp, were reduced to about 600dbhp a few months later. Porta carried out modifications to some of these engines, including improved exhaust and valve setting, with the very successful result that the dbhp of the 2—6—4 tank locomotives so modified was increased to 1,200 with much less falling off in service. Further, the modified 2—6—2 tank engines were more powerful than the unmodified 2—6—4 type and could therefore be used on the more exacting services.

Porta now undertook a much more radical rebuilding of a 2—6—2 tank locomotive, using Chapelon techniques. The original design incorporated features which, indeed, were almost the opposite of those to be found in a Chapelon engine: the firebox volume was inadequate, the steam space was restricted, steam passages were long and of small cross-sectional area, the superheat was low, frames were weak, and lubrication was poor. To remedy these defects, Porta raised the boiler pressure, increased the superheat, augmented the steam chest volume, redesigned and renewed the reciprocating parts, fitted specially designed piston valves to improve the steam flow and enable higher steam temperatures to be used, reinforced the frames, improved the lubrication of cylinders and running gear, and redesigned the oil-burning equipment. In addition he fitted the Kylpor exhaust, which was derived from the Kylchap (but which did not appear to be an improvement on it.)

The results with the rebuilt engine were excellent. The maximum dbhp was 1,400, nearly double that of the original engine and was about the same as that obtained with the much larger PS.11 class three-cylinder Pacifics built by the Vulcan Locomotive Works in 1926. It could, in fact, take over the trains normally worked by these Pacifics and work them at a fuel consumption which was lower by some 30–40 per cent.

In all nine different classes of locomotive on three different gauges were rebuilt, and one of the most striking was the conversion of the 2—10—2 locomotives running on the narrowest gauge of all, the 2ft 5½in of the Rio Turbio Railway. The Rio Turbio is a mineral line in the south of Patagonia and by far the most southerly of any railway in the world. It runs for 160 miles from the Rio Turbio mines to the port of Gallegos, carrying coal for shipment. The track is light with rails of 35lbs per yard and axle weight is limited to 7½ tons. In spring and autumn operating is hampered by the constant very strong winds with frequent gusts of up to 100mph. Loaded mineral trains may total up to 1,700 tons and these are hauled by 2—10—2 locomotives built in Japan, and delivered in two batches of ten each in 1956 and 1964 respectively. Porta modified three of the first batch by fitting the Kylpor exhaust and his gas producer combustion system in which the bulk of the air required was admitted as secondary air above its fire, with the object of attaining high power outputs without lifting the fire. As this modification resulted in the maximum sustained dbhp being raised from 700 to 1,200, Porta incorporated the same modifications and one or two others in the second batch.

Perhaps the most controversial part of Ing. Porta's paper was his look into the future and his idea of a general-purpose steam locomotive which would be suitable for countries which had plentiful supplies of cheap lower-grade fuel. Design of such an engine would have to take into account the lack of skilled fitters and it would have to be simple and robust, with ample bearing surfaces and accessible mechanism. He thought the engine should be a 2—8—0 with mechanical firing to deal with very low grade coal or wood fuel. The design that he proposed was a two-cylinder compound locomotive with inside cylinders and piston valves operated by external Walschaerts gear. He chose inside cylinders because if they were outside it would make the locomotive heavier and subject to greater inertia forces; in addition there would be higher radiation losses. His compound engine would have both HP and LP superheaters, like Chapelon's No. 160.A.1. The boiler would have a pressure of 285lbs per sq in and a gas producer firebox.

Chapelon paid tribute to this conception, but, whilst he agreed that a two-cylinder compound drive was the best solution from the point of view of thermal efficiency, he thought that the diameter of LP cylinder necessary for the locomotive to attain the power of 2,000hp which Porta wanted, even with the pressure of 285lbs per sq in and improved steam distribution, might be too large to be accommodated within the frames. In addition, he did not think that this cylinder arrangement was advisable because at the power output envisaged the crank would be at the limit of forces which it could withstand. It was these problems, experienced with crank axles of the largest four-cylinder compounds, that had induced him to adopt the three-cylinder compound drive, the single-throw crank axle being much more robust. There were various other aspects of the design which Chapelon believed might require revision and he was sure that the prototype locomotive would need a tuning-up period on the test bed and running in on the line before being given a full trial in service.

Chapelon has a very high opinion of Porta as a locomotive engineer and regards him as 'eminent amongst those who believe in the further development of the steam locomotive'.

14

The Chapelon Steam Engine

AT THE END of 1967 André Chapelon resigned from GELSA, nearly 43 years after his arrival on the Paris-Orléans Railway. His influence on the design of the steam locomotive had been tremendous; but it is curious that, in spite of the almost universal acceptance amongst locomotive engineers of his pre-eminence in their field, practically none of them believed him right in his insistence on the superiority of the compound over the simple expansion locomotive. In face of the rival claims of other forms of traction, many of them believed and said that the steam locomotive had nearly reached the limit of possible development. They could not grasp the tremendous possibilities that lay in the compound. And so Chapelon was almost alone in his stand on the continuing superiority of the steam locomotive for main-line operation, except where such special circumstances as shortage of water made it uneconomic. The final evaluation of the tests carried out with No. 160.A.1 came when the battle for steam had already been lost.

It was Chapelon's fate that practically all the steam locomotives for which he was responsible were either rebuilds or improvements of existing engines. The sole exceptions were the locomotives he designed for the Brazilian Railways, and these, to meet the requirements of the purchasers, were simple expansion. But this is of course to his credit, rather than the reverse, for in designing the engine he wanted, he was hampered by the necessity of fitting his plans to the limitations imposed by an existing locomotive. It is a great tribute to his success that the Nord should have ordered new Pacifics identical with Chapelon's rebuilds, though the engines from which they had been rebuilt were then over 25 years old.

The prejudice against the compound steam locomotive is a little difficult to understand, but it is probably due mainly to the number of compounds which have produced insufficient savings in consumption to offset the additional complication in construction and extra costs in maintenance. The main reason for this has probably poor design, resulting, amongst other things, in the low pressure cylinders not doing their fair share of the work. An additional factor was probably that many engineers preferred just two outside cylinders, and they believed that a two-cylinder compound produced uneven distribution of power between the two sides of a locomotive. There was, in fact, little foundation for this belief. In the first (1938) edition of Chapelon's book, *La Locomotive à Vapeur*, there are reproduced calculations made by M. Wantz, Chief of Studies on the PO-Midi, which show that even in a two-cylinder simple expansion engine, with cranks placed at 90deg to each other, the effort to which the frame on the right side is submitted is 15 per cent greater than that on the left side. For example, in the PO simple expansion Pacifics of the 3591–3640 class, working at slow speeds with 35 per cent cut-off and 175lbs per sq in pressure in the steam chests, there appeared this difference of 15 per cent, a difference which is not always found in a two-cylinder compound.

The first real compound locomotive did not appear till 1876, and it was invented, as is fitting, by a French engineer, Anatole Mallet, who built three two-cylinder compound engines for the little Bayonne-Biarritz Railway. They had two outside cylinders, one HP and one LP, and for starting live steam could be admitted to the LP cylinder whilst the HP cylinder exhausted directly to the atmosphere. The change from simple to compound working was under control of the driver. But Mallet is most famous for his articulated compounds, and in fact he is remembered more by his system of articulation than by his method of compounding. Two little Mallet compound tank engines with the 0—4—0+0—4—0 wheel arrangement and weighing 12 tons each were built in 1887 for goods traffic on the 2ft gauge railway running from Pithiviers (half way between Orléans and Fontainebleau) over a distance of 19 miles to Toury and operated by the Decauville Company. They had four outside cylinders, two HP and two LP. The HP cylinders were fastened to the rear part of the main frame and drove one set of wheels, whilst the LP cylinders were carried on a leading bogie truck and drove its four wheels. Similar engines worked all trains on another Decauville 2ft gauge light railway from Caen to Dives and Luc-sur-Mer, a total distance of 23½ miles.

This was the classic wheel arrangement that produced the enormous compound locomotives in the United States. The first of these was put into service on the Baltimore and Ohio Railroad in 1905; it had two sets of six-coupled wheels, the large grate area of 70sq ft, a pressure of 238lbs per sq in, and a weight of 152 tons. It was used as a banking engine and, over the period January 1905 to December 1910, it showed a fuel economy of 38 per cent as compared with the 2—8—0 locomotives on the same duty.

Eventually engines of this type were built of such a size that the compound arrangement had to be abandoned, because, the LP cylinders having reached a diameter of 4ft, no further increase in size could be fitted inside the loading gauge. When the Chesapeake & Ohio introduced in 1924 some 2—8—0+0—8—2 engines articulated on the Mallet system, but of simple expansion, other railways followed. But not all of them did so because of the size of the LP cylinders; some of them just did not like compounds. It was said that the rotating masses were too heavy and difficult to balance, resulting in heavy maintenance costs, and that the high back pressure in the LP cylinders increased so much with speed that unequal power was developed in the two units with consequent loss of adhesion, which could only be remedied by introducing live steam at reduced pressure in the intermediate receiver.

The Norfolk & Western Railroad did not agree, however, with these criticisms of Mallet compounds and they went on building them. Batches of 2—8—0+0—8—2 compounds were turned out in 1938, 1942, and even 1952. They were used for working heavy freight trains over the steeply graded lines, notably those crossing the Alleghany Mountains. They were preferred to simple expansion Mallet type engines (which the Norfolk & Western also had) because, contrary to the opinion given above, they had better adhesion, and also because they had a reserve of power, obtained by exhausting the HP cylinders directly to the atmosphere and admitting live steam to the intermediate receiver. Their maintenance costs were little different to those of the simple articulated engines.

Not long after Mallet, A. von Borries of the Prussian State Railways built in 1880 a two-cylinder 2—4—0 compound locomotive. For more than 20 years engines of this type (though with a leading bogie from 1893) operated all the express passenger trains on the Prussian State Railways. In 1889 von Borries incorporated an automatic starting arrangement by which live steam was admitted to the intermediate receiver until the pressure in the latter, through the HP cylinder exhausting into it, rose sufficiently high to cut the live steam off. It was not altogether successful and von Borries reverted to a non-automatic arrangement.

T. W. Worsdell of the North Eastern Railway produced his own version of the von Borries system. For starting, Worsdell provided a handle in the cab, by means of which the driver, if he had difficult, could admit live steam into the LP cylinder whilst at the same time cutting communication between this cylinder and the receiver. Change to compound working was effected automatically, after a few strokes of the piston, by the pressure of the HP exhaust in the receiver. Bowman Malcolm adopted Worsdell's method for the Belfast & Northern Counties Railway. The North Eastern engines ran extremely well once they got going, but the automatic starting system was a failure and Wilson Worsdell, in due course, converted his brother's compounds to simple expansion.

But where non-automatic starting arrangements were used the two-cylinder compounds worked well, and better than simple expansion engines of similar type and size. The Prussian State Railways alone had 6,400 locomotives of the von Borries compound type. But, to meet the demands for an increase in power, von Borries had changed to a four-cylinder compound system. This was unlike the du Bousquet de Glehn arrangement because the cylinders were placed in line, with the LP outside, and all drove the same axle. At the same time the valve gear was simplified; the motion of the inside cylinder valves being derived from the Walschaerts gear of the outside cylinder valves, with the LP cut-off from 10 per cent to 20 per cent greater than that of the HP. The possible differences between HP and LP cut-offs was of course very much less than with the de Glehn system in which there were separate valve motions to each cylinder.

The PLM chose the von Borries arrangement in 1914. Since 1898 that railway had adhered to a LP cut-off fixed at a 63 per cent, following trials carried out from 1894 to 1896 on the four-cylinder compound 'wind-cutting' 4—4—0 No. C.21. Eventually in 1941, at Chapelon's suggestion, equal HP and LP cut-offs were adopted for the 141.P class 2—8—2 locomotives, with the inside LP valves operated by a motion derived from the exterior HP mechanism.

During the same period as von Borries, the Prussian engineer Borodine had followed Mallet by rebuilding, from 1880, simple expansion engines as two-cylinder compounds, with very satisfactory results.

In France A. Herdner, Engineer-in-Chief of Rolling Stock and Motive Power on the Midi Railway, advocated the adoption of the two-cylinder compound system for engines of lower power. He rebuilt a number of Midi simple expansion outside cylinder 0—6—0 engines (a type known in France as *Bourbonnais*) into two-cylinder compound 2—6—0s. This rebuilding was so successful that Herdner's example was followed by the PO, Etat, Ouest, and Est Railways. Herdner then rebuilt as two-cylinder compounds 22 of the 38 1600 class 2—4—0 express engines of 1885–9. The PO followed his example again by converting into a two-cylinder compound 2—4—2 No. 85 of E. Polonceau's 77 class express engines, and then by rebuilding some of Forquenot's excellent little simple expansion 2—4—2 express engines as two-cylinder compound Atlantics.

In 1900 J. Nadal, Engineer-in-Chief of the Etat Railway (who introduced the Pacific type on to that line with his engines of 1909 and 1914), completed his *Mathematical Theory of Cylinder Wall Effect in Steam Locomotives*; an authoritative work which was con-

confirmed by experience on locomotives and which threw much light on this complex and extremely important phenomenon. In addition he made a complete analysis of the general functioning of the locomotive, as Herdner had done for counter-pressure braking, double-heading (the safety of which was questioned by some), and the value of high centres of gravity to reduce the extent of lateral thrust on the track by the axles of an engine's rigid wheel base. This last point was confirmed on the PO by the Engineer Manzier, who was charged with research into the causes of track deformation in the electrified zone. He concluded that the locomotives which did not damage the track were those with characteristics that included a high centre of gravity. This was manifestly contrary to the aims pursued by Crampton, but then his engines did cause wear on the rails (on the other hand they did generally remain upright after derailment which was much appreciated by the Motive Power department).

The great Austrian locomotive engineer, Carl Gölsdorf had a very effective starting device on his own two-cylinder compound engines. In the valve face of the LP cylinder were very small ports for live steam which were only uncovered when the engine was working in full gear. The first reduction in the cut-off shut them off. Although most of Golsdorf's engines were two-cylinder compounds, his later and larger locomotives had four cylinders, two HP and two LP.

In 1882 F. W. Webb of the London & North Western Railway built the first of a long line of compound engines, of which the earlier had three cylinders and the later four. For upwards of 20 years he built nothing else for express passenger services, and practically all his eight-coupled goods engines were compounds. Webb's compound engines were noteworthy for having no arrangement for admitting live steam to the LP cylinders, so that they worked compound under all conditions. Nor could the cut-off in the HP and LP cylinders be operated independently. Webb's compounds could hardly be called a success; in fact their drivers found them so unreliable that the compound system acquired a permanently bad reputation on the L.N.W.R.

Really successful modern compound locomotives owe their origin to five great engineers: Edouard Sauvage then of the Nord, W. M. Smith of the North Eastern, Gaston du Bousquet of the Nord; Alfred de Glehn of the Société Alsacienne, and A. Henry of the PLM.

Sauvage in 1887 built a three-cylinder compound 2—6—0 locomotive in the Nord workshops with one inside HP cylinder and two outside LP cylinders. It was the only one of its type and was used for the haulage of fast freight trains, a duty which it performed with great success. It was not the first three-cylinder compound of this type, for three-cylinder compound 2—6—0 locomotives with a similar arrangement of HP and

LP cylinders had been built by Weyerman for the Swiss Jura-Simplon Railway, and the first of no less than 147 of them appeared in 1886. They were successful engines but they were inferior to the Sauvage design, partly because of the arrangement of the cranks. Whereas the Swiss engines had these set at 120deg from each other, Sauvage set the outside cranks at 90deg to each other whilst the inside crank bisected the obtuse angle between them.

But although Sauvage's engine was a solitary example, his idea was taken up by W. M. Smith, Chief Draughtsman of the North Eastern Railway. In 1898 he rebuilt a Worsdell-von Borries two-cylinder compound 4—4—0 engine as a three-cylinder compound, adopting Sauvage's disposition of the cranks and arrangement of the cylinders. Smith's engine, too, was a solitary example (though he built two excellent four cylinder compound Atlantics on the same principle for the North Eastern in 1904), but in 1901–03 S. W. Johnson of the Midland Railway built five 4—4—0 engines at Derby as compounds on the Sauvage-Smith system. Like the engines of both Sauvage and Smith, they had independent reversing gears and could be worked as simple, semi-compound, or compound. At starting, live steam entered the LP steam chest at a pressure controlled by the driver, and when the pressure in the steam chest reached the maximum allowed the live steam supply was automatically cut off. But in an emergency the driver could work the engine on simple expansion, and when climbing a steep gradient or hauling a heavy train he could switch to semi-compound working by admitting extra steam from the boiler to the LP cylinders.

These Midland engines were very good, and Deeley later successfully simplified the Smith arrangement. All subsequent compounds for both the Midland and London, Midland & Scottish Railways were built to the Deeley modification. They were economical and adequate for the light trains of the Midland, but, after the formation of the LMS, they were in difficulties with the much heavier trains worked over the old L.N.W.R. lines. Nevertheless, tests carried out later showed them to be capable of a greater power output than had at first appeared.

In 1905 J. G. Robinson built four three-cylinder compound Atlantic locomotives for the Great Central Railway on the modified Smith system, but they do not appear to have been better than his simple expansion Atlantics. In 1932 Beyer Peacock built five three-cylinder compound 4—4—0s (*Eagle, Falcon, Merlin, Peregrine,* and *Kestrel*) for the Great Northern Railway (Ireland) to the design of G. T. Glover, who adopted a modification of the Sauvage-Smith system. Those were fast and powerful engines and were probably the best compounds ever to run in the British Isles; but they were spoilt when, for maintenance reasons, their boiler pressure was dropped from 250lbs per sq in to 200.

The four-cylinder systems designed by Henry and jointly by du Bousquet and de Glehn have already been dicussed in these pages.

Chapelon, as we have seen, was concerned first with the du Bousquet de Glehn system on the PO, then with the Henry system when he was designing the 141.Ps for the SNCF, and lastly with the Sauvage-Smith system which he selected for No. 242.A.1. As already mentioned, his reason for the selection was to avoid the weakness caused by the two cranks on the driving axle which were necessary with a four-cylinder engine. We have noted that he did not object to a single reversing gear to operate the HP and LP cut-offs together, but that he insisted on independent operation in a prototype locomotive until the fixed relationship beteen the HP and LP cut-offs had been established. He had shown that, given such proper relationship and with a design that ensured approximately equal work in the HP and LP cylinder groups, the compound was superior in both power and economy to the best-designed simple expansion engine of similar dimensions—the most striking example being the comparison between the 141.P and 141.R 2—8—2 locomotives. The design of the 141.P class was, in fact, a notable triumph of improvement combined with simplicity, for this engine embodied all those principles that Chapelon had incorporated in his PO rebuilds, combined with a single reversing gear and having all the gear outside the frames. Essential to their success were the wide cross-sections of the steam passages and the correct proportions of the cylinder clearance volumes.

In the design of locomotives generally, Chapelon considered that there were certain essential features. Some of these were generally recognised, whilst others had received surprisingly little attention from many locomotive engineers.

On the boiler depends the amount of steam that can be produced and, in consequence, the power that the engine can develop if furnished with the proper mechanism. But there have been locomotive engineers who have spoiled a good engine by providing it with an inadequate boiler. Daniel Gooch and Archibald Sturrock recognised the importance of the boiler in comparatively early days. So probably did Patrick Stirling, but the weight limitations of the poor Great Northern track prevented him from building big enough boilers for his engines. In the boiler the dimensions of the firebox, tubes, etc. determine the quantity of heat produced, and the most important of these dimensions is the area of the grate. Du Bousquet knew this at the turn of the century when he gave his Atlantics a grate area of 29·7 sqft. Other important dimensions affecting the boiler are the size and of the air and hot gas passages and the efficiency of the exhaust. Poor combustion due to an inadequate air supply was probably the cause of the comparative failures of some British 4—6—0 designs in the early years of this century.

Once the heat is produced it must, of course, be used for raising steam, and for this purpose the heating surface should ideally be about 75 times the area of the grate, and, of even greater importance, the area of the tube surface in contact with the hot gases should be 400 times the cross-sectional area of their passages, and more if the exhaust allows. But the narrow limits of weight and dimensions imposed on locomotives often present these proportions being attained, particularly the former when the grate is very large. Part of the heating surface is, of course, required for superheating the steam.

The size of the cylinders depends on the tractive effort required and is related therefore to the diameter of the driving wheels, but the boiler must be big enough to supply them with the steam they need. Again, the adhesive weight should be related to the tractive effort, because if it is insufficient the driving wheels will slip.

Engines which have to run fast must ride well and be able to take curves easily, and they must also be able to run over poor tracks without undue rocking and plunging. These are factors which ensure safety and which require the greatest competence in design.

The builder of a locomotive must make it simple, robust, and convenient. He must never lose sight of the work which it will be required to do and the conditions under which it will have to do it. He should avoid all complications and sacrifice all gear which is not indispensable; thus the chances of damage will be reduced and both the maintenance and the operation of the engine will be easier. Inspection, lubrication, and cleaning should be easy; the controls should be grouped so that they are under the hands of the crew; the crew should be comfortable; pipes exposed to frost or which disfigure the appearance of the engine should not be multiplied without good cause.

These are the basic factors of good design; but they are not in themselves sufficient to produce a really good engine. For instance, the PO Pacifics, before Chapelon rebuilt them, fulfilled most of the above conditions, but their exhaust was poor, their degree of superheat was too low, and the cross-section of their steam passages was inadequate. It will be remembered from Chapter 2 that Chapelon decided that three main improvements must therefore be incorporated in the rebuilding of the engines:

(a) An exhaust which would both increase the power of the boiler and diminish the back pressure against the pistons; thus increasing both power and efficiency.

(b)   A higher degree of superheat so that the LP as well as the HP cylinders should benefit from superheated steam.

(c)   An increase in the cross section of the steam circuit from regulator to exhaust to reduce throttling and so allow the locomotive to reach the highest speeds.

He calculated that these three measures would permit the development of 3,000 cylinder horsepower by an engine which had been designed to develop 2,000 (but which in practice, because of bad adjustment, could not even sustain that).

The exhaust problem he dealt with by the introduction of his outstandingly efficient Kylchap arrangement as described in Chapter 2 —an arrangement which still remains unsurpassed in efficiency although it is some 45 years since Chapelon designed it.

With the existing superheat temperature of 300deg C it was easy to obtain gains in power of 20 per cent as compared with saturated steam, but at this temperature the LP cylinders were themselves still operating almost entirely on saturated steam. Chapelon decided to double the effective degree of superheat by increasing the temperature to 400deg C, and so ensure that there remained 100deg C of superheat for the LP cylinders. However, it would have been difficult to increase the temperature of the superheat any further because in 1926 400deg C seemed to be the maximum which the best cylinder castings and the best lubricating oils could withstand. In fact, there was little change in this position when construction of steam locomotives in France ceased. But of course the evaluation of the results achieved by No. 160.A.1 changed the position as regards superheat, and doors which had been closed to further development were once again thrown wide open.

Throttling of steam was a problem which had occupied the attention of engineers since at least the middle of the nineteenth century, because, particularly at high speeds, it was responsible for a considerable reduction in the power and efficiency of locomotives. But most of these engineers had confined their attention to the reduction of throttling during the period of admission of live steam to the cylinders, and this led to the design of various arrangements to replace the standard slide valves, on the ground that the latter did not allow full port openings sufficiently rapid for the pressure to remain constant during the admission period. This too limited approach had the effect of actually retarding the development of the express locomotive. Indeed, engineers in busying themselves over the problem of a sudden port opening were wasting their time, because it is easy to prove that the only really effective way of countering throttling through the steam ports is to increase their size, and no rapidity of opening or closing can compensate for an error in the dimensions of the ports. The reason for this is that the speed of the piston varies at each part of its travel.

In any case, throttling during admission only accounts for a small proportion of the total losses of pressure to which the steam is liable during its passage between the boiler and the exhaust. On a great number of engines the loss between regulator and cylinder at high speeds may be as much as 50lbs per sq in. In fact the exhaust side of the cylinder is infinitely more important than the inlet side.

It is probable that no aspect of Chapelon's work impressed locomotive engineers, both in France and overseas, so much as his demonstration of the importance of ensuring that the steam had an unrestricted flow from the regulator to its exit from the chimney. The part that this played in the rebuilding of the PO Pacifics was so striking that from the 1930s onwards few express locomotives were built in Europe or North America that did not have steam circuits designed in the light of Chapelon's teaching.

A different consideration in locomotive design is the problem of the locomotive crew. For a long time in all countries it was the practice for an engine to be allotted to a single crew, as it was held that this gave the best results. The effect was that an engine only ran the mileage of which its crew was capable, and this was normally about 6,000 miles a month. Because this was a very uneconomic use of an engine, certain railways tried double manning, i.e., allotting two crews to each engine. By this method the average monthly mileage was increased to 9,000. The next step was to try a common-user system. This generally gave deplorable results because the men lost interest in the engine and maintenance suffered.

In the United States, where regular crews were still considered essential in 1905, a method was found of making the common-user system work. Responsibility for maintenance was removed from the drivers and transferred to the staff at the sheds. As soon as a locomotive entered its shed it was taken over by three examiners, of whom one was responsible for the boiler, one for the mechanism, and one for the brakes. The engine was thus submitted to a most minute examination. The engine crew pointed out any faults that they had noticed and the examination disclosed others that would not normally come to the notice of the footplate men.

This system was found very satisfactory, but, in addition, these frequent inspections soon pointed to ways in which the utilisation of locomotives could be increased still more by incorporating into their construction devices which would reduce to a minimum the causes of deterioration and facilitate maintenance. The measures taken included the following: the use of monobloc chassis which cannot be deformed and which removed the work of taking frames to pieces; the incorporation of roller bearings in axle boxes and coupling rods to prevent heating and reduce wear; the introduction of automatic wedges to stop axle box play and suppress shocks; the use of wheels with rims which were immune to deformation and so prolonged the life of tyres and stopped them from becoming loose; automatic lubrication throughout; and purification of water, which is essential to maintain the boiler in good condition. These measures increased the mileage run by locomotives very considerably, and the last American steam locomotives, such as the 4—8—4 'Niagara' class of the New York Central Railroad, achieved a monthly average of 24,000 miles.

The common-user system was introduced into France with the entry into service of the 141.R class 2—8—2 locomotives. As compared with the average running of French locomotives, which had regular crews, the mileage of the 141.Rs was 2·4 times greater. Under the same conditions, the average running of the electric locomotives was about 2·7 times that of the regularly manned French steam locomotives; so that if the average utilisation of steam locomotives had been brought up to that of the 141.R 2—8—2s it would have been necessary to provide nearly one electric locomotive for every steam engine replaced. This is far from the common assumption that one electric locomotive can do the work of from two to three steam locomotives. Such an assumption is based, indeed, on a comparison of modern electric traction with old and obsolescent steam power. In addition, experience with the 141.Rs showed that their maintenance costs per 100km running were about one-third of those of the steam locomotive stock as a whole, and were very similar to the maintenance costs of the electric locomotives. There were of course wide differences in such costs over the whole range of French steam locomotives. The 141.R figures were, for instance, half of those for the simple expansion 2—8—2s of the Etat and the PO (of which the latter were built in America during World War I), and rather less in relation to those of the 141.P class (2/3.5). But as compared with these last engines, the 141.Rs consumed about 40 to 50 per cent more fuel, and in normal service, with trains of 600 tons, the total costs of the 141.Rs were about 30 per cent higher than those of the 141.Ps, even though the latter were operating under easier conditions, because, as pointed out in Chapter 7, only about 25 per cent of their duties were on express trains as compared with 84 per cent on express work of the 141.Ps.

The common user system was also applied to older locomotives which had never been designed for this form of manning. But even so, when the compound 2—8—2 tender and 4—8—4 tank engines of the Sud-Est Region (old PLM) were operated under this system the daily mileage of the former was doubled and that of the latter increased by about 50 per cent, whilst both maintenance costs and fuel consumption were reduced by about 25 per cent. Some of these coal-fired 2—8—2s were operated from Roanne depot in the same link as oil-fired 141.Rs and did well, running 200kms per day as compared with the 300kms of the latter—the difference being due in part to two methods of firing. (Throughout the whole SNCF system the coal-fired 141.Rs averaged 175kms per day as compared with the 230 for the oil-fired.)

In running faults and in the necessity for calling on locomotive reserves, electric traction compared very badly with steam, whatever the age of the engines. As compared with the steam locomotive stock (of an average age of 40 years), the number of faults per million km running with electric traction were about twice those with steam, with diesel railcars about one and a half times the steam figure, and with diesel locomotives considerably more than all forms of traction. (Of the electric faults, 21 per cent were due to the traction motors and 45 per cent to electric apparatus).

From the above considerations and those discussed in Chapter 12, Chapelon was convinced that steam remained the most economical form of railway traction. Nor could electric or diesel operated trains claim superior speed, because the faster passenger services of today are not due to the type of traction but to modern signalling and track.

In the choice of steam locomotives it has often been argued that the two-cylinder engine costs less to maintain than the four-cylinder one, particularly a four-cylinder compound. This opinion seems to be supported by the almost universal dislike of inside cylinders on North American railways, in spite of the compound's economy in fuel. But in the United States and Canada economy in combustion was of lesser importance because the low price of coal made the four-cylinder compound, with its higher maintenance costs, more expensive to operate than the two-cylinder engines, from which the power demanded was low enough not to require maximum power outputs. This is, in fact, the nub of the matter. There is a power beyond which two cylinders will no longer suffice for the task without working under very poor economic conditions. This is why in Europe, where the low axle weights allowed do not permit components as large as in the United States, a critical point is soon reached when three or four cylinders become preferable because, in spite of the greater number of mechanical parts, the cost of maintenance becomes lower than that of a two-cylinder simple engine working too near the limit allowed by its components. The Americans themselves encountered this trouble, but thanks to their less stringent weight and gauge restrictions they were able, even with a rigid frame, to put all their cylinders outside.

But apart from the number of cylinders and its greater economy in consumption, the compound system does result in less strain on the working parts. If one compares two European locomotives, say Pacific or Mikados, two cylinders will prove superior from the point of view of maintenance as long as the power demanded of the engine does not exceed a certain figure, which might, for example, be 1,500hp. If the power to be developed is increased beyond that, there will come a stage (say at 2,000hp) where the two-cylinder engine will be working above its true capacity. Damage to coupling rod bearings and axle boxes will then begin to appear. The four-cylinder compound, on the other hand, will absorb this increased effort without any strain or harmful effect. There was a typical example of such a comparison on the Paris-Orléans Railway when, because there were insufficient rebuilt compound Pacifics available, it was necessary to have a number of the more easily scheduled expresses worked by the American-built two-cylinder simple expansion Pacifics. As compared with the rebuilt compounds they had 50·4sq ft grate area instead of 46·6, and 171lbs per sq in boiler pressure instead of 245. In running these trains, not only was their fuel consumption per 100 ton/km 40 per cent more than that of the rebuilt compound Pacifics, but it was necessary to carry out on them 14 hours or more of small maintenance jobs for every 625 miles of running; and it was also necessary to carry out supplementary intermediate repairs on the boiler. In spite of a simpler mechanism therefore, the maintenance costs were very much higher.

Owing to the limitations of the standard gauge there are difficulties, as we have seen, when power rises above a certain level in having two cylinders driving the same axle inside the frames, and so, as stated above, Chapelon chose three cylinders for his projected fleet of locomotives for the SNCF. Giving evidence before the Gauge Commission in 1846, Daniel Gooch said, "I do not think we have any too much room on the Wide Gauge for the power we are requiring". It was just 100 years before that remark was justified.

The evaluation of the tests with No. 160.A.1 showed how compound engines could be built which would be far cheaper to operate and maintain than two-cylinder simple expansion engines. Looking ahead to the next generation of steam locomotives Chapelon had designed a triple expansion 4—8—4 express passenger engine. It was derived from No. 242.A.1 and was something of a combination between that engine and No. 160.A.1. In front of 242.A.1's existing three cylinders there was to be a high pressure cylinder fed with saturated steam at 584lbs per sq in and with a steam jacket. The original high pressure cylinder was now a medium pressure cylinder supplied with steam superheated between the HP and MP stage. From the medium pressure cylinder the steam passed to a re-superheater and then to the two low pressure cylinders. The boiler to carry this very high pressure followed a design prepared by Lawford H. Fry, from 1943 to 1948 Director of the Steam Locomotive Research Division at The Locomotive Institute in America. This had a water tube firebox because of the very high pressure. As in 160.A.1, the front part of the boiler barrel was to be a simplified form of the Franco-Crosti pre-heater, separated from the boiler proper by an intermediate tube plate. This new engine, says Chapelon, would have been able to sustain 6,000hp at the drawbar, as compared with the 4,000 of No. 242.A.1, which, he says, "shows the development of the *classic* steam locomotive that was still possible if work had continued since 1945 during these 25 years that have been wasted on the Diesel".

15

The Locomotive Engineers

WHERE DOES Chapelon stand amongst the great designers of steam locomotives? In answering this question one is confronted with certain difficulties. Many locomotives have been designed by a team, and this probably applies to most of the engines designed by the great locomotive firms, and hence to the vast majority of steam locomotives that ran on American railways; just as it applies to the diesel and electric locomotives running on British Railways today. Design, too, has often been attributed to a particular chief mechanical engineer, or equivalent, because the locomotives concerned appeared during his tenure of office; although he took no part in the design at all. This implies no criticism of such a CME, because design of locomotives was often quite a minor part of his many responsibilities. Amongst those CMEs who personally directed design there were obviously wide differences in practice between, on the one hand, some who preferred to issue general directives and, on the other, men who took charge of every detail.

Nevertheless, in the history of the steam locomotive certain names stand out. Some are connected with outstanding locomotives, whilst others are noteworthy in relation to some particular feature which was a milestone in locomotive development.

In the very early period of the steam locomotive ungainly engines with primitive single or double flue boilers clanked slowly over the mineral lines of North-East England hauling trains of coal wagons at a speed not much above that of a man walking. The first advance which made possible the fast passenger trains that drove the stage coach off the road was the invention of the multi-tubular boiler which was patented by the French engineer Marc Séguin on December 20th 1827. In the locomotive which he built in 1828 this boiler took the form of return tubes, so that the chimney was at the same end as the grate as in the single return flue engines of Timothy Hackworth. Séguin used a forced draught provided by a bellows driven from one of the tender axles which blew air under the grate. Marc Séguin had in fact realised that the strong resistance of small diameter tubes to the passage of the hot gases (to which as explained later he owed his high thermic efficiency) could only be overcome by a forced draught. From the first trials of the engine the efficiency and productive capacity of this boiler impressed observers. For every kilogramme of coal the boiler vaporised 7 litres of water and produced 1,500kg of steam per hour, as compared with the 500kg which the engines of the period could manage with difficulty. As a result Seguin's engine could run considerably faster than had been practicable hitherto.

But the first engine to make a really effective use of the multi-tubular boiler and the acknowledged ancestor of the modern steam locomotive was George Stephenson's *Rocket*. According to George's son, Robert, the tubular boiler was due to a suggestion by Henry Booth, the Secretary of the Liverpool and Manchester Railway. However, Booth was wrong in thinking that the substitution of the return flue, used in many engines of the period, by a number of tubes going direct from the firebox to the chimney would provide a better draught; and according to Clark, author of the celebrated *Railway Machinery* of 1850, the *Rocket*, in grave difficulties with steaming, had to be fitted on the eve of the Rainhill contest with Timothy Hackworth's exhaust, and it was to this that it owed its success.

Whether George Stephenson knew of Séguin's invention it is now impossible to say, but the latter did visit the Stephenson's Newcastle works in 1828. The *Rocket*, nevertheless, was the first to embody those essential features and layout which characterised the steam locomotive till the age of its decline some 140 years later. They were the tubular boiler, separate firebox, cylinders with a direct drive on to the wheels, and blast pipe.

Almost as astonishing as the original concept was the speed with which the Stephenson locomotive, in its development, acquired those other characteristics which remained basically similar in all subsequent 'conventional' steam locomotives. The first alteration was the lowering of the cylinders to a more horizontal position. The next engines had smokeboxes and those following them had internal fireboxes. Before the end of 1830 the *Planet* had appeared, with inside cylinders disposed horizontally and enclosed within the smokebox; it also had sandwich frames—the first use of true frames on an engine, indeed, for up till that time the boiler was itself the structure to which the mechanism and bearings were attached. In fact the *Planet* was the model upon which the vast majority of succeeding locomotives were built.

According to Robert Stephenson, the arrangement of inside cylinders within the smokebox was due to a statement made to him by Trevithick. The latter had to repair one of the old Cornish mine engines which, unlike most of this type, did not have a steam jacket to the cylinder. Trevithick rectified this deficiency by constructing an outer brick casing round the cylinder, leaving an air space which he heated by fire. The result of this was that he reduced the fuel consumption to a fifth of what it had been before he repaired the engine. Robert Stephenson was so impressed by this that he provided a heat jacket for the *Planet's* cylinders by putting them inside the smokebox, and found as a result that he got considerable increase in power.

The passage of the years has done nothing to dim the remarkable achievements of the two Stephensons (for it is difficult to separate father and son). Their inventive genius was most brilliantly displayed, perhaps, during the year 1829–30, but this was by no means the end. They put their final seal on the shape of the locomotive when in 1833 they added a pair of carrying wheels behind the firebox to produce the first 2—2—2 engine 'Patentee'. This became a standard passenger type in both France and Great Britain and was built in the latter country until 1894. Their last major contribution was in 1842 when they were the first to provide engines with a link motion valve gear, a wonderful invention which was so eminently suitable for locomotives that it was still being used for new construction in the last great days of steam.

George Forrester of Liverpool was perhaps the next to have a major influence on locomotive design. He saw the advantage of horizontal cylinders but was convinced that instead of having cylinders beneath the boiler they should be outside so as to be easily accessible. In 1834, therefore, he built some 2—2—0 locomotives which were the first to have outside horizontal cylinders. Forrester's ideas inspired the choice of engines for the Grand Junction Railway, and they were echoed by Joseph Locke, the engineer of that line, who in giving evidence before the Gauge Commission of 1846 said: "I directed my attention to simplifying the engine itself; and the result of that was that, instead of wanting space under the boiler, we now have no machinery there at all except the eccentrics. We now place the cylinder outside the engine. We have got rid of a very great deal of complexity in the machinery itself, and the complexity which remains is on the outside of the engine and not under the boiler."

Comparatively little known, perhaps, is John Gray, Locomotive Superintendent of the Hull & Selby Railway, and yet he was one of the engineers who were was considerably ahead of their time. His 2—2—2 engines of 1840 constituted an advance on several accounts. They had the high boiler pressure for the period of 90lbs per sq in, and he appears to have been the only locomotive engineer of the time who realised that it was not necessary to keep the centre of gravity low, and it was not till much later that this was generally recognised. In addition his engines were fitted with his patent expansion gear (known as the horse-leg motion) which was the earliest to be used on locomotives, and his reversing lever had a notched sector.

Daniel Gooch of the Great Western was probably the first of the great railway company locomotive engineers. In the years 1840–2 105 six-wheeled tender engines were built for his company to his own designs, the first standardisation on an extensive scale for any railway. Of these, 62 were 2—2—2 express passenger locomotives with 7ft driving wheels, which were derived from the earlier Star class engines supplied by Stephenson. They put the Great Western ahead of any other company in Great Britain in locomotive power. In 1846 he produced the first of his famous 8ft singles which were the most powerful express passenger engines in the country and which hauled the most important express trains on the broad gauge until its abolition in 1892. When they were built Gooch's eight-foot single drivers were ahead of any other locomotives in the world and they put his company in the forefront of railway speed.

Thomas Russell Crampton was a genius who received far more recognition abroad than he did in his own country. He believed, like so many other engineers of the time, that to obtain a very steady engine the centre of gravity should be as nearly as possible on the same horizontal line as the drawbar—a theory which was subsequently shown to be wrong (see Chapter 14). To get this low centre of gravity, combined with a large heating surface, he put a single pair of large driving wheels behind the firebox and supported the forward part of the engine on two carrying axles. The outside cylinders were near the middle of the engine, between the carrying axles. Critics maintained that the rear-mounted driving wheel would be subject to very heavy tyre wear, but Crampton was probably the first engineer to point out that the rearmost axle of an engine, when going round a curve, moves away from and not towards the outer rail. However, although the truth of this was immediately appreciated by French locomotive engineers, it was a long time before it was accepted in Great Britain. But the most important aspect of Crampton's work was never recognised in Great Britain; this, as stated in Chapter 2, was his realisation of the importance of having steam passages of large cross-sectional area, and it was their excellent steam passages which made Crampton's engines the enormous success they were in France and Germany. Comparatively few Crampton engines ran on British railways and they did not have a long life. But over 300 were built for use on the Continent between 1846 and 1864, and some were running on the Est Railway until well on in the present century. During trial runs on the PLM after the 1889 Paris Exhibition a single-driver Crampton, hauling a First Class carriage, reached a speed of 89·5mph, which was faster than that reached by any other of the engines tested.

The earliest locomotives running on French railways were built in

Great Britain and were identical with those running on British railways. The few that were built in France were similar in design and appearance to those made by British firms. In 1850 a remarkable man, Camille Polonceau, became Contractor of Motive Power and Works on the Paris-Orléans Railway, having come from the Alsace Railway. He was already well known as the co-author of a treatise on locomotives which was for many years regarded as an authority and ran into many editions. He arrived on the PO just when there was a need for new motive power owing to the rapid increase in the Company's route mileage. Polonceau arranged for the construction of a complete range of locomotives for express, mixed traffic, freight, and shunting work. Some of them had had an extraordinarily long life, witnessing to the excellence of their design and construction, and for the first time on the PO engines appeared which had a French and not a British look. His 0—6—0 shunting tank engines were copied by the Ouest and Est, and three were still running in 1953, after nearly a century, with their original boilers. Polonceau did much to improve locomotives and in 1858 he introduced a distribution with two superposed valves and steam jacketed cylinders to counter the cooling losses incurred from cylinder walls.

The importance of an adequate boiler has often been too little appreciated by locomotive engineers. One of the earliest recorded comments on the matter came from J. E. M'Connell, then Locomotive Superintendent of the Birmingham & Gloucester Railway, when giving evidence to the Gauge Commission in 1846. He said: "My opinion is, that with respect to the power, which is in other words speed, that depends upon the amount of evaporating surface in the boiler." In a letter, which came into the possession of the late E. L. Ahrons, written by Archibald Sturrock, Locomotive Engineer of the Great Northern Railway, he said: "The success of the GNR was nearly entirely due to the introduction of fireboxes of about double the area of those in use on the narrow gauge in 1850, and the raising of the steam pressure from 80lb to 150lb. . . . Engines, like horses, go well in many shapes, sizes and colours, but no variation such as position and diameter of a wheel or diameter of cylinder are worth anything unless there be plenty of steam *at a high pressure*, which gives economy by expansion. The finest gun is of no use unless there be plenty of powder".

John Ramsbottom of the London & North Western Railway was one of the greatest locomotive engineers of his day. His DX class 0—6—0 goods engines, which were built from 1858 to 1872, numbered more than any other steam locomotive class in British history. The DX was an extremely light engine which could run anywhere on the system and it had the screw reversing gear which Ramsbottom was the first engineer to use. He produced a noteworthy class of 2—4—0 express locomotive which as continued and modified by his successor Webb made the fastest running in the railway races from London to Aberdeen in 1895. Because, at the time these engines first appeared in 1866 many engineers held that only engines with single driving wheels were suitable for fast running, it is likely that Ramsbottom had discovered that a good steam circuit was of greater importance.

In 1860 Victor Forquenot succeeded Camille Polonceau, becoming Engineer-in-Chief of Rolling Stock and Motive Power on the Orléans Company in 1859. He held the appointment until his death in 1885, 26 years later. For the first time in France he introduced standardisation on a large scale. Of the 19 classes of locomotive which he introduced, most were of the same basic design. Some of his engines were still being built after his death up till 1894, and his seven main types (2—2—2, 2—4—0, 0—6—0, 0—8—0, 0—6—0T, and 0—10—0T) numbered more than 1,000. In 1914 all his engines were still in service (including 128 which had been rebuilt), and the SNCF inherited 502 of them when it was formed in 1938. In fact at that time the depot at Bergerac, which worked the services on short-distance routes running eastwards from Bordeaux, had nothing but Forquenot locomotives. And, as M. L. M. Vilain comments in his book *Un Siècle de Matériel et Traction sur é le Réseau d'Orleans*, it was remarkable that engines designed and constructed between 1875 and 1880, on the basis of a prototype of 1863, should still be running express trains in 1939–40 at speeds of from 56 to 62mph or even more, on a fuel consumption of 18 to 20lbs per 100 ton/miles. When the first du Bousquet de Glehn compound 4—4—0s arrived on the PO in 1899–1900, it was found with dismay that they performed little better than these redoubtable Forquenot 2—4—2 locomotives. Forquenot's engines were two-cylinder simple expansion with all their mechanism outside to facilitate maintenance.

Patrick Stirling of the Great Northern Railway provides, perhaps, the nearest British parallel to Forquenot. Stirling became Locomotive Superintendent in 1866 and remained in office until he died in 1896. Like Forquenot he created a stud of locomotives which had many parts in common and a great similarity of appearance. Again like Forquenot, he was noted for the uniform excellence of his work. Unlike Forquenot his engines (with a notable exception) had inside cylinders. Also unlike Forquenot his engines had a remarkably austere, though handsome, appearance; whilst Forquenot's, with everything on the outside and a polished brass boiler covering, were certainly not austere and were attractive but not handsome. But perhaps Patrick Stirling's chief claim to fame was that he was the first locomotive engineer to fit an express engine with a leading bogie, and his bogie singles with their eight-foot driving wheels, built from 1870 onwards, were probably the most beautiful and most famous engines of their day. In spite of their single driving wheels they hauled trains in their early days of greater weights at faster speeds than locomotives of any other railway, and never, until the end of the century, were they double-headed on a train.

Stirling's chief difficulty was the very poor Great Northern track. This necessitated low axle loads and in consequence his engines had too small boilers and it was only their good design and free steaming that enabled them to accomplish their fine performances.

William Adams, who became Mechanical Engineer of the London & South Western Railway in 1878, was a contemporary of Stirling's, as locomotive chief of a large railway, during the latter's later years, for Adams retired in 1895. It is probable that Adams's express locomotives were the best in Great Britain; they were certainly the most powerful. He designed the first efficient bogie in Great Britain in 1864 and this was fitted to his famous 4—4—0 tank engines for the North London Railway in 1868. His excellent 'Vortex' blast pipe is mentioned in Chapter 2.

The first British engineer to insist on the necessity of a really large boiler was J. F. McIntosh of the Caledonian Railway. His famous 4—4—0 engine No. 721 *Dunalastair*, completed in 1898, had a boiler of 4ft 9½in diameter, which was larger than that of any other contemporary British four-coupled passenger engine.

A. Henry of the PLM was mentioned in the last chapter in connection with his compounds. But he had another claim to fame for his notable work on boiler proportions. He had an eminent successor on the PLM in Baudry, who was Engineer-in-Chief of Rolling Stock and Motive Power on that railway until 1907.

Du Bousquet of the Nord has been mentioned in the last chapter and also elsewhere in this book. He was such a great engineer that he probably occupied the same pre-eminence in France as Churchward did in Great Britain. It would be appropriate, therefore, to consider them together. They were very much contemporaries. Gaston du Bousquet, however, came into prominence earlier, for the first compound engine, which he designed jointly with Alfred de Glehn, appeared on the Nord in 1891. At that time, of course, de Glehn's engine with his compound system had been running on the Nord for five years. The two collaborated so closely that 'du Bousquet de Glehn' is almost a hyphenated word; and it is difficult to determine the extent to which each was responsible for the original designs. But it seems probable that de Glehn designed the detail and dimensions of the compound system and that du Bousquet dealt with the rest of the engine. But although du Bousquet is perhaps remembered mostly in connection with this four-cylinder compound arrangement, it was only a small part of this work. He insisted on really excellent workmanship, and it was perhaps this aspect of the French Atlantics which most impressed Churchward when they arrived on the Great Western. But of greater importance was du Bousquet's work on the steam circuit and the resulting outstanding work of his 4—6—0s. He died before the first of his great 4—6—4 engines was finished, so where his work would have eventually led him is unfortunately unknown.

It is probably because Churchward's steam circuit was better than that of du Bousquet's at the time of the comparison between the French Atlantics and his own engines, that the Star class four-cylinder locomotives were simple expansion and not compound. Churchward's contribution to British locomotive engineering was gigantic. The principal reason for the success of his locomotives was the excellence of the valve gear characteristics and steam distribution; but in addition there were the first-class boiler design, the high standard of workmanship on which Churchward insisted, and the meticulous maintenance to which Great Western engines were subjected under his regime.

It was many years before the secret of Great Western standards of performance were appreciated by the locomotive engineers of other British railways. R. E. L. Maunsell of the South Eastern and Chatham learned it first through the importation of Great Western men on his staff, and his Mogul of 1916 resulted. Sir Nigel Gresley only learned it when Pacifics failed to match the much smaller Great Western 4—6—0s in 1925. Sir William Stanier, a Great Western man, took the Churchward way of doing things to the London Midland & Scottish Railway in 1932.

Unfortunately Churchward's designs were so good that they were ahead of the traffic requirements; with the result that all subsequent 4—6—0 engines built for the Great Western by either Churchward or his successors were either modifications or enlargements of his original four-cylinder and two-cylinder locomotives. It is perhaps permissible to doubt whether Churchward, great engineer that he was, had the imagination to press forward, as du Bousquet pressed forward in his improvements to the steam circuit, in his investigations into water tube fireboxes, and in his conception of the 4—6—4 express engines.

During the period that we have been considering, superheating of locomotives had made such rapid strides that before the outbreak of World War I it had become accepted as an essential component of almost every new steam locomotive. Schmidt's great invention and its impact has been mentioned in Chapter 1. Using Schmidt superheaters the very able German engineer, Garbe, provided the Prussian State Railways with a fine stud of locomotives. Indeed, he established a design practice which was subsequently adopted as a national standard; so that the locomotives of the Reichsbahn were as clearly influenced by Garbe as were those of the London Midland & Scottish and British Railways by Churchward.

In the last chapter Carl Göldsorf's compound engines were discussed. The particular genius of this great Austrian engineer lay in designing large engines to run over winding tracks with a permitted axle load of only $14\frac{1}{2}$ tons. By economising in weight, by distributing loads, and by making his locomotives sufficiently flexible, he was extremely successful in providing engines powerful enough to cope with heavy trains over the difficult Austrian routes. Gölsdorf held office from 1891 till his death in 1916.

Sir Nigel Gresley is a very difficult engineer to assess. That he was very able is unquestioned. His early designs were by no means outstanding, but he always displayed a great willingness to learn from other engineers. From H. Holcroft he got the idea for the valve gear of his three-cylinder engines; from trials against a Great Western *Castle* he found what was wrong with his Pacifics; and from Chapelon he learned how to improve the steam circuit and he benefited from the Kylchap exhaust. The end result was an A4 class streamlined Pacific which achieved the world speed record for steam: a brilliant performance, but its validity as a record is somewhat dubious because the engine was running downhill. Gresley was a broad-minded man. Locomotives from the constituent companies of the London & North Eastern Railway had a long life under his rule and construction of some of them was continued. He did not really go in for standardisation and his own engines were often 'tailor-made' for the job. He left the LNER with a large stock of capable engines but also with a great number of different classes. He was a very great figure in the locomotive world but much of his practice was discarded by his successors.

Sir William Stanier was a vastly different engineer to Gresley, both in outlook and practice. It was under his regime on the LMS, and not on the Great Western, that the natural development of Churchward's ideas took place. There was a massive standardisation and much scrapping of obsolescent locomotives. Under Stanier the LMS rapidly acquired a fleet of engines which could more than meet all traffic requirements and which, as a whole, were the most capable and modern in the country. He was a keen observer of Chapelon's practice and adopted the Chapelon type of steam circuit for his own locomotives.

R. A. Riddles became responsible for the steam locomotives of British Railways during the difficult period following the end of World War II. It was a time when conditions required engines that should be simple to drive, easy to maintain, and able to run with indifferent fuel. The stud of locomotives that Riddles provided met these requirements brilliantly. They were rugged machines with two outside cylinders, with a maximum route availability, and embodying all the modern techniques that were commensurate with their essential simplicity. That they were remarkably free-steaming is shown by the performance of the Riddles 2—10—0 heavy freight engine which could, and did, run at over 90mph—a speed far higher than many express engines designed for the job have been able to manage. Riddles's last engine, a three-cylinder Pacific with poppet valves, was not given time to prove itself before all steam production and progress on British Railways was abruptly stopped.

It is now time to consider Chapelon's position amongst all these eminent designers of steam railway locomotives. Such a consideration falls naturally under three headings:

(a) What he did;
(b) What he proposed to do;
(c) How he influenced other locomotive engineers.

André Chapelon's five major achievements were the Pacifics, the two series of 4—8—0s, the 2—12—0 No. 160.A.1, the 141.P class 2—8—2 locomotives, and the 4—8—4 locomotive No. 242.A.1. All these were rebuilds, but, as pointed out before, this does not detract from the achievements but rather enhances them, because he was restricted from giving free rein to his ideas by having in every case to retain a large part of the original engine (or original design in the case of the 141.P). For instance, he was, as we have seen, by no means wedded to the du Bousquet de Glehn compound system and he would have preferred to have built the 240.P class 4—8—0 locomotives as as three-cylinder compounds, for the same reason as he chose this system for No. 242.A.1. But so brilliantly was the rebuilding conceived that in none of these engines did difficulties of operation or maintenance arise from the alterations made to obtain such vast increases in power. Minor problems were dealt with without difficulty. The trouble with the lubricator pads on the bogie axle boxes of the 240.As is discussed in Chapter 3. The only problem ever experienced on 242.A.1 was in connection with the HP crosshead pin on account of the high temperature communicated to it by the piston rod, which was periodically plunged into a highly superheated steam. This problem was completely resolved by replacing the too-fluid oil of the motion by a superheater oil supplied by a special lubricator. (Rather strangely a story has been told that the inside motion was so difficult of access that only a short and slim driver could get at it. In actual fact Driver Robert of the Sud-

Est and Driver Bondu of the Sud-Ouest who drove the engine, both very good and highly qualified men, had figures which testified to the excellence of French cooking, and Locomotive Inspector Deschamps who was responsible for the engine had no difficulty in inspecting the lubrication of the inside motion. Chapelon, who had himself stood in a pit under the engine, says that it was far less encumbered between the frames than the four-cylinder engines.)

The amazing thing about all these engines is that each made every other locomotive of their type in France appear obsolete. It is amazing because there seems to be no similar parallel in the whole range of locomotive history. Stephenson's *Rocket* was in a class by itself but it did not make the return flue freight engines of the Stockton & Darlington obsolete; Daniel Gooch's broad-gauge engines were better for a time than any possessed by the standard gauge, but they were not strikingly better; du Bousquet's designs were pre-eminent in France, but on their first appearance on the PO they were scarcely better than Forquenot's; Churchward's engines were the best in Great Britain, but there were those who would stoutly maintain the superiority of the Ivatt Atlantics.

If Chapelon's designs for the future range of French steam locomotives had been built, the SNCF would have had engines for all types of traffic which, whilst being considerably cheaper, would have rivalled diesel and electric traction in power, speed, and economy of operation. Most locomotive engineers, after launching such a steam fleet based on the superlative 242.A.1 as a prototype, would have rested content for at least a period. But not Chapelon; he was already looking ahead to yet a further generation of locomotives with 242.A.1 married to 160.A.1 to produce a triple expansion 4—8—4 as the first of the line.

The majority of chief mechanical engineers, having designed a satisfactory stud of locomotives, have not undertaken a further ambitious range of designs; few have even taken one step into the future once they have satisfied the existing needs of the traffic. Churchward's Pacific was a step which neither he nor his successors pursued; de Bousquet's 4—6—4s might have led him further, but because he died we shall never know; Bulleid had ideas, but they did not start from a sufficiently firmly established base to be successful; Stanier's projected 4—6—4 was frustrated by the outbreak of war; and Riddles's further progress through his promising three-cylinder Pacific was stopped by the order ending steam in Great Britain.

The pages of this book have already borne witness to the influence of Chapelon's designs on other railways and engineers, and again there seems to be no historical parallel. All the railways of France either acquired Chapelon-built engines or rebuilt many of their own in accordance with his ideas, or did both. In Great Britain every Chief Mechanical Engineer from the 1930s onwards incorporated Chapelon's ideas into his new construction or rebuilding. In Czechoslovakia three 4—8—2 three-cylinder compound locomotives with Kylchap exhausts were built in 1948 as a result of the trials of No. 242.A.1. The Kylchap exhaust has been used in Great Britain, Czechoslovakia, Spain, Algeria, and other countries. Engines built or rebuilt by Chapelon run in Brazil and Argentina; and in the latter country Ing. L. D. Porta, an enthusiastic disciple of Chapelon, is still designing engines on his principles.

It is a brilliant and a unique record, and in the light of the evidence one must conclude that André Chapelon is the most outstanding locomotive engineer in the whole history of the steam engine.

Appendix A

The Table below was prepared by Chapelon in connection with his plans to rebuild PO Pacific No. 3566

15—12—26: Improvements that one could hope to obtain by the modifications proposed for the second 3500 class engine with Lentz valves (rotary cams)*

Objects	Means Employed	Modification Proposed	Increase in power with constant fuel consumption[2]	Precedents
(a)	(b)	(c)	(d)	(e)

A.
Increase in thermal efficiency
1.
From the boiler

(a) Improvement of the efficiency of combustion by better mixing of the gases	Lengthening of the brick arch	3%	Trials of engines 4597 and 4528 in 1926	

(b) Improvement in steaming efficiency by increasing the activity of the circulation of the water close to the heating surfaces	Installation of a Nicholson syphon	4%	In America the builder announced a 10% economy	

2.
From the mechanism

(a) Improvement of the thermic cycle by:

(i) increasing the temperature of the steam from 300°C to 350°C and 400°C	Number of large tubes increased from 24 to 40. Superheater elements, at the return bend to the smokebox, shortened/stopped at $\frac{2}{3}$ of the length of the tubes from the termination at the firebox[3]	350°C 400°C 5% 9%	Following Strahl (German trials) real economies achieved in fuel consumption in raising the temperature from 300° to 350°C were 9%	

151

(a)	(b)	(c)	(d)	(e)
(ii)	always running with the greatest possible pressure in the steam chest (regulator wide open)		10%	
(b)	Improvement of the actual cycle by:			
(i)	increasing the degree of superheat, the condensation due to the action of the cylinder walls should be nearly totally suppressed, even in the LP cylinders			
(ii)	diminishing throttling thanks to:	**(a)** Increase in section of: Regulator, Admission pipe, Superheater, Inlet & Exhaust ports of the four cylinders HP/LPcomn pipe, Inlet & Exhaust poppet valves of the four cylinders	mph mph 25–37 44–56 mph 62–75	Lentz Ltd claim economies of the order of 10% with engines with oscillating cams & ports of normal section
(1)	the increase in section of the whole steam circuit from the regulator to the exhaust			
(2)	improvement in shape of the steam pipes	**(b)** Increase in volume of: HP steam chest, Intermediate receiver, Admission & comn HP & LP pipes		
(3)	the use of poppet valves.			
(4)	rapid raising of poppet valves			
(5)	greater fluidity of very highly superheated steam and its lower specific mass			
(6)	less variation in steam pressure in the HP steam chests by increasing the volume of chests and admission pipes			

(a)	(b)	(c)	(d)	(e)
3. From the boiler and mechanism together	Extraction of steam from the intermediate receiver to heat the feed water[4]	An injector worked by the steam thus extracted[4]	7%	The theoretical economy would be about 12%. An economy of 10% was achieved on the Est Railway
B. **Increase in the steaming capacity of the boiler**	Increase in the hourly rates of combustion per sq.m. of the grate area by 50% (600kg instead of 400)	Fitting a 1K/1C type double exhaust (A Kylala nozzle followed by a cylindrical nozzle with conical pipe)	25% with 50% better fuel consumption	The multiple exhaust is due to Geoffrey who applied it in 1865 to a Crampton engine of the Nord (4 chimneys). It was adopted in 1925 by the Americans and fitted in 1925 to a Flamme Pacific of the Belgian Etat by Legein

(a)	(b)	(c)	(d)	(e)

C.
**Special arrangements
made in view of the
high superheat**

1.

Cylinder lubrication	Visible mechanical greasing, with special delivery to each greasing point	High pressure Michalk mechanical greaser[5] with valves to maintain uniform pressure		

2.

Steam tightness of:

(a) pistons	Increase in the number of piston rings	4 rings on the HP piston 3 rings on the LP piston		
(b) glands	Labyrinthine glands with cast rings	Hauber glands		
(c) shunt valve (used at starting to isolate HP and LP cylinders)		Addition of rings and grooves		

3.

Reduction of losses due to external radiation of superheated steam°	Very complete insulation of all parts of the steam circuit, admission pipes, steam chests, cylinders, HP/LP comn. pipe			Visible loss of pressure (0·5 to 1kg) at the front of the cylinder: investigations made for the Nord Co. in 1892 and for the PO in 1903 (classes 3000 & 4000) and in 1926 (class 4500) on saturated engines. With superheat of about 300° a loss of pressure was still found.

(a)	(b)	(c)	(d)	(e)

D.
Other arrangements

1.
Lessening of fatigue on the crank axle in view of the extra effort which will be required from the engine | Axle with balanced cranks | | | |

2.
Perfect lubrication of the axle box bearings | Mechanical greasing | | | |

3.
Temporary increase of adhesion | Sanding the six coupled wheels with an air sander | | | |

Notes

The fitting of rotary cams having been found inconvenient, oscillating cams with Walschaerts distribution were adopted at Chapelon's request.

[2] These figures are valid for 1500–2000 indicated horsepower, which was developed by the original engine with piston valves and unmodified. The increase in power was such that the volume of the cylinders, which was not changed, should always be sufficient for whatever effort was realisable. It was considered extremely probable that this requirement would always be met at high speeds (70–75mph).

[3] After the trials of the Schmidt superheater with shortened loops on No. 3566, at first with 40 large tubes and then with 32, the Houlet superheater with 28 large tubes (of which two contained ordinary Schmidt elements so as not to exceed 400degC) was fitted to Nos. 3702/3721.

[4] This arrangement was not adopted and the fingines were fitted with an ACFI type feed water heater.

[5] This lubricator was not used; the Bosch type, with its greater precision, was adopted.

[6] Imperfect insulation can cause the loss of all the benefits of high superheat; because the number of calories needed to produce this superheat is relatively low.

FINAL CALCULATED RESULT

I. Indicated Horsepower				II. Consumption of Fuel per Indicated hp		
Running Conditions	Present Engine	Projected Engine	Increase of Power (per cent)	Present Engine	Project Engine	Increased consumption of fuel of present engine compared with projected engine (per cent)
(a)	(b)	(c)	(d)	(e)	(f)	(g)
1. Cut-off 60/70; pressure 142–166psi in the steam chests; temperature of the steam at HP admission 300°C	1500–1600hp			1·25kg		
Speed 44–56mph		1750hp	15 %		1·085kg	15
Speed 62–75mph		1850hp	20		1·040kg	20
2. Wide open regulator; pressure 213psi in HP steam chest; temperature of the steam at HP admission						
(a) 350° Speed 44–56mph		2150hp	40		0·9kg	40
Speed 62–75mph		2250hp	45		0·865kg	45
(b) 400° Speed 44–56mph		2250hp	45		0·865kg	45
Speed 62–75mph		2350hp	50		0·830kg	50
3. Use of whole boiler power thanks to double exhaust; pressure 213psi in HP steam chests; temperature of the steam at HP admission						
(a) 350° Speed 44–56mph		2700hp	75		1·075kg	16
Speed 62–75mph		2850hp	80		1·040kg	20
(b) 400° Speed 44–56mph		2850hp	80		1·040kg	20
Speed 62–75mph		3000hp	90		1·000kg	25

Note
The figures contained in these tables, being purely an estimate, can only be given with every reservation. (Signed) A. Chapelon 15-12-26

Additional Notes

In practice, on trials with brake locomotives, two engines of the first series to be rebuilt (Nos. 3075 and 3718) gave figures for fuel consumption per ihp which were better than those in section 3 of the Final Calculated Result. Instead of 1·075, 1·040, 1·040, and 1·000kg, they were, respectively, 0·863, 0·990, 0·960, and 1·000kg (with an average steam temperature of 385deg C and a pressure of 247lbs per sq in in the boiler), which represented an average economy greater by 8 per cent.

One of the Pacifics rebuilt in 1934 with certain improvements gave still better results. This was No. 231.726 which had LP cylinders with 10 per cent increase in volume, together with increases in the LP ports of 22 per cent at admission and 31 per cent at exhaust, and a 25 per cent greater cross-sectional area for the passage of the steam through the superheater. On test the above figures fell to 0·730, 0·766, 0·770 and 0·760kg of coal respectively (with an average steam temperature of 380deg C and a pressure of 247lbs per sq in in the boiler). This was a further increase in fuel economy of about 20·5 per cent, giving a total improvement on the calculated figures of 1926 of 27·5 per cent. This highly satisfactory result was due to economy in the use of steam and the increased efficiency of the boiler which led to a lower rate of combustion on the grate.

Appendix B

IN THIS APPENDIX are listed some dimensions and additional particulars of the more important locomotives mentioned in the preceding pages. (All weights, as throughout the book, are in tons of 1,000kg.)

1. The Du Bousquet de Glehn Atlantics

These famous locomotives appeared on four railways in France (the Nord, the Midi, the Etat, and the Paris-Orléans), one in Great Britain (the Great Western), and one in the USA (the Pennsylvania). There were two types, the original one of the Nord and an enlarged version for the Paris-Orléans. The Midi engines belonged to the former type, as did one of those acquired by the Great Western, whilst the larger PO design was adopted by the Etat, the Great Western (two engines), and the Pennsylvania (one engine). The PO Atlantics were 13 per cent more powerful than those of the Nord as originally built, but they were never superheated whilst the Nord Atlantics were.

The first Nord engines were built in 1900 and the PO in 1903. These Atlantics were perhaps the first really great locomotives of the twentieth century.

Nord type (superheated) dimensions: cylinders, HP 13·4in × 25·2in, LP 22in × 25·2in; coupled wheels 6ft 8½in; grate area 29·7sq ft; pressure 228lbs per sq in; adhesive weight 37 tons, total weight 70·6 tons.

PO type dimensions: cylinders, HP 14·2in × 25·2in, LP 23·6in × 25·2in; coupled wheels 6ft 8½in; grate area 33·4sq ft; pressure 228lbs per sq in; adhesive weight 35·6 tons, total weight 72·9 tons.

2. Nord 3513 (later 230.D) class 4—6—0

These engines, first built in 1907, had boilers identical with those of the Atlantics. Dimensions (when superheated in 1911): cylinders, HP 15in × 25·2in, LP 21·7in × 25·2in; coupled wheels 5ft 9in; grate are a 29·7sq ft; pressure 228lbs per sq in; adhesive weight 51 tons, total weight 70·8 tons.

3. Paris-Orléans 4000 Class 4—6—0 (1903)

A 4—6—0 version of the PO Atlantics, they had the same boiler, pressure, and cylinders as the latter engines; other dimensions were: coupled wheels 6ft 3¾in; adhesive weight 54·6 tons, total weight 75·3 tons.

4. Midi 4000 class 2—8—0

In 1900 the Midi asked the Société Alsacienne to design for them a powerful four-cylinder compound freight locomotive to work trains over steep gradients. The 2—8—0 type was selected and 18 engines were built; the first being delivered in 1901 and the last in 1907. They sere not only the first of their type but also the most powerful engines built in France up that that time. The HP cylinders were inside and all cylinders were in line. Stephenson's valve gear was used for the HP cylinders and Walschaerts for the LP. After the amalgamation of the Midi with the PO, all these engines received the Kylchap 1K/1C exhaust.

Dimensions: HP 15·6in × 25·6in, LP 24in × 26·5in; coupled wheels 4ft 8in; grate area 30sq ft; pressure 213lbs per sq in; adhesive weight 65·7 tons, total weight 72·8 tons.

5. Paris-Orléans 5000 class 2—8—0

The class consisted of 67 engines, Nos. 5001–5167. They were four-cylinder compounds derived from the Midi 4000 class but with the boiler fitted to the PO Atlantics. The HP cylinders were inside, with Stephenson's valve gear, and the LP outside, with Walschaerts gear. Nos. 5001–5012 were built in 1904–5; Nos. 5013–5152 were turned out in 1905–9, but with cylinders of larger volume; and Nos. 5153–5167, which appeared in 1910–11, had the large cylinders and were also superheated and had piston valves. From 1926 a certain number were given the Kylchap 1K/1C exhaust, and a little later the superheated engines were equipped with feed water heaters.

Dimensions: cylinders (according to whether saturated or super-heated), HP 15·4in, or 16·4in × 25·6in, LP 23·6in × 25·6in coupled, wheels 5ft 2in; grate area 34sq ft; pressure 228lbs per sq in; adhesive weight 66·3 or 67·1 tons, total weight 74·6 or 75·8 tons.

6. Paris-Orléans 4500 class Pacifics

This was a joint design by the PO and the Société Alsacienne. The first two, Nos. 4501 and 4502, went into service in July and September 1907. In 1908–9 there were 4503–4570, and of these 4530–4540 had the shapely capped chimney which became so characteristic of the later PO engines, and which was later fitted to the other engines of this class. Nos. 4571–4600 were superheated and had the capped chimney from the start. After 1918 all engines were fitted with a Davies &

Metcalfe exhaust steam injector. HP cylinders had piston valves, LP balanced slide valves.

Dimensions: cylinders, HP 15·3in (saturated) and 16·5in (superheated) × 25·6in, LP 25·2in × 25·6in; coupled wheels 6ft $\frac{3}{4}$in; grate area 46·6sq ft; pressure 228lbs per sq in; adhesive weight 52 tons, total weight 90 tons (saturated) 92·2 tons (superheated).

7. Paris-Orléans 3500 class Pacifics

The first of this class was built at Belfort by the Société Alsacienne in 1909 and the remainder of the first 50 (3501–3550) were turned out during that year and 1910. Of these, the Société Alsacienne built the first 20 as saturated engines and the remaining 30 were built from 1910 by Fives-Lille as superheated. Nos. 3551–3589 of 1912–14 had the larger-diameter HP cylinders fitted to the superheated 4500s. All engines had Davies & Metcalfe exhaust steam injectors.

The 3500 class only differed slightly from the 4500; boiler, cylinders, exhaust, pressure and valves were identical, and there were only slight differences in the coupled wheelbase and the weights—the main difference being the larger coupled wheels of 6ft 4$\frac{3}{4}$in diameter.

8. Paris-Orléans 6000 class 2—10—0 (1910–12)

Design of this class (Nos. 6001–6070) took place at the same time as that of the two Pacific classes, but, in order to keep the axle weight down to the desired limit, they had to be given a rather smaller boiler and the thickness of the frame plates was reduced from 32 to 30mm. This latter weight saving led to trouble and the frames had to be strengthened. In general arrangement they were very similar to the 5000 class 2—8—0s. The cylinders were in line, with the inside HP driving the second coupled axle and the outside LP the third axle. From 1931 a large number had feed water heaters of various patterns.

Dimensions: cylinders, HP 18·1in × 24·3in, LP 26in × 25·6in; coupled wheels 4ft 7in; grate area 40·9sq ft; pressure 228lbs per sq in; adhesive weight 77·7 tons, total weight 85·2 tons.

9. Great Western Railway, 'The Great Bear'

G. J. Churchward's solitary Pacific locomotive, *The Great Bear*, of 1908 was basically an enlargement of his four-cylinder Star class 4—6—0s. Its principal features were the large boiler and wide Belpaire firebox. The axle load of 20$\frac{1}{2}$ tons restricted its running to the London-Bristol main line.

Dimensions: cylinders (4) 15in × 26in; coupled wheels 6ft 8$\frac{1}{2}$in; grate area 41·79sq ft; pressure 225lbs per sq in; adhesive weight 62 tons, total weight 98·8 tons.

10. Du Bousquet's Nord 4—6—4 (1910)

The LP cylinders, between the frames, were placed in a disposition due to Maurice Demoulin, one being behind the other to allow for their being made of the requisite diameter without having to widen the frames at the front. The steam circuit gave the LP group a 10 per cent relative increase in cross-section as compared with the Atlantics.

These engines had been designed by du Bousquet to haul 400 tons at 74·5mph on the level and 59mph up gradients of 1 in 200. A total of 2,800ihp was obtained on several occasions, but the various troubles which occurred prevented such figures from being maintained for any lengthy period.

The official conclusions drawn from the tests were that after the engines had been put into proper order they could have hauled 800-ton trains at 78mph on level track in normal service. They would have been the most powerful passenger locomotives in the world.

Dimensions: cylinders, HP 17·7in × 25·2in, LP 24·4in × 28·7in; coupled wheels 6ft 8¼in; grate area 46·1sq ft; pressure 228lbs per sq in; adhesive weight 55·5 tons, total weight 113 tons.

11. Nord 3.1151 class Pacifics (1912)

These engines had a narrow grate, piston valves to the HP cylinders, and compensated slide valves to the LP cylinders. One of them, No. 3.1160, was at first given HP piston valves of a larger diameter but these were not retained.

Dimensions: cylinders, HP 16·2in × 26in, LP 23·6in × 26in; coupled wheels 6ft 8¼in; grate area 34·7sq ft; pressure 228lbs per sq in; adhesive weight 49·2 tons, total weight 85·6 tons.

12. Nord 3.1200 class Pacifics ('Superpacifics') 1923

The famous Nord Superpacifics, the finest express engines in Great Britain or France in their day, were derived from du Bousquet's 3513 class 4—6—0s, and hence had a particularly well-designed steam circuit. Like the 3.1151 class Pacifics, they had a Belpaire firebox with narrow grate, but it was of the exceptional length of 11ft 8in.

The first 40 engines (3.1201–3.1240) went into service in 1923. In 1930 another 8 were produced, Nos. 3.1241–3.1248. They were followed by Nos. 1249 and 1250, of which the first had Dabeg (RC) poppet valves and the second Caprotti poppet valves. Later they were rebuilt as two-cylinder simple expansion engines with piston valves and Cossart valve gear, identical with that fitted to the 4.1200 class 2—8—2 tank locomotive, and showed themselves as very inferior to the compounds.

Maintenance of these engines proved rather costly, partly due to trouble with the LP valve motion. M. de Caso, the new Chief Engineer of the Nord Locomotive Studies Division, accordingly designed some notable improvements which were incorporated in a new batch of these engines, Nos. 3.1251–3.1290, built in 1930–1. At the same time the boiler pressure was raised from 228lbs per sq in to the 245lbs already used for the two simple expansion engines. The results were very successful.

Dimensions: cylinders, HP 17·3in × 26in, LP 24·4in × 27·2in (simple expansion engines, 25·6in × 28in); coupled wheels 6ft 2·8in; grate area 37·7sq ft; pressure 245lbs per sq in; adhesive weight 56·8 tons, total weight 100·5 tons.

13. PLM Pacifics

The first two PLM Pacifics were No. 6.001, a four-cylinder saturated steam compound with 232lbs pressure and No. 6.101 a four-cylinder simple expansion with Schmidt superheater and 174lbs pressure. Except for their boiler pressure and mechanism the two engines were otherwise identical. In 1910–11 70 more of the simple version were built, Nos. 6.102–6.171, and in 1911 20 more compounds with 232lbs per sq in pressure, but superheated (Nos. 6.011–6.030). In 1912 another 20 simple expansion engines were built, but with the higher boiler pressure of 203lbs (Nos. 6.172–6.191). No further simple expansion locomotives were constructed, all further PLM Pacifics were compounds, and the existing simple Pacifics were rebuilt as compounds. The original superheated compounds became in due course class 231.C, the converted simples with the higher boiler pressure became 231.B, and the converted simples with the lower pressure became 231.E. The single saturated compound, No. 6.001, was superheated and became eventually No. 231.C.1.

All the Pacifics constructed before 1914 had four separate valve gears and the LP cut-off remained constant at 63 per cent. Later Pacifics (classes 231.D and 231.F) had two sets of Von Borries gear and there was a constant difference in cut-off between HP and LP of from about 10 to 20 per cent.

In the subsequent rebuilding, 27 of the 231.Bs and 231.Es became 231.H; whilst 190 of the 231.Ds became 231.G and 79 of the 231.Cs were converted to 231.K.

Various dimensions were:

CLASS 231.B Cylinders, 18·5in × 25·6in; coupled wheels 6ft 6¾in; grate area 45·8sq ft; pressure 203lbs per sq in; adhesive weight 55·5 tons, total weight 95 tons.

CLASS 231.C Cylinders, HP 17·3in × 25·6in, LP 25·6in × 25·6in; coupled wheels 6ft 6¾in; grate area 45·8sq ft; pressure 232lbs per sq in; adhesive weight 55·5 tons, total weight 91·2 tons.

CLASS 231.H Cylinders, HP 15·8in × 25·6in, LP 25·6in × 25·6in; coupled wheels 6ft 6¾in; grate area 45·8sq ft; pressure 292lbs per sq in; adhesive weight 57 tons, total weight 104·8 tons.

CLASS 231.G Cylinders, HP 17·3in × 25·6in, LP 25·6in × 25·6in; coupled wheels 6ft 6¾in; grate area 45·8sq ft;pressure 232lbs per sq in; adhesive weight 55·5 tons, total weight 96·7 tons.

14. Paris-Orléans 3600 class two-cylinder simple expansion Pacifics

During World War I, to simplify the provision of express passenger locomotives, it was proposed that a standard simple expansion Pacific should be constructed for all the big railway companies. Nothing came of this, but the PO whose needs were urgent, ordered in 1920 fifty simple expansion Pacifics from the American Locomotive Company, which were delivered in 1921. They had bar frames and the bissel truck that was fitted to the first 141.R locomotives 23 years later.

Between 1927 and 1930 they all received the Kylchap 1K/T exhaust, and at the same time 37 of them were given feed water heaters of various types. The PO type smoke deflectors were also fitted. Later they became class 231.D.601–650 of the Sud-Ouest Region.

Dimensions: cylinders 24·4in × 25·6in; coupled wheels 6ft 4¾in; grate area 50·4sq ft; pressure 171lbs per sq in; adhesive weight 53·5 tons, total weight 93·3 tons.

15. Paris-Orléans 3700 class Pacifics

These, and all other locomotives designed by Chapelon have been very fully covered in the main body of the book and it is only necessary to add a few details. The prototype was No. 3566, rebuilt at Tours in 1929, and it was followed by the rebuilding in January–May 1932 of the 1909 saturated Pacifics Nos. 3501–3520. The 21 engines were renumbered 3701–3721. With the adoption of the new numbering after the amalgamation of the PO and the Midi they became Nos. 231. 701–721, and after the nationalisation of 1938 they were designated the 231.F class of the Sud-Ouest Region.

On rebuilding the pressure was increased to 247lbs, the adhesive weight to 57·3 tons, and the total weight to 101·8 tons.

In 1934 twenty more engines from the series 3.521–3.589 were rebuilt for the Nord and put into service on that railway as Nos. 3.1171–3.1190. The Nord then built new exactly similar locomotives, of which 8 were delivered in 1936 and numbered 3.1191–3.1198, and 20 more soon followed with numbers running from 3.1111–3.1130. After the formation of the SNCF they became class 231.E.1–48, Nord Region, of which 1–20 were rebuilt by the PO and 22–48 were the new engines.

Also in 1934 the PO rebuilt 10 more engines for its own use and these received the new numbering (the first locomotives to have it) and became Nos. 231.722–731. They later became class 231.H of the Sud-Ouest Region. Certain improvements were incorporated in them which were the result of experience. They included an increase in the LP poppet valve openings (22 per cent for admission and 30 per cent for exhaust) and an increase in the volume of the LP cylinders by 10 per cent. The remaining 23 engines of the 3500 class (15 had been rebuilt as class 3800) were rebuilt for the Est in 1935 on the same lines as the 231.722 class. These eventually became the 231.C.51–73 class of the Est Region.

16. Est 4—8—2 Locomotives

Est 4—8—2 No. 41.001, which appeared in 1925, was a de Glehn compound with the HP cylinders outside driving the second coupled axle and the LP cylinders inside driving the leading coupled axle. The engine had a Belpaire firebox and a combustion chamber and was fitted with a Duchatel-Mestre pattern superheater.

The comparative tests which took place in May 1928 between No. 41.001 and Nord 4—6—2 No. 3.1214 resulted in the former locomotive being supplied with larger cylinders, improved steam passages, and higher boiler pressure. It was this improved type which was ordered by the Etat.

After the competitive trials on the Nord in 1932–33 several of these engines were tested on the Vitry bank and on the road over the next two years to try and find the best ways of strengthening the frames and of improving the steam circuit, exhaust, and other matters. The final type which evolved from these investigations had a greater weight, higher pressure, piston valves with double admission and double exhaust for the LP cylinders, and a variable exhaust with a large cross sectional area. The rebuilt engines produced no less than 40 per cent more drawbar horsepower than even the improved version of 1928.

Dimensions: Est 41.001, 1925—cylinders, HP 17·7in × 28·4in, LP 26in × 28·4in; coupled wheels 6ft 4¾in; grate area 47·7sq ft; pressure at first 232 and later 242lbs per sq in; adhesive weight 74·9 tons, total weight 114·7 tons.

Est 241.A.1–90—cylinders, 16·8in × 28·4in, LP 26in × 28·4in; coupled wheels 6ft 4¾in; grate area 47·7sq ft; pressure at first 290lbs per sq in and later 261; adhesive weight 77·4 tons, total weight 121·6 tons.

17. P.L.M. 4—8—2 No. 241.C.1

Delivered from the Schneider works at Le Creusot on December 30th 1930. The inside HP cylinders drove the third coupled axle and the outside LP drove the second. The boiler was that fitted to the 241.A class 4—8—2s but the combustion chamber was longer and the pressure (290lbs per sq in) higher. It originally had a Prandtl ovoid smokebox front and a single chimney, but in 1932 smoke deflector plates and a double chimney were substituted.

Dimensions: cylinders, HP 17·7in × 25·6in. LP 26·8in × 25·6in; coupled wheels 6ft 6¾in; grate area 53·8sq ft; pressure 292lbs per sq in; adhesive weight 78·8 tons, total weight 126·1 tons.

18. P.L.M. 241.A class 4—8—2

No. 241.A.1 was built in 1925. It had a round top firebox with a combustion chamber. The inside HP cylinders drove the second coupled axle and the outside LP the leading axle. In 1927 the PLM began to put into service 145 similar engines, of which the last was delivered in 1932. They all originally had the ovoid smokebox front but this was later replaced by smoke deflectors. At the Liege Exhibition of 1930 one of them was shown beside No. 241.001 of the Est.

Dimensions: cylinders, HP 20·1in × 25·6in; LP 28·4in × 27·6in; coupled wheels 5ft 10¾in; grate area 53·8sq ft; pressure 228lbs per sq in; adhesive weight 74 tons, total weight 114·6 tons.

19. Paris-Orléans 3800 class Pacifics

These were the 3500 class Pacifics which were modified in a less extensive way than those in the 3700 class. They embodied improvements which could be carried out fairly cheaply. The first engine treated was No. 3583 in 1931. In the following year Tours Works modified 16 more, of which 14 were of the 3500 class and two of the 4500 class (No. 4578 and 4587). The 3500 class engines were divided into two series, differentiated by the sizes of the HP piston valves; Nos. 3801–3806 coming from the 3521–3550 batch and Nos. 3821–3829 from the 3551–3589 batch.

As compared with the unmodified 3500s the 3800 engines produced a much greater effort at the draw bar; whereas at 56mph the original engines recorded 1,750dbhp the 3800s could manage 2,150.

The 3800 class Pacifics became the 231.800 class after the new PO-Midi numbering was introduced, and after nationalisation they were the 231.G class of the Sud-Ouest Region.

20. The 240.A and 240.P 4—8—0 Locomotives

The first engine to be converted from a PO 4500 class Pacific to a 4—8—0, No. 4521 (which became No. 4701) was put into service on August 16th 1932. The following 11 engines were completed over the period February to May 1934, and the whole 12 became Nos. 4701–

4712—later 240.701–712, and ultimately 240.A.701–712 of the Sud-Ouest Region. In the rebuilding the HP cylinders were increased in diameter from 15·3in to 17·3in, the adhesive weight was increased from 52·3 tons to 74·6 tons and the total weight from 90 to 109 tons. The boiler pressure was 292lbs per sq in.

A further 25 engines were rebuilt in 1940 from the unsuperheated 4500 class Pacifics for the PLM (later Sud-Est Region) as class 240.P. In these the LP cylinders were increased in volume from 25·2in × 25·6in to 25·6in × 27·2in as in the second series of Pacific rebuilds.

21. LNER P.2 class 2—8—2

The P.2 class was designed by Sir Nigel Gresley to work heavy passenger trains north of Edinburgh. Of the first two, built in 1934, one, *Cock o' the North*, had Lentz RC poppet valve gears and the other, *Earl Marischal*, had Walschaerts gear with piston valves. Both engines had a semi-streamlined casing and *Earl Marischal* had deflector plates as well. Four further engines were built in 1936—*Lord President, Mons Meg, Thane of Fife*, and *Wolf of Badenoch*. These had the streamlining with wedge front that Gresley had adopted for his Pacifics and all had Walschaerts valve gear. They also had the larger steam passages which resulted from the trials in France. In 1936, also, *Earl Marischal* was given the same external form as the latter engines and in the following year *Cock o' the North* was partially rebuilt with the same streamlined casing and valve gear as the others.

Dimensions: cylinders (3) 21in × 26in; coupled wheels 6ft 2in; grate area 50sq ft; pressure 220lbs per sq in; adhesive weight 81·8 tons total weight 112 tons.

22. Etat Pacifics

The first Etat Pacifics were put into service in 1910 and were numbered 231.011–231.060. All of them were saturated engines. They were superseded on the principal duties by the 231.500 class Pacifics of 1914 onwards. The Paris-Orléans received 40 of them in 1923 (Nos. 3641–3680) and designated them class TP (i.e. *Travaux Publique*, or Public Works) because they were part of the number ordered by the Ministry. In 1929 Nos. 3661–3670 were transferred to the Alsace-Lorraine and in 1934 they were followed by Nos. 3671–3680. They eventually became 231.B.351–370 of the Est. Also in 1934 Nos. 3641–3660 went to the Etat and were eventually 231.C.401–420 of the Ouest Region.

Of the 231.500 class Pacifics rebuilt by the Etat some (rebuilt as classes 231.D, 231.F, and 231.G) were on the lines adopted by Chapelon for the PO 3700 and 3800 classes, whilst others (231.H) received new

HP cylinders (retaining the original LP cylinders) and were fitted with the Kylchap exhaust.

Dimensions of the 231.500 class were the same as those of the PO 3500 class.

23. Est 4—6—0

The first of the Est 20th Century fleet of 4—6—0 express passenger locomotives were Nos. 3.101 and 3.102 constructed in 1903. These were followed in 1905 by the first of a long series which were built up till 1925. From 1910 all new engines were superheated. There were eventually 180 of these engines. The last 50 (230.231–230.280) were rebuilt in 1934 on Chapelon lines and most of the others were either rebuilt or modified.

Dimensions: cylinders HP 15·4in (series 3.211–3.230) and 14·6in (series 3.213–3.280, rebuilt) × 26·8, LP 23·2in × 26·8in; coupled wheels 6ft 10¼in; grate area 34 sq ft (3.211) and 33·8 (3.231); pressure 228lbs per sq in (3.211) and 260lbs per sq in (3.231); adhesive weight 54 tons (3.211) and 57 tons (3.231), total weight 78.8 tons (3.211) and 82·18 tons (3.231).

24. Alsace Lorraine experimental Locomotives

It had been intended that the two S.16 Pacifics and the two G.16 2—10—2s should be the forerunners of new classes. In fact orders for 8 more of the G.16 had been prepared and these were to be followed by a further 10. But a decision as to valve gear held things up, and the outbreak of war stopped production immediately because they were to be built at the Graffenstaden works of the Société Alsacienne.

Dimensions: S.16—cylinders, 22·6in × 28·4in; coupled wheels 6ft 4¾in; grate area 48·5sq ft; pressure 292lbs per sq in; adhesive weight 60 tons, total weight 107·4 tons. G.16—cylinders, 22·6in × 28·4in; coupled wheels 4ft 11in, grate area 53·8sq ft; pressure 292lbs per sq in; adhesive weight 100 tons (119·9 tons with booster), total weight 135 tons.

25. No. 160.A.1 2—12—0

This engine is fully described in Chapter VI.

Dimensions: cylinders, HP 20·5in × 21·3in, LP inside 20·5in × 21·3in, LP outside 25·2in × 25·6in; coupled wheels 4ft 7in; grate area 47·4sq ft; pressure 261lbs per sq in; adhesive weight 120 tons, total weight 137·5 tons.

26. Nord 5.1200 class 2—10—0

Dimensions: cylinders, HP 19·3in × 25·2in, LP 26·8in × 27·6in;

coupled wheels 5ft 1in; grate area 37·7sq ft; pressure 261lbs per sq in; adhesive weight 90 tons, total weight 104 tons.

27. Class 141.P 2—8—2

The dimensions of the various types of 2—8—2 leading up to and including Chapelon's 141.P design were as follows:

PLM CLASS 141.A AND 141.C 2—8—2 Cylinders, HP 20·1in × 25·6in, LP 28·4in × 27·6in; coupled wheels 5ft 5in; grate area 44·7 sq ft; pressure 228lbs per sq in; adhesive weight 70 tons; total weight 94·7 tons.

SNCF CLASS 141.E 2—8—2 (*234 engines*) Cylinders, as for 141.C; coupled wheels, as 141.C; grate area 46·2sq ft; pressure, as for 141.C; adhesive weight 74 tons, total weight 98·5 tons.

SNCF CLASS 141.P 2—8—2 (*318 engines*) Cylinders, HP 16·2in × 27·6in, LP 25·2in × 27·6in; coupled wheels, as 141.C; grate area, as 141.E; pressure 292lbs per sq in; adhesive weight 75·8 tons, total weight 112 tons.

28. Class 241.P 4—8—2 Express Locomotive

Dimensions: cylinders, HP 17·6in × 25·6in, LP 26·6in × 27·6in; coupled wheels 6ft 7½in; grate area 54·3sq ft; pressure 292lbs per sq in; adhesive weight 81·6 tons, total weight 131·7 tons.

29. Classes 232.R, S, and U 4—6—4 Express Locomotives

Dimensions:

(1) 232.R three-cylinder simple expansion Cylinders, (3) 21·2in × 27·6in; coupled wheels 6ft 6¾in; grate area 55·7sq ft; pressure 292lbs per sq in; adhesive weight 66 tons, total weight 125·3 tons.

(2) 232.S four-cylinder compound Cylinders, HP 18·2in × 27·6in, LP 26·8in × 27·6in; coupled wheels, grate area, and pressure as for 232.R; adhesive weight 66 tons, total weight 131 tons.

(3) 232.U four-cylinder compound Cylinders, HP 17·6in × 27·6in, LP 26·8in × 27·6in; coupled wheels, grate area, and pressure as for 232.R; adhesive weight 66 tons, total weight 133 tons.

30. 4—8—4 Express Locomotives No. 242.A.1

The dimensions of No. 241.101, from which No. 242.A.1 was built, were as follows: cylinders (3) outside 21·2in × 30·4in, inside 22·8in × 26in; coupled wheels 6ft 4¾in; grate area 54sq ft; pressure 292lbs per sq in, adhesive weight 80·8 tons, total weight 126·8 tons.

Compared with these, the dimensions of the three-cylinder compound locomotive No. 242.A.1 were: cylinders, HP (1) 23·6in ×

28·3in, LP (2) 27in × 29·9in; coupled wheels 6ft 4¾in; grate area 54sq ft; pressure 292lbs per sq in; adhesive weight 84 tons, total weight 148 tons.

31. LMS 'Coronation' class Pacifics
These locomotives were the most powerful express locomotives in Great Britain, and were probably as fast as Gresley's A4 Pacifics, but the LMS did not have track as suitable for high-speed tests as that possessed by the LNER. In the light of numerous dynamometer trials carried out with this class of locomotive, Chapelon considered that they could have probably developed 2,900dbhp on the level with 35 per cent cut-off at 60mph.

Dimensions: cylinders (4) 16½in × 28in; coupled wheels 6ft 9in; grate area 50sq ft; pressure 250lbs per sq in; adhesive weight 68·1 tons, total weight 106·9 tons.

The dimensions of R. A. Riddles's Pacific *Duke of Gloucester*, which would have been even more powerful, make an interesting comparison: cylinders (3), 18in × 28in; coupled wheels 6ft 2in; grate area 48·6sq ft; pressure 250lbs per sq in; adhesive weight 66 tons, total weight 101·25 tons.

31. Locomotives for Brazil
Dimensions:
(a) 2—8—4: cylinders, 17in × 22in; coupled wheels 4ft 2in; grate area 43sq ft; pressure 210lbs per sq in; adhesive weight 40·4 tons, total weight 69 tons.
(b) 4—8—4: cylinders, 17in × 25in; coupled wheels 5ft; grate area 58sq ft; pressure 290lbs per sq in; adhesive weight 32 tons, total weight 91 tons.

32. Projected 2—10—4 Locomotives
It is fitting to close this appendix with the principal dimensions of the great 2—10—4 freight locomotive, the construction of which had already been started. They were:
Cylinders, HP (1) 23·2in × 30in, LP (2) 26in × 30in; coupled wheels 5ft 5in; grate area 65sq ft; pressure 318lbs per sq in; adhesive weight 100 tons, total weight 154 tons.

TYPE 232
TYPE 242
TYPE 142
TYPE 152

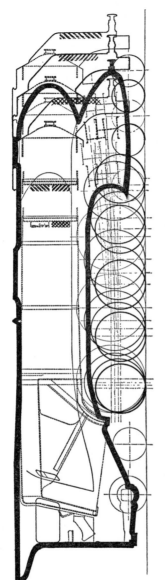
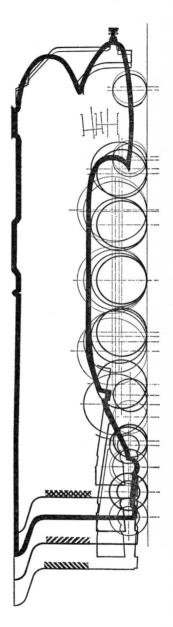

Figure showing how the larger projected SNCF locomotives were entirely standardised. Only the chassis, the wheels, the coupling rods, the tube plates, and the shape were different.

[Sud-Est

Index